POW #3959

POW #3959

*Memoir of a World War II Airman
Shot Down Over Germany*

RALPH E. SIRIANNI

with PATRICIA I. BROWN

McFarland & Company, Inc., Publishers
Jefferson, North Carolina, and London

Library of Congress Cataloguing-in-Publication Data

Sirianni, Ralph E., 1923–
    POW #3959 : memoir of a World War II airman shot down
over Germany / Ralph E. Sirianni with Patricia I. Brown.
        p.   cm.
    Includes index.

    ISBN 0-7864-2297-1 (softcover : 50# alkaline paper) 

    1. Sirianni, Ralph E., 1923–   2. World War, 1939–1945 —
Prisoners and prisons, German.   3. World War, 1939–1945 —
Aerial operations, American.   4. World War, 1939–1945 —
Personal narratives, American.   5. Prisoners of War —
Germany — Biography.   6. Prisoners of war — United States —
Biography.   I. Title: Pow number 3959.   II. Brown, Patricia I.,
1931–   III. Title.
D805.G3S518   2006
940.54'7243092 — dc22   2005030256

British Library cataloguing data are available

On the cover: Ralph Sirianni's POW identification

Manufactured in the United States of America

McFarland & Company, Inc., Publishers
   Box 611, Jefferson, North Carolina 28640
      www.mcfarlandpub.com

To the American veterans of all wars,
and especially to Ralph's ten-member crew,
who flew with him in their B-17 named *Heaven Can Wait*:
Lieutenant George McFall, pilot
Lieutenant Frank Irizarry, copilot
Lieutenant Edward Brazies, navigator
Lieutenant Roy Eggman, bombardier
Sergeant William Kemp, top turret gunner and first engineer
Sergeant Ernest Alcorn, radio operator
Sergeant William Krupitsch, ball gunner and armorer
Sergeant Alan Grimshaw, left waist gunner
Sergeant Ralph Sirianni, right waist gunner and second engineer
and
Sergeant Walter Pawlesh, tail gunner.

Acknowledgments

Ralph Sirianni would like to acknowledge the support and cooperation of his four queens, who make him feel like a king: his wife, Mary; his daughter, Kris Mazzone; and his granddaughters, Jamie Mazzone and Krisy Mercer.

We would both like to thank Roger Hathaway for his assistance. Roger is a U.S. Army Korean War veteran, a former commander of VFW Post 460 in Winthrop, Massachusetts. Roger is also the current historian of American Legion Post 146, Winthrop. He is a member of the Disabled American Veterans (DAV) and currently has a TV show called *Veterans Forum*. We also wish to thank Larry Holmes for his help. He is a Marine Corps veteran of the Vietnam War and is currently the veterans agent for the town of Winthrop. Larry Holmes cohosts *Veterans Forum* with Roger Hathaway. We would like to acknowledge and thank all veterans, past and present — those who have served and those who are now serving our country.

R.E.S. and P.I.B.

Table of Contents

From High School Quarterback to Aerial Gunner

My name is Ralph Sirianni, Jr. In 1941 I was seventeen, living a nice, quiet life with my family in Winthrop, Massachusetts. My mother, Ann Sirianni, was a homemaker. My father, Ralph Sirianni, Sr., was a food broker for several fruit and vegetable distributors in Boston Market Terminal. He traveled around the country visiting farms to search for quality fruits and vegetables for his distributors to purchase. Part of his job was to choose the fruits and vegetables and then call his distributors to arrange for them to purchase the goods. Sometimes he stayed at the farm, supervising the cutting, washing and packing of the merchandise to ensure excellent quality for his distributors. He also arranged for the shipment of the goods. Because his job required so much traveling, my father was often away from home. In spite of his extensive traveling, we still remained a very close family. I had a younger brother, Michael, fifteen years old, who was in Winthrop Junior High School.

I remember, as a youngster, my main ambition was just to hurry and grow up, to become a man. I guess many young boys have that ambition. We just couldn't wait until we grew up, went to work, and got a car. I used to lie on the grass in a field near my house and look up at the sky, just doing nothing but dreaming. We lived near the Boston airport, now called Logan Airport. I loved to lie on the grass and watch the planes flying overhead. I liked to watch all the different planes flying, but the trimotor planes were my favorites. The trimotor plane had three engines, two under the wings and one in front on the main fuselage. They were passenger planes, carrying about twelve people. I was impressed with the trimotor plane because, at that time, it was one of the biggest planes I ever saw.

Gradually I began to realize that flying interested me. I wondered what it was like to fly all around the country. I had never been in a plane before. One day, as I was watching the planes, it suddenly dawned on me that I wanted to be a pilot. I knew that I really wanted to fly.

I was thrilled when I heard that Eddie Rickenbacker was going to land his plane at the Boston airport. Captain Eddie Rickenbacker was a World War I hero. In 1918 he was assigned to the 94th Aero Pursuit Squadron. In the war against the Germans, Rickenbacker became America's best-known flying ace. He shot down 26 enemy planes, more than any other America pilot had done. In May of 1918, he was awarded the French Croix de Guerre. Twelve years later, in 1930, President Hoover awarded Rickenbacker a belated Medal of Honor for his services. For me, Rickenbacker was a hero, and I wanted to be a flier just like him.

1941. I was quarterback for the Winthrop High School football team.

I convinced Warren Harding, a friend, to go with me so we could watch Rickenbacker land his plane and visit with the people. There was a huge crowd in the field near the landing site, all eagerly waiting to cheer for Rickenbacker. Warren and I managed to squeeze in among the crowd. It was very exciting to watch that plane slowly descend to the field and make a perfect landing. Rickenbacker climbed out of the plane. He was dressed in his World War I flying suit, with his helmet and goggles on. As he stepped on the wing of the plane and dropped to the ground, he pushed his goggles back and removed his helmet. The crowd cheered when Rickenbacker approached them. I was one of those cheering the loudest. I was so thrilled to see a World War I hero in person. He was my hero, and I was now surer than ever that I wanted to fly. But for now, it was time to return to school.

Everything was going well for me. I was passing all my classes in school. I was the first-string quarterback for the Winthrop High School football team, and I had a part-time job at the Winthrop Movie Theater. And then one Sunday in December everything changed.

Sunday, December 7, 1941, was a typical Sunday for me. I went to church and then to my part-time job at the Winthrop Theater. It was my job to sweep up and clean the theater to be ready for the Sunday matinee. Warren was the usher that afternoon, and I was scheduled to usher for the evening show. In the afternoon I played touch football with friends until it was time to go home to supper.

When I arrived home, my parents were listening to the radio. As I entered the room, they turned to me and told me that Japanese planes had bombed American army and navy ships at Pearl Harbor. The three of us listened with disbelief as more and more news came over the radio about the destruction at Pearl Harbor. It was indeed a sad day for my family and me, and for all Americans. When I left my house that night to usher at the theater, I did not realize how much my life would be changed by the bombing of Pearl Harbor.

On Monday, the day after the Japanese attacked Pearl Harbor, I was in class at the high school when Mr. Davis, the principal, had all of us go to an assembly in Osborn Hall at noontime. Mr. Davis had a radio on top of a table on the stage. He said that President Roosevelt was about to make an important speech, and he wanted us to hear it. We sat there shocked and saddened as President Roosevelt announced the following: "Yesterday, December 7, 1941, a date which will live in infamy, the United States of America was suddenly and deliberately attacked by naval and air forces of the Empire of Japan." We sat there spellbound as the president concluded his speech by saying, "With confidence in our armed forces, with the unbounding determination of our people, we will gain the inevitable triumph, so help us God. I ask that the Congress declare that since the unprovoked and dastardly attack by Japan on Sunday, December 7, a state of war has existed between the United States and the Japanese Empire."

For the next few weeks, my friends and I watched the bombing of Pearl Harbor over and over again on the screen at the Winthrop Theater. As patriotic Americans, we felt we had a duty and an obligation to serve our country. I talked to my mother and father about quitting school and joining one of the military services. They did not exactly jump for joy at my wanting to enlist. Since I was only seventeen and still in school, I was not eligible for the draft, so my parents wanted me to wait until later to enlist.

On December 24, 1941, I turned eighteen, and on January 2, 1942, four of my friends and I went to our local draft board in Winthrop and filled out applications for voluntary induction to get into the Marine Corps. A week later we picked up our approved papers at the Winthrop Town Hall. With voluntary induction papers in hand I did not need my parents' permission because I was now eighteen years old. Five of us, all close friends, decided to skip school and go enlist in the Marines. We rode the Narrow Gauge Railroad from Winthrop to East Boston, where we boarded the ferryboat to Boston. Then we rode the streetcar to Kenmore Square. We got off the streetcar at Kenmore Square in front of what once was the Buick building. It was no longer being used to sell cars; the Marines had taken it over.

I looked up at the giant sign on the front of the building which read, "United States Marine Corps Recruitment Station." As I watched the hundreds of other men entering the building, I was not nervous or scared. My four friends and I were full of what we called "fire and brimstone." We thought to ourselves that we, and all these hundreds of thousands of men like us, were going to end this war as soon as we started fighting the enemy. Little did I know that my fighting in the war was going to be delayed for a while.

After we gave the recruiting sergeant our induction papers, we filled out the enlistment applications and began our physical exam. The five of us were able to stay together during the process, walking from room to room carrying our clothes wrapped up in a ball. Four of us passed the eye test, but one flunked. We stood there together, still with only our shorts on, and when our friend was told he failed the eye test and had to leave, we were all upset. Even though we were almost finished with the physical, we decided that if we could not join together, none of us would enlist in the Marines. We got dressed and left. I was glad to be loyal to my friends as we left the Marine Recruiting Center, but at the same time, I was disappointed to not be joining the Marines. I have often wondered what my life would have been like had we all joined the Marines that day.

I was not sure what I wanted to do next. The start of the war had changed things drastically for me. I did not want to go back to school while our country was at war. I was in my senior year in high school, but I quit school because I wanted to help the war effort. I went to work for General Ship and Engine Works in East Boston. I was thinking of joining the Army Air Corps. But on January 21, 1943, at the age of 19, I was drafted for active duty by the United States Army, with orders to report on January 28, 1943.

I reported to the local draft board and was taken by bus to the Fort Devens Reception Center in Ayer, Massachusetts. Except that I had lived

App. not Req.

Prepare in Duplicate

Local Board No. 162   13
Suffolk County   025

JAN 12 1943   162

Town Hall
Winthrop, Mass.
(LOCAL BOARD DATE STAMP WITH CODE)

January 12, 1943
(Date of mailing)

ORDER TO REPORT FOR INDUCTION

The President of the United States,

To ___RALPH___________________ ___EDWARD___________ ___SIRIANNI, JR.___________
(First name)   (Middle name)   (Last name)

Order No. ___11394___

GREETING:

Having submitted yourself to a local board composed of your neighbors for the purpose of determining your availability for training and service in the armed forces of the United States, you are hereby

notified that you have now been selected for training and service in the ___Army_______
(Army, Navy, Marine Corps)

You will, therefore, report to the local board named above at ___Town Hall, Winthrop, Mass.___
(Place of reporting)

at _7:45 A._ m., on the ___21___ day of ___January___, 19_43_
(Hour of reporting)

This local board will furnish transportation to an induction station of the service for which you have been selected. You will there be examined, and, if accepted for training and service, you will then be inducted into the stated branch of the service.

Persons reporting to the induction station in some instances may be rejected for physical or other reasons. It is well to keep this in mind in arranging your affairs, to prevent any undue hardship if you are rejected at the induction station. If you are employed, you should advise your employer of this notice and of the possibility that you may not be accepted at the induction station. Your employer can then be prepared to replace you if you are accepted, or to continue your employment if you are rejected.

Willful failure to report promptly to this local board at the hour and on the day named in this notice is a violation of the Selective Training and Service Act of 1940, as amended, and subjects the violator to fine and imprisonment.

If you are so far removed from your own local board that reporting in compliance with this order will be a serious hardship and you desire to report to a local board in the area of which you are now located, go immediately to that local board and make written request for transfer of your delivery for induction, taking this order with you.

____
Member or clerk of the local board.

D. S. S. Form 150
(Revised 7-15-42)

☆   U. S. GOVERNMENT PRINTING OFFICE : 1942   16—18271-4

1943. My induction papers.

in California with my family until I was seven years old, I had never been farther from Winthrop than about 10 miles in any direction. Here at Fort Devens, I was about 25 miles from home. Although that was not very far, I knew that eventually I would be sent overseas.

We were ushered into a large hall where an army captain gave us the oath of allegiance, and we were now officially sworn into the United States Army. After the swearing-in ceremony, we were divided into groups and led into separate barracks. Each man was assigned a bunk. We were told to leave our personal effects on our bunks and proceed to the mess hall, where we ate lunch. After lunch we were escorted to another building to prepare for our physicals.

I had no idea what this physical was going to be like. In our Marine Corps physical we only got as far as an eye test and a lot of health questions before we left. As I mentioned earlier, when our friend flunked the eye test at the Marine recruitment center, the four of us decided not to sign up and left with him. But now, as an officially sworn in soldier, I had no choice. I would be taking the complete physical.

I was a little uncomfortable at first, as we had to undress and stand around in groups of 30 to 40 men. However, I was too busy to stay uncomfortable as the doctors began probing all parts of my body. When the probing phase was finished, I was given several different shots, supposedly to protect me from almost every kind of disease known to man. Somehow I managed to survive the physical, get dressed, and move on to another room.

The next room had chairs and I could finally sit down. What a relief that was. A doctor, standing at the front of the room, was preparing to give a lecture about diseases. He talked about some diseases I had never heard of, and I listened intently. The doctor warned against the various social diseases that we might encounter later in our army careers. After a brief discussion, we watched two movies. The movies showed every stage of gonorrhea, syphilis, and other venereal diseases. The pictures were so vivid that they scared me. The demonstration was meant to shock and frighten us, and it accomplished its mission. I was definitely frightened.

The next day we were issued our uniforms and other gear necessary for basic training. We took aptitude tests, and then they asked us what branch of the Army we wanted. I had always wanted to fly, so I requested the Army Air Corps and hoped that my request would be granted.

The stay at Fort Devens lasted a week. As anybody who was in military service can tell you, rumors often start in the latrine and spread rapidly. The rumors spread about different locations we were being sent to, but just like most rumors, no one got it right. We were being sent to Miami

1943. Parade ground at Miami Beach, Florida.

Beach, Florida, and no one had guessed it. I think security was pretty good at Fort Devens. The chance to leave the snow, sleet, and freezing weather of Fort Devens behind for the warm, sunny climate of Florida made me happy.

We arrived in Miami in February 1943. Basic training was scheduled for six weeks. We were housed in fancy, plush hotels on Biscayne Boulevard on the waterfront of Miami Beach. Unfortunately, there were no bellhops and there was no room service. Two double bunks in each room accommodated four men. It was great to live in such a fine hotel rent-free and with free meals. On thirty-two dollars a month, we could never have afforded such rich accommodations.

Basic training was not easy, but I was fortunate because I had played football in high school and was in better shape than some of the men. But even I was shocked when we were told that our days were to start at 4:30 A.M. I soon began to learn the army way to tell time. Four-thirty A.M. was 0430, and we did not end our day until 1800 hours (6 P.M.), which was after supper. We finished dressing, making our beds, and checking to make sure everything was clean and neat. And then we marched to breakfast. By 5:30 A.M. breakfast was over, and they ordered us to march to the field for physical exercise first and then to the obstacle course for more strenuous training. We also did a lot of running around the track. By the end of the morning's six-hour training session, all of us were pretty tired. We marched to the mess hall for lunch. With all the marching we did, it did not take us long to become expert marchers. After lunch some of us were assigned to KP (kitchen police) duty, while others were assigned to afternoon or evening guard duty.

Guard duty was mostly walking the beach near our hotel. Guard duty on the beaches was necessary because we had been warned that German submarines might be off the Atlantic coast. Our orders were to watch for the subs as well as for any German spies trying to come ashore. All the buildings facing the water were required to maintain a strict blackout to prevent German submarines from using the lights as a target.

I got a chance to see many of the beautiful golf courses in the Miami Beach area. But we were not playing golf. The golf courses were being used for physical training, obstacle courses, and marching. Sundays we could relax, and go to the PX or rec hall, but we were not allowed to leave the base. Some of the men moaned and groaned about basic training, but I enjoyed it. Basic training was getting us into the best possible physical condition for whatever was awaiting us in the future.

During basic training, all the trainees were required to attend lectures on army life and military conduct. After finishing the aptitude tests, we had a chance to say in which branch of the Army we would like to serve. As I had written on my earlier papers, once again I wrote Army Air Corps. Passing the tests did not mean that we would get what was requested, but at least it showed what branch of the service we would prefer.

Toward the end of basic training, the postings were listed. I had been accepted in the Army Air Corps and was being sent to aerial gunnery school at Tyndal Field in Panama City, Florida. I was very excited. This was what I had been waiting for.

At last it was graduation day. We were standing at attention on one of the golf courses. The band was playing as we marched past the reviewing stand. This was strictly a military graduation, and no civilians were present. The commanding officer approached the microphone and announced over the loudspeaker, "All those marching here today have successfully completed basic training, and have been given new assignments. We wish you all well in your new assignments."

We were then dismissed, and could return to our barracks. It was a couple of days before we packed and left Miami Beach for Panama City. The bus ride from Miami to Tyndal Field in Panama City took about seven hours. I was very happy to be on my way to aerial gunnery school.

Two hundred and sixty of us disembarked from the buses at Tyndal Field. No one was there to greet us, so we just stood there waiting for further orders. We were tired, dirty, and hungry. Some of us sat down on our barracks bags. Just as we sat down, I saw a greenish army car speeding toward us. The car screeched to a stop in front of us. A tall giant of a man got out of the car and walked over to a nearby platform. He stared down at us with his hands on his hips and yelled in a booming voice, "Who told you to sit down on your barracks bags?" His voice got louder as he yelled, "Pick them up now. While you are here at this gunnery school, you are not to do anything unless you are ordered to do it! As of this moment, you are aerial gunnery school cadets. You will be given demerits when you foul up. When you receive a certain number of demerits, you will wash out of gunnery school!" He ended his short speech with these words, "Your heart and soul belong to God, but your ass belongs to Sgt. Cherry."

I stared somewhat fearfully at that tall man in his impressive uniform. I had immediately stood and lifted my barracks bag when he said to pick them up. This was my introduction to Master Sergeant Cherry, who was our head instructor. And, believe me, I never forgot his warning or his name.

The next day we learned that the commanding officer of the aerial gunnery school was Colonel Leland S. Stranathan. Our instruction started the next day with physical training, the obstacle course, marching, and drills every morning after breakfast. Reveille was at 5 A.M., and we did not stop until it was time for taps at 10 P.M. We were there with one goal in mind, and one goal only, to become expert aerial gunners. Our training was thorough and intensive. Our first job was to learn about the .30-caliber and the .50-caliber machine guns. We had to know the name of every part of the .50-caliber. Training consisted of taking the machine gun apart and naming all the parts, then putting it back together so it would fire. We had to do the same with the .45-caliber automatic. We called the classroom instruction "chalk talk" because it consisted of lectures and illustrations on the blackboard.

After about a week or ten days of instruction on machine guns, we went on the firing range to learn to shoot the stationary .50-caliber machine guns. Later we practiced shooting the twin .50-caliber machine guns from a moving turret that worked electrically and hydraulically. Even if we did not become turret gunners, we had to know how to repair the equipment in an emergency situation. As part of the training, we also practiced skeet shooting. Skeet shooting was fun, and I enjoyed it, but it was also important because it taught me how to track and lead a target. Each phase of training was a part of the total picture of becoming an aerial gunner, as well as training us in all the necessary skills for combat.

Training was hard work, but we also had some moments of humor during the training. One time a cadet asked the instructor for permission to use the latrine located in the middle of the field. The instructor nodded his permission, and the cadet began to run. As soon as the cadet headed for the latrine, we began to make bets with each other as to whether he would make it in time. The latrine was about 200 yards down the field. As the cadet got closer he began to run faster. We now realized that he had diarrhea, which we called the GI's. When he was about 20 yards from the building he slowed down to a walk, dragging his feet as he walked into the latrine. He did not seem to be happy. The instructor announced to us in a deep voice, "He didn't make it. He waited too long." We felt sorry for the cadet, but we couldn't help bursting out laughing.

We had also begun classes in plane identification. Black silhouettes of enemy fighters and American fighters were projected on a screen for a split second. We had to identify them. The German FW-190 and the American P-47 were close in appearance, and the American P-51 and German ME-109 looked a lot alike. We had to be able to identify every fighter that Germany, Japan, the United States, and England had in this war. It was necessary for us to be able to identify the planes correctly. We certainly did not want to shoot down our own fighter planes that were sent out to protect us.

AT-6 trainer at Tyndal Field, Florida.

The next phase of our training was different. It was exciting and challenging because we were now going to practice firing from an airplane. I was extremely excited and looked forward to it. We were finally going up in an airplane to test our skills. A plane was flying ahead of us towing a large sleeve-like target. It was our job to get as many hits as possible on the target. I had never been in an airplane before. The highest I had ever been was at the top of the Custom House, which was the tallest building in Boston at the time. I was 19, but the pilot flying the AT-6 trainer that I was in wasn't much older, maybe 22 or 23.

The AT-6 only had room for the pilot in front and a trainee in back. The canopy was removed, so it was an open cockpit. I had to stand in the open cockpit of the plane wearing a parachute strapped to my chest. The harness had a heavy webbed strap attached to an eyebolt on the floor of the plane. This strap was the only thing that kept me from falling out of the plane when the pilot did some dives and rolls, or took evasive action. These maneuvers were necessary because enemy planes would be moving also. The twists and turns of the plane made it more difficult for us to shoot at the target. I had to adjust to wearing a helmet and goggles and to the earphones that enabled me to maintain contact with the pilot. We used a .30-caliber machine gun that could swing up or down, but it was strictly limited in the use of a sideways swing. The pilots did not want the trainees to accidentally shoot the rudder off the aircraft.

Just before we took off, the pilot asked me if I had flown before. I told him this would be the first time I had ever been in a plane. We took off and headed out over the Gulf of Mexico. When we reached the target area, an AT-6 was already there, towing a white target sleeve. The object of the exercise was to shoot at the target, which was about 300 yards away, and hit the sleeve being towed by the plane. I heard the pilot's voice over the intercom. "Remember to hit the target without hitting the tow plane," he warned me with a chuckle. Maybe it was funny to him, but this was not only my first time flying in a plane, but also my first time shooting at a moving target in the air. I was already nervous enough without worrying about hitting the tow plane by mistake. The ammunition had red paint on the tips of the bullets. This allowed me to get a look at my "hits" and see how many times I hit the target.

On the way back to the base my pilot did loops, rolls, dives, and every conceivable maneuver an airplane could do. It's difficult to describe the ride that this pilot gave me. I enjoyed all these fancy maneuvers. It was exhilarating. I was sure he did it because this was my first time in a plane, and he wanted to see how I would react to these types of maneuvers. Maybe he just wanted to give me a thrilling first ride I would never forget. No matter what his reason was, I positively enjoyed my first plane ride. The only time I became a little concerned about the ride back was when he flew under a bridge along the Gulf coast. Remember, I was standing in an open cockpit. It seemed to me he flew just a little too close to the bridge. But we made it OK and finally landed back at the airfield. The gunnery instructor and I inspected the target sleeve. I had more than enough hits to qualify as an aerial gunner.

I wrote to my mother and father at least twice a week during basic training and gunnery school, and I heard from them regularly. When I was about halfway through gunnery school, my mother wrote to tell me that my father was going to be in Sanford, Florida, which was about 300 miles away from Tyndal Field. She said he planned to drive from Sanford to Tyndal Field to see me. He made a business trip to Sanford once a year for his job as a food broker. My father was fortunate to have a high-priority gas ration because he dealt with food. We made arrangements for him to visit me at Tyndal Field, and two weeks later he arrived. I had already received permission to see him, and we were able to spend a couple of hours in the day room talking together. My father gave me all the news from Winthrop and greetings from family and friends. Even though I

1943. Graduation from gunnery school. I am the last one on the left in the back row.

missed my family and friends, I explained to my father how much I liked being in the Army Air Corps, and how pleased I was to be in gunnery school. We had a great afternoon just talking, and I felt a little less homesick. It was a great experience for both of us. He said he would call my mother as soon as he got back to Sanford and reassure her that I was fine.

The big day finally arrived for graduation. Like our earlier graduation from basic training, this one was strictly military also. No friends or relatives were there. Our graduating class was number 43–16. This meant that we were the sixteenth class to graduate in 1943. Two hundred and fifty nine of us graduated that day. What a proud day that was for me. I received my first stripe, private first class, and I wore my new silver gunnery wings with pride.

I received my graduation book, which included pictures of each member of the Army Air Corps' gunnery school graduating class, 43–16. There was also a special poem printed in the book. This poem, "A Gunner's Vow," had been posted on the walls of all the barracks for us to read. It was an inspiration for us to become the best gunners in the Air Force.

A GUNNER'S VOW

I wished to be a pilot
And you along with me,
But if we were all pilots
Where would the Air Force be?
It takes guts to be a gunner,
To sit out in the tail
When the Messerschmitts are coming
And the slugs begin to wail,
The pilot's just a chauffeur,
It's his job to fly the plane,
But it's we who do the fighting
Though we may not get the fame.
If we all must be gunners,
Then let us make this bet:
We'll be the best damn gunners
That has left this station yet.
Author Unknown

CHAPTER TWO

Combat Training

After graduation from aerial gunnery school at Tyndal Field, we were assigned to Sheppard Field in Wichita Falls, Texas, for training at the Army Air Force Technical School. Sheppard Field was over 600 miles from Florida, and we had to make the trip by train. The train that we rode was so old that it looked like it had been built in the late 1800s during the time of Billy the Kid. We joked about it, and agreed that Billy the Kid may have even held up this same old train. The seats in the coaches were made of straw and were hard as hell. The train even had the old gas fixtures still in place. We commented that they must have dug this train out of the archives.

All we carried with us were the clothes and gear from gunnery school. The word "crowded" doesn't even begin to describe the way we were packed on this train. But we always managed to find the room and the time for card games and crap games. We walked to the mess car, picked up our food, and then went back to sit in our coach car to eat. When we finished eating, we went back to the mess car and dipped our mess kits in a trash barrel filled with boiling water.

That's me receiving my wings after finishing gunnery school.

Then we rinsed the kits in a second barrel of boiling water. Hopefully this procedure was sanitizing our mess kits. Imagine, if you will, what it was like after a couple of days of spilling food on our clothes and in the coaches. The odor of the food crumbs, combined with the fact that we were not able to take a shower, filled the coaches with a strong raunchy smell. We had to suffer for the day and a half it took for the train to arrive at Wichita Falls. It was late in the afternoon on a very hot day when we arrived.

Sheppard Field was one of the largest Army Air Force technical training bases in the country, and it also included a basic training center. Since we already had basic training at Miami Beach, we were here only for technical training to learn the operation of the aircraft. The training was scheduled for four months. We attended the aircraft and radial engine school to learn everything about American airplanes. We had to learn about the mechanics of the radial Pratt and Whitney engine and the various operations of the airplanes. There were classroom sessions, and we also had hands-on instruction to become aerial engineers. I was very interested in learning everything I could about airplanes, and so I enjoyed all the training.

There were many different phases of study. We had to learn about all types of aircraft that the Army Air Corps was using in World War II. Instructors taught us about the structure of the planes, and about the engines, the carburetor, and the flight instruments. We had to know how the hydraulics functioned in the operation of the engine. All this training was necessary for us to be prepared for an emergency, in case we had to fly the plane or repair damaged equipment. Our gunnery school training was

Keeping in shape at Sheppard Field, Texas.

finished, and our training as flight engineers was about to begin. We were expected to be experts at both positions. Because we were being trained as flight engineers, we were given more time in the cockpit along with instrument training. Cockpit training was necessary for flight engineers. If the pilot or copilot was injured during combat, the flight engineer was expected to help fly the plane.

One time we were put in a decompression chamber to simulate how it felt to lose your oxygen at twenty thousand or thirty thousand feet. If you lost your oxygen at that altitude, you would pass out in one minute and die in five minutes. Another memorable event, which I did not enjoy, was our experience with gas masks. We had to walk through a tear-gas chamber, stand inside for a short time, then take off the gas mask and inhale a whiff of gas. The sudden whiff of the gas made us come out choking. This little exercise ruined our appetites for supper because it made us sick to our stomachs. We only had to go into the tear-gas chamber one time. That was good. None of us were eager to go through the gas chamber again.

In addition to the special technical training we were receiving, we needed to keep in shape. Part of our everyday routine included running the obstacle course and participating in training exercises. With all the things we had to learn, I could understand why the training would take four months. Our training began in June and was scheduled to end by the middle of September.

Summer was not the best time to be training in Texas. I came from New England, where the temperature never reached 105. It was difficult for me to adjust to the temperature in Texas because it would often rise to 100 and 105 degrees for weeks at a time. The red dust of Texas was also an unpleasant new experience for me. After a violent windstorm, the dust would get into the barracks through the windows. The dust covered the floors, the bunks, and even our clothes. At times the dust was so thick on our bunks that it took hours to clean off the bunks before we could go to sleep. We were completely exhausted by the time we finished cleaning the floors and the bunks. In spite of the Texas heat and red dust, the food here was a lot better than it was at Tyndal Field. But the water in Texas tasted terrible. It was warm and smelled like bleach. But it was all we had so we forced ourselves to drink it.

Learning to repair airplanes was another part of our training. We marched into the desert to a bivouac area where we pitched two-man tents for our sleeping quarters. The officers told us that we would be in this bivouac area for three days. As I looked around this desert land, I saw that the ground outside the bivouac area was filled with all different types of airplanes. There were B-17s, B-25s, B-26s, and some fighter planes. It had been a five-mile march to the field training area, and the cooks, who were permanent personnel, prepared our lunch. After lunch the training began.

We knew it was going to be our job to repair these bombers and fighters just as if we were working under combat conditions. Before actually working on the planes, we were told to sit on the ground. An officer stood in front of us and gave a lecture on what was expected of us. In the middle of the lecture a dog with a dead six-foot rattlesnake in his mouth ran through our group and disappeared at the far end of the field. We scattered in all directions and let the dog go by. I do not fear many things in life, but I do have a deadly fear of snakes, scorpions, and tarantulas. I stayed far away from the running dog. After this experience, I wouldn't enter my tent until the airman who shared it with me checked first to make sure there were no snakes inside. He checked every night for me, but I still did not sleep very well those nights in the desert. I told myself that I would rather go on a mission in combat over Germany than stay where there were snakes. We found out later that the dog belonged to one of the sergeants. As we settled back down on the grass, the officer calmly resumed his lecture.

The next two days we were very busy working on the planes and learning how to do the repair work that might be needed in an emergency. Finally, in September, our class graduated from the Army Air Force Technical School, and I received two more stripes. Rising from private first class, I was now a buck sergeant. I couldn't wait to go to a tailor in town to have my new stripes sewn on my uniforms because I was very proud to display my new rank.

Now that we were finished at Sheppard Field, our orders were to make preparations to be shipped to another base for more intensive training. With all the training I had endured so far, I felt that at last I was getting closer and closer to joining the fighting overseas. They told us our next training assignment would be to actually go up in the planes and practice flying missions. This was what I had been waiting for. It was my hope and my dream to go up in combat planes. I had no idea which type of bomber I would be flying in; we hadn't been told yet. Right at this moment, I just wanted to get into a plane. Some men from our class were sent to different bases to fly in B-25s and B-26s. I and some other members of my class were assigned to a base in Ephrata, Washington. As soon as I heard the words "Ephrata, Washington," I felt sure that I was going to fly in a B-17. There was a Boeing factory located nearby in Everett, Washington, and they manufactured B-17s.

There were 200 airmen in our troop train heading for Ephrata. It took us two and one half days to get there. Unfortunately, I had the same type of accommodations on this train that I had on my previous two government-sponsored train rides. It was not exactly a pleasure trip. I wasn't even sure where Ephrata was, but after my arrival, I learned that it was located between Seattle and Spokane. This is where I first met some of the members of our crew.

Lieutenant George McFall was our pilot. He was from Wisconsin, where he had lived on the family farm. McFall had already been in the Air Corps for a year and a half. Early in his service career he had been trained as a flight engineer. At his request, McFall asked for a transfer to flight school. It was granted, and he finally achieved what he really wanted, to be a pilot.

Our copilot was Lieutenant Frank E. Irizarry from Florida. Frank was born in Puerto Rico, but had moved to Florida many years ago. He had been a civilian pilot for a small airline. When Frank first joined the Army Air Corps, he was immediately sent for training as a fighter pilot. And that was exactly what he wanted. But unfortunately for Frank, there was a shortage of bomber pilots. He was reassigned to our bomber group as a copilot. From day one, Frank made it plain to us that he was very unhappy about the transfer to bombers. But like all of us in wartime, he eventually adapted to the situation.

Our aerial gunner and first engineer, Staff Sergeant William P. Kemp, was from Kennesaw, Georgia. Bill had been through gunnery school and had also passed at the top of his flight engineer class. I soon discovered that Bill talked funny. He had a very pronounced Southern accent. I told him he talked like a Rebel. He always used the phrase, "You all," even when talking to one person. That made me laugh. In spite of our different backgrounds and accents, we became very close friends.

And then, of course, there was me, Sergeant Ralph E. Sirianni, aerial gunner and second engineer. I was nineteen years old, from Winthrop, Massachusetts, and I had never been out of Winthrop until I joined the Army Air Corps. Now it seemed as if I was on the move all around the country every few weeks.

In the ten days we spent at Ephrata, Lieutenant McFall, Lieutenant Irizarry, Sergeant Kemp, and I worked closely together so we got to know each other pretty well. We became very good friends, and were gradually learning to depend upon one another in our training sessions. Trust in the ability of each crewmember to do his job well was essential if we were to survive. I was really happy to meet some of my crewmembers, and to get to know them before we went into combat. I could sense the friendship and trust being shared by the four of us. However, we were still short six men. Ten men were needed to complete a B-17 crew. We were told that the other members of our crew would be joining us in Ardmore, Oklahoma.

At the mess hall, we had a chance to chat with other airmen who had been in Ephrata for a while. From them we learned that Ephrata, and the surrounding area, was noted for its great apple crops. Because of that, we had plenty of apples and apple butter at our meals. I had never tasted apple butter before. In fact, I had never even heard of it. After sampling the apple butter at the mess hall, I was not impressed. When we began our flights, I saw the apple orchards for myself as we flew over them. There were so many orchards that the whole countryside seemed filled with them. Even though I did not like apple butter, I discovered that the many miles of orchards below us was a beautiful sight.

We were assigned a B-17 to begin our practice flights. There were only the four of us instead of the usual ten men, but we still flew our scheduled training flights These flights in the B-17 were designed to familiarize us with the controls, and to help us become skillful in flying the plane. The training flights usually took from three to four hours to complete. Bill Kemp and I also actually flew the plane along with our pilot and copilot. As first and second engineers, we were the ones who had to be ready to step in and help fly the plane if the pilot or copilot was injured in combat. As the second engineer, I would only be called in if the first engineer was unable to perform his duties. By the third training flight, I realized that I did not want to be a first engineer. I was satisfied to be a gunner and second engineer.

Since we did not have all the members of our crew yet, I had my choice of which gunner's position I wanted. I chose to be the right waist gunner. I definitely did not want to be the ball turret gunner or the tail gunner. I felt claustrophobic in those two positions. It would be very difficult for me to stay in the narrow, confined spaces in the ball turret or tail-gun position. I was extremely grateful when McFall said I could be the right waist gunner.

In the ten days at Ephrata Air Base, we flew six training flights of three to four hours' duration. We often flew around Mount Rainier. The snow-covered top of Mount Rainier was beautiful. I just stared at the beauty of the mountain every time we flew near the top of it. We also flew over Grand Coulee Dam, which was another awesome sight. Until I got into the Air Corps, I had never traveled and had never seen such wonderful sights before. It was like the whole country was opening up to me, and my hometown seemed smaller and smaller. But, of course, I still wanted to eventually get back home to my family and friends.

After the ten days of training at Ephrata Air Base were over, we were assigned to the 395th Combat Training School in Ardmore, Oklahoma. The train ride to Ardmore was boring and uneventful. We certainly did not have first-class accommodations in this vintage train that was classified as a troop train. The Washington to Oklahoma trip took us a couple of days to complete, and I, for one, was glad when it was over.

At the combat training school in Ardmore, we met four more members of our crew. Lieutenant Roy E. Eggman, our bombardier, was from Indiana. Roy told us that he graduated from bombardier school at the top of his class. He proudly showed us a special bracelet that had been awarded to him in honor of being first in his class at bombardier school. In response to his news about being at the top of his class, we reminded him that he was only a passenger on our plane. It was our job to fly him to the target so he could drop his bombs, and then we would fly him back to England. He enjoyed the joke and laughed along with us.

Staff Sergeant Ernest Alcorn, our radio operator, was from St. Louis, Missouri. Ernie was a great guy and easy to get along with. Every position on a B-17 was important, and Ernie was a very good radio operator. We could trust him to make sure we kept in contact with each other on the plane as well as with the other planes and with the base.

Sergeant Willy Krupitsch was the ball gunner and armorer. He was from New York. The ball gunner was located in the ball-turret compartment underneath the plane. Willy was also the armorer, who was responsible for arming the bombs in the bomb bay when it was time for the bomb run.

Lieutenant Robert White was our navigator. He was from New York. I didn't know too much about his background at that time.

Sergeant Alan Grimshaw was our left waist gunner. He was originally from New Bedford, in Massachusetts, my home state. But he had moved to California and had made his home there. Grimshaw was thirty-five years old, the oldest member of our crew. So naturally he got tagged with the nickname "Pop." He was the "Dapper Dan" of our crew. All his uniforms were tailored and form fitted. When Pop got dressed to go into town, he looked like a model who had just stepped out of a magazine.

Out of the nine crewmembers we now had, I was the youngest at nineteen, and Alan Grimshaw was the oldest at thirty-five. There were separate barracks for the NCOs and the officers. The officers ate together in the officers' mess hall, and we ate in the regular mess hall with the other noncoms. We now had nine crewmembers and only needed one more to complete our crew. Even with a nine-member crew, we were able to begin flying our combat training missions.

The missions were usually scheduled for four hours each. We did practice bombing runs and celestial navigation flights to learn to navigate at night. So far in these training missions, we gunners were only passengers learning to adapt to our flying positions and to become more experienced in flying together as an efficient crew. Our special training would come later.

Before any training mission began, we reported to the briefing room. There were usually eight to ten crews, which meant between eighty to one hundred men at one time in the briefing room. The purpose of most of the briefings during these particular training sessions was to tell the pilots, navigators, and radio operators their flight course and radio frequencies. The rest of us were just like visitors listening to the briefing. Sometimes even on our actual training missions, I felt as if I was just a passenger. I loved flying and just being a passenger was fun and exciting. Of course, these were only training missions. It would be different when we began our combat mission briefings. I would not be a passenger, but someone actively participating in protecting our plane and its crew.

We were leaving the briefing room and heading out to the flight line when a man came running up to us and asked, "Is this Lieutenant McFall's crew?" George McFall replied, "Yes, it is."

Our B-17 crew. Left to right, first row: Lt. Robert White, Lt. Roy Eggman, Lt. Frank Irizarry, Lt. George McFall. Second row, Sgt. Walt Pawlesh, Sgt. Ralph Sirianni, Sgt. William Kemp, Sgt. Alan Grimshaw, Sgt. Willy Krupitsch, Sgt. Ernest Alcorn.

"I'm Sergeant Walter Pawlesh, sir," the man said. "I've been assigned to your crew."

McFall welcomed Walt to the crew. And we now had our new tail gunner, and a full ten-man crew. When we asked Walt where he was from, he replied, " McKees Rocks, Pennsylvania." He told us he had been waiting to be assigned to a crew. We were out at the airfield and preparing to get on our plane, when Walt asked Lieutenant McFall if he could fly with us on this night's mission. The lieutenant said no, he couldn't fly with us yet because he was not dressed to fly and he did not have orders for this flight. I could see from the look on Walt's face that he was disappointed as he watched us walk to our plane.

McFall taxied our plane to the runway to get in line for takeoff. Just as we began to lift off, the plane ahead of us crashed on a small hill. As we flew over the plane, it exploded in a ball of flames. Walt, who was watching from the ground, could not see which plane had crashed, and he was fearful that it might have been ours. All planes were called back and we landed safely. The field was shut down for the night.

Walt saw us coming back into the briefing room and ran to catch up with us. He was so happy to see that it wasn't his new crew that was involved in the terrible wreck. Ten men were killed in the plane that crashed just ahead of us. We were never told what caused the crash.

After this flight, Sergeant Pawlesh officially became a member of our crew as our tail gunner, and he was able to fly with us on all our training flights. Walt was shorter than any of us, so naturally, we called him "Shorty." Walt was nineteen years old, but I was still the youngest member of the crew at nineteen because Walt was about six months older than me. Walt was married. We became good friends and, very early on, Walt and I made a pact that we would check on each other during combat. As the right waist gunner, I was the only one who could see Walt in his tail-gunner position.

From the end of September through the middle of December at Ardmore was really the best time I had in my military life. Within that short time, the ten of us became like a very close family, and we worked well together on our training missions. These training missions consisted of night celestial navigation flights, formation flying, and simulated bombing runs. The bombardier got his practice by dropping 100-pound practice bombs in the desert. I loved flying, especially with this great crew. We were concerned for each other, and intent upon doing our best on every mission. We went on so many practice missions that it seemed as though we were always in the air.

Lieutenant McFall was a very competent leader, and he made sure we were well trained for combat. On our training missions, he had every crewmember take a turn flying the plane from the copilot seat. For me, flying the aircraft was the most enjoyable part of our training. McFall told us that this training was necessary because if he or the copilot were disabled, one of the crewmembers would be able to fly the plane.

On one of our training flights, Walt and I had nothing to do as yet, and we were both sitting down, looking out of my right waist-gun position. Pop turned from his left waist-gun position and listened to our conversation. Walt looked at me and asked, "Would you like to bail out?" Even though we had talked about bailing out several times before, I just smiled at Walt and did not answer him.

Pop spoke up and said, "Let's knock it off. This is nothing to joke about."

"I am serious," Walt replied.

"Walt," I said, "we just can't bail out without asking Mac."

We really wanted to see what it was like to bail out of the plane, so I picked up the intercom and asked the lieutenant if it would be OK for Walt and me to bail out. We thought the plane was going to blow up from the force of his angry reply. He yelled a loud, emphatic "No!" over the intercom. Then he added grimly that he would deal with Walt and me when we got on the ground.

When we landed, McFall pulled Walt and me aside, and gave us our first ass chewing. McFall stared hard at us, and said, "I thought you both were more intelligent than that. You should have known that asking to bail out was a stupid idea. I don't want members of my crew clowning around."

McFall continued berating us, as Walt and I stood almost at attention, not daring to say a word. McFall said that everything we did in the performance of our duty as crewmembers was extremely important to the safety of our entire crew and to the successful completion of our mission. Then he abruptly turned and walked away from us.

From this episode I learned, the hard way, that McFall did not like joking around when we were flying missions. Neither Walt nor I dared to volunteer the information that we had not been joking, but had been very serious. Some things are best left unsaid.

We had been at Ardmore for about ten days when we were issued our first passes. We were fortunate to get two-day passes. For our first two-day pass, all of us, including our officers, went into the town of Ardmore, which was only about five or six miles from the base. Public buses ran daily from the base to the town and back again.

In Ardmore we met Marge Pawlesh, Walt's wife, and Judy Eggman, Roy's wife. Walt, Roy, and Frank were the only married men in the crew but Frank's wife was not here. Pop Grimshaw had been married and was divorced. During the four months we were in Ardmore, Marge and Judy each had a small apartment. While we were in Ardmore, we all hung out together. Even the two wives went with us everywhere when we were off the base. Marge and Judy would go skating, out to dinner, and even to the local pubs with us. They were practically honorary members of the crew. We had a lot of good times together and became very close friends. This friendship is how we developed a close bond and became like a family. I felt very strongly that this sense of family unity would be one of the reasons we would survive the war. When we went back to the base at night, Roy and Walt would stay in town with their wives and return to base in the morning when the two-day pass was over.

When our short leave ended, we went back to concentrating on our combat training. Combat training was not always easy. Sometimes things go wrong. I enjoyed most of the training flights, but sometimes a flight would put us into the middle of that dual experience of fright and excitement. I can't explain how an experience can be both frightening and exciting at the same time, but that's exactly what happened.

For example, one night we were on a celestial navigation flight from Ardmore to Dallas, Texas, to Oklahoma City and back to Ardmore. We called flying this route a triangle mission because we had to navigate correctly over three specific areas—Ardmore, Dallas, and Oklahoma City— and then back. They were called celestial navigation flights because we flew at night. On this particular flight it was a very dark night. The moon and stars were hidden by dark clouds. We had been up in the air for a few hours. As gunners we had nothing to do, so we used our parachutes as pillows and tried to grab a little sack time.

I was awakened by a sudden surge of the plane as it began to climb. I wondered why we were climbing, but I wasn't worried. Suddenly the four engines started to stall, and the plane began to fall off and fall backward. Now I was worried and so was Walt. In fact, the sudden downward spiral of the plane nearly scared us to death.

As the plane was falling, we were floating inside the plane away from the earth's gravity. It only lasted a few seconds, but it was long enough for Pop, Walt, and me to fly up and hit the top of the fuselage and then fall back down to hit the floor with a bang. We were in the back of the plane, so we had no idea what was happening or why we were being violently bounced around. For all we knew, the plane was about to crash. The pilots got the plane under control a few minutes later, and we prepared for landing. Everything had happened so fast that there was no time for communication between the pilots and us. We were shaken up by the way we had been bounced around on the plane, but no one was injured. I left the plane on shaky legs that night.

Later, Lieutenant McFall explained to us what had happened. He had given Frank control of the plane so he could close his eyes to rest them. Lieutenant Frank Irizarry, our copilot, had always wanted to be a fighter pilot, and he reminded us of that fact as often as he could. When McFall gave him control of our plane, he decided to try to execute a chandelle while piloting the four-engine bomber. To execute a chandelle maneuver, the aircraft is put into a shallow dive, then with a pull-back on the controls, the aircraft attempts to go straight up in a steep climb. It's like doing a loop in a fighter plane. Fighter pilots often needed to execute the chandelle maneuver to escape an enemy plane. Needless to say, a larger, heavier four-engine B-17 bomber with ten men on board would not react like a fighter plane would with one man on board.

McFall had been suddenly awakened by the erratic action of the plane. His hat had been on the shelf over the instrument panel, but now it was floating through the air toward him. He was startled by what was happening. All the instruments indicated a stall. McFall took back control of the airplane. With his right hand he pushed forward to full throttle, then he pushed the superchargers forward. With his left hand he pushed forward on the yoke, trying desperately to gain control of the plane. McFall finally brought the plane under control and we landed safely. I have no idea why Frank suddenly decided to execute a chandelle maneuver, unless perhaps he envisioned himself as a fighter pilot for that one time.

When we got out of the plane, McFall took Frank aside and talked to him. We couldn't hear what was being said, but it looked like McFall was upset and was letting Frank know just how wrong he was in attempting the unscheduled maneuver. When they rejoined us, the incident was not discussed, and it was never mentioned again. As far as McFall was concerned, he had his say and the incident was closed.

I had seen other plane crashes resulting in loss of life, and throughout my flight training, I had personally been in close calls and near-crashes. Nevertheless, this episode was still a very scary and unsettling experience. Naturally these events concerned me. I knew that one day our turn might come, and there was a possibility that we might not walk away from a crash. But none of those events made me fearful enough to change my mind about flying. I still had not wavered in my desire to fly with my crew into combat as an aerial gunner. I was proud to serve my country in the Air Corps, and I wanted to continue to serve even though the scary moments kept coming.

For example, I vividly remember an incident while on another training mission at Ardmore. It was December 24, 1943, my twentieth birthday. The bad weather had been the major topic of discussion for several days. We were scheduled to fly another of the triangle missions from Ardmore to Dallas, to Oklahoma City, and back to Ardmore. It seemed to be clearing up when we took off, and we rose up above the clouds without any problems. We made it to Oklahoma City all right, but on the return trip, when we were about halfway back to Ardmore, the weather took a dramatic turn for the worse. We were pounded by heavy rain. Lightning streaks were lighting up the sky all around us. We were listening on the intercom as McFall explained our situation to the base. The control tower operator said it was safer for us to land there rather than try another field. Suddenly, an extreme cold front developed when we were about a half-hour away from Ardmore. It was too late now for us to even think of trying another field. We did not have enough fuel to change our course. It was Ardmore or else. It wasn't easy to land, but we did manage to make it down safely.

Our training planes were old and beat up. They were only used for practice. As we began our descent, the leading edges of the wings began to ice up. McFall tried the deicers, but they did not work. The same problem occurred with the windshield deicer. It didn't work either. McFall and Irizarry couldn't see out of the windshield at all.

McFall called over the intercom, "Anyone who has his helmet and goggles, bring them to me." Walt had his, and worked his way up to McFall and gave him the helmet and goggles. McFall banged the inside of his window to break the outside ice off of it, so he could open the side window. Frank took over the controls. With the helmet and goggles on, McFall put his head out the open side window so he could see the runway. He held one of the intercoms in his hand and used it to yell instructions to Frank.

The plane was extremely difficult to control because it was so heavy from the ice buildup on the outside of it. Visibility was very poor, and the runway below was like a skating rink covered with sheets of ice. We landed with such a powerful impact that a lot of the ice that had formed on the plane broke off into smaller pieces. The runway was so icy that our plane skidded uncontrollably over the sheets of ice. Our plane was out of control and kept skidding off of and onto the runway. I was afraid that we were never going to stop until we crashed into something. McFall and Irizarry had a tough struggle with the controls, but finally they were able to stop the plane about four hundred yards beyond the runway in an open field. When we came to a stop, the tension that had gripped us disappeared with one big collective sigh of relief. How McFall and Irizarry landed our plane without crashing was as close to a miracle as I had ever seen. There was another plane right behind us trying to land. That plane hit the runway so hard that it broke in two, and some of the crewmembers were injured in the crash. We were happy to hear later that there were no fatalities.

That night our whole ten-man crew, officers and non-coms alike, went into town to celebrate my twentieth birthday, and perhaps partly to celebrate the survival of another close call. After surviving that frightening episode, we all felt in our hearts that McFall and Irizarry would bring us back from the war. After four months of training and flying together, we had confidence in each other. We had become like family and had a mutual trust in each other's ability to do their job properly. We did not know what would happen in the future, but we were ready to trust each other in order to survive. When in our plane, the ten of us were dependent upon each other, and we wanted to be the best combat crew to fly a B-17 into enemy territory. We came from different parts of our country, from different family backgrounds, from different religious beliefs, and we were of different ages. But none of that mattered here. We were one, one unit, one crew. It was time to move on and do the job we had been trained for.

During our earlier orientation, we had been taught that our main objective was to remain in formation and to drop our bombs on such targets as munitions factories, fuel depots, trains, railroad stations, submarine pens, and any and all military targets that would help to bring the war to an end. Our missions were never planned to target areas populated by civilians. Unfortunately, some civilians were bombed accidentally.

In attempting to accomplish our missions, we were warned to be prepared to face bad weather, mechanical problems with our planes, and flak from antiaircraft fire, as well as German fighter planes swarming all around us, shooting their machine guns. I would be less than honest if I said I felt no apprehension whatsoever. We all did.

Before we were to go overseas, it was time to get a ten-day furlough. I was positively ready for that if I could raise the money for the train fare to Boston and back. I had been sending half of my pay home to help my family. The other half I spent for cigarettes and small necessary items. I also needed to keep some money to spend for when we went out on a pass. But now it was close to the end of the month. We had not been paid yet and I was broke. My next monthly pay was not due for another week. So when I received my ten-day furlough, I did not have enough money for a trip home. I went to the Red Cross to see if I could get some money for a train ticket to Boston. Even though I was scheduled to leave for combat after my furlough, the Red Cross wouldn't lend me the money to go home.

I did not know what to do. I thought for sure I was not going to see my family. I went to the commanding officer's headquarters, and spoke to a lieutenant in the office. I explained my predicament to him and asked if there was anything else I could do. The lieutenant suggested going to the Salvation Army for help. They had an office on the base. I did as he suggested and applied for the money needed for my trip. The Salvation Army person on duty called the train station to find out how much the roundtrip ticket would cost. When he got his answer, without any further delay, the Salvation Army representative gave me the money to get the ticket. They never even asked me about paying the money back. I can tell you now, that for the past 60 years, I have tried to be very generous with donations to the Salvation Army year-round, and more so at Christmas time.

I left the base on December 26, 1943. This would be my first time home since January 1943. It took two and a half days by train to get back to Winthrop, and I arrived home too late to celebrate Christmas with my family. But it was great to see them again. My mother, father, and little brother were very happy to see me, and they were proud to see me in my uniform. I was happy to be with my family, but the first day home was rather uncomfortable for me, and I believe for my family also. We all knew that when I got back on duty, my next stop was overseas in preparation for combat. And my family and friends were not sure what to say. They asked how I liked the Army Air Corps, and I said that it was nice and I liked it a lot. But how could I tell them about the plane crashes, the near-misses, the deaths, or the gunnery training where I was being trained to shoot down planes with living men in them, even if they were the enemy? How could I explain what our bombs would do to the enemy's cities and how innocent civilians might also be killed? I knew that all this training had been necessary for us to beat the enemy, but I could not discuss it with my family. And so, after we went through the usual small talk about friends and relatives and what was happening in Winthrop, there was not a whole lot more to talk about.

That night I slept in my own bed for the first time in nearly a year. Having a room all to myself was a luxury to me now. Actually, it even felt strange not to have my crewmembers around. I soon put those thoughts aside, and was pleasantly surprised the next morning when my mother and father came into my bedroom with a breakfast tray filled with food. I thanked them very much for their love and care for me, but I told them that I would rather get up and have breakfast in the kitchen with them, so we could talk to each other about what I called "the good old days." It wasn't easy to talk about what was ahead of me, but it was fun to reminisce about the wonderful things that we had all done.

I went out later that day to walk around Winthrop just to look at all the old familiar places and to find old friends. I could not find many of my high school friends. Most of them were off in the military somewhere, but I did meet other townspeople that I knew. They greeted me warmly, and I stopped for a few minutes of conversation.

Back at the base I had celebrated my birthday on December 24, 1943. I was now twenty years old, no longer a teenager. My whole life was changed and, even though I was enjoying this short furlough home, sometimes I felt that I no longer belonged in Winthrop. I was looking forward to getting back to the base and joining my crew for the overseas assignment.

My parents wanted to celebrate my birthday with a belated birthday party. I agreed to the party if they would only invite a few relatives and close friends. I also asked them if they could have the party on New Year's Eve because I had to leave New Year's Day to get back to the base on time. We did have the party on New Year's Eve and celebrated my birthday and the arrival of the new year of 1944. It was nice to visit with aunts and uncles, my next-door neighbors, and other close family friends. That party was the last one I would have for a long time.

As my trip was coming to an end, I became even more conscious of how drastically things had changed in my life. I knew I was ready to return to my crew and do what the Air Corps had trained me to do, fly combat missions over Germany. No matter what the outcome, I was ready to do my duty. It was a good feeling to know that I would soon be back with the members of my crew, who were almost like my substitute family. We non-coms ate together, slept in the same barracks together, and hung out together. With our officers we worked together, trained together and flew our aircraft together. Our lives were dependent upon each other, and we had vowed to watch out for each other in combat.

On New Year's Day my family was up early. I was packed and ready to leave. After saying my goodbyes to the family, my father drove me to South Station in Boston where I took the train for Chicago. I had to change trains in Chicago to get to Oklahoma City, and from there, take a bus to get back to the Ardmore base. My ten-day furlough was over. Out of the ten days, I had spent five days traveling back and forth, and only five days at home. In spite of the short time I had at home, the remembrance of the warmth, love, and friendship that greeted me during the visit was to remain with me during the dark days ahead.

Chapter Three

Going Overseas

When we got back to Ardmore, Oklahoma, from our furloughs, the instructors began preparing us for our trip overseas. We attended orientation sessions and received more shots to protect us from the various diseases and illnesses that can often occur in wartime. Mostly, we just waited impatiently for our next assignment. Rumors were rampant throughout the base. Many different destinations were named, but we still were unsure where we were going. Everyone guessed correctly that our final destination would be England, but nobody guessed exactly where we would be sent in England.

At the end of January 1944, we boarded a very crowded troop train and were on our way to Grand Island, Nebraska. We arrived on February 4. Our crew was assigned to the transit barracks. The transit barracks were for airmen who were only going to be here for a few days from the time they arrived at the base to the time they left for their new assignments.

We received all of our new flying equipment. Our high-altitude clothing consisted of heated suits and gloves and heated felt booties. This type of clothing was designed to keep us warm while flying on our missions. We also received our oxygen masks, parachutes, and a heavy cloth satchel that was our flight bag. The flight bag was extremely heavy when it was filled with our flying equipment. Our barracks bags were filled with our regular uniforms and miscellaneous items. Then, as if the flight bag and the barracks bag were not enough to carry, we had to carry our parachutes separately. I was five feet nine and weighed 155 pounds. It was a struggle to carry everything at once, but I managed to do it.

A new silver B-17G was assigned to our crew. Hopes were high that maybe this was going to be our regular plane. The plane was not camouflaged because the Air Corps had stopped using camouflage paint by this time. A couple of days later we received our overseas orders. The

```
                    R E S T R I C T E D

                ARMY AIR BASE HEADQUARTERS
                  Grand Island, Nebraska

370.5 # 140 (106-39)                          8 February 1944

SUBJECT:  Movement Order, Heavy Bombardment Crew Number FG-200-AA113, to Overseas
          Destination.

TO:     P     2nd Lt  McFALL, GEORGE K.          0748444
        CP    2nd Lt  IRIZARRY, FRANK E.         0813901
        N     1st Lt  BRAZIS, EDWARD G.          0670712
        B     2nd Lt  EGGMAN, ROY J.             0689141
        MG    S/Sgt   Kemp, William D.           14138665
        ROG   S/Sgt   Alcorn, Ernest M.          17161142
        AG    Sgt     Krupitsch, Willy (NMI)     32818164
        G     Sgt     Sirianni, Ralph E., Jr.    31271422
        G     Sgt     Grimshaw, Alan (NMI)       39553674
        G     Sgt     Pawlesh, Walter (NMI)Jr.   33439816


        1.  You are assigned to Shipment FG-200-AA, as crew number FG-200-AA113, and
to B017 Airplane number 42-97059, on aircraft project number 92456-R.  You are
equipped in accordance with subject movement order.

        2.  You are relieved from atchd, unasgd 9th Heavy Bomb Proc Hq, this station,
and WP via mil acft and/or rail to Presque Isle Army Air Field, Presque Isle, Maine,
or such other ATC, Air Departure Station, as the CG, ATC, may direct, thence to the
overseas destination of Shipment FG-200-AA.

        3.  This is a PERMANENT change of station.  Personnel involved in this move-
ment will not be accompanied by dependents; neither will dependents join personnel
at any assembly point, nor at the ATC, departure station.  Except as may be necess-
ary in the transaction of official business, you will not discuss this movement.
```

The crew receives orders for overseas destination.

orders were very brief and rather vague so that the enemy could not use the information. Our orders simply read: "Movement Order. Heavy Bombardment crew, number FG-200-AA113, to overseas destination."

While we were at the Grand Island air base, and about to ship out for overseas, our navigator, Lieutenant Robert White, became ill and had to go to the base hospital. Lieutenant McFall was notified that White was too sick to remain with our crew. Lieutenant Edward Brazies was assigned as our replacement navigator. We were sorry that Bob White was sick, but Ed Brazies seemed to fit right in with the rest of our crew. All of us were pleased to have another well-trained navigator.

On February 8, 1944, we flew the new B-17G out of Grand Island. Our orders were to report to the Presque Isle Army Air Field in Presque Isle, Maine. As we got closer to Presque Isle, the weather got worse. McFall was notified not to proceed to Presque Isle because of the bad weather there. Instead we were diverted to Grenier Field in Manchester, New Hampshire. At Grenier Field, I was less than fifty miles from my home in Winthrop,

Massachusetts. Unfortunately, we were not allowed off the base and could not make phone calls. We were leaving the next day for Goose Bay, Labrador, in Canada. Early the next morning we took off in the B-17G and headed for Goose Bay. It was a short flight of about two or three hours.

As we approached the field at Goose Bay, Lieutenant McFall radioed the control tower for landing instructions. The air traffic controller gave McFall the landing instructions, and ended his communication with the words, "I just want to let you know that it's 30 degrees below zero at ground level. Tell your crewmembers to dress warmly."

McFall quickly responded, "They're already dressed as warmly as they can be. It's 35 degrees below zero up here."

We landed without incident, and the ground crew immediately began to put heavy canvas covers over the four engines of the plane. These form-fitted heavy canvases were especially made to protect the engines in this extremely cold weather. We helped the ground crew throw a canvas over each engine so that the canvas reached the ground on each side of the engine. The canvas covers fit perfectly over the tops of the engines, and went right down to the ground. The ground crew placed a small heater on the ground under each of the four canvas covers. The warmth from the small heaters would help to prevent the oil in the engines from congealing.

When we finished helping the ground crew, we went right to the barracks. We wanted to get our gear put away before we went to the mess hall. The snow in the alleys between the barracks was almost up to the roof. The ground crew had cleared most of the walkways and pushed the snow in between the buildings. W had been told that we were restricted to the base and no passes were going to be issued to us. Even if passes had been granted, there was no place to go and nothing to do. Anyhow, I was too cold to go anywhere.

Goose Bay was extremely cold and very boring. To kill time while waiting for our next assignment, we played cards and got as much sack time as we could. The first night at the base I went to a movie. It didn't matter to me what the movie was. Like most of the airmen, I went just for something to do. On our second day at Goose Bay we met with our officers, who told us our orders had come through, and it was time to go. We were ordered to fly the B-17G to the Nuts Corner Air Base in Ireland. The snow had stopped, and the weather was clear, but strong winds prevailed, and taking off could be dangerous. In spite of the strong winds, we got the signal to go and managed to take off successfully. The two boring days in Goose Bay were over, and we were glad to be on our way to Ireland.

The flight to the Nuts Corner Air Base took us six to seven hours.

When we landed at the air base, they had assigned barracks all ready for us. We had just settled into the barracks when we were notified that our crew was being issued a one-day pass for the next day. This was good news for all of us. At the other stopovers, we were hustled in and out so fast that no passes were issued. I was happy to be able to get off any base for a short leave. It would give me a chance to relax and see something of Ireland. The city of Belfast was only four or five kilometers from the Nuts Corner Air Base. My crew, including the officers, decided that Belfast was where we should spend the day.

Before leaving the base, we exchanged some of our American money for British currency, and then the ten of us headed for the bus stop at the front gate. There were so many airmen waiting for the bus, that we figured we would make better time if we walked the four or five kilometers to Belfast.

On the way to Belfast, I noticed the thatched roofs on many of the small farmhouses that we passed. I wondered if the thatched roofs were strong enough to keep the rain out. I did not see any telephone poles or electrical wiring, so I assumed that they did not have telephones or electricity. Near one of the houses five young children were leaning on the fence watching us walk down the road. We were happily singing as we walked along. The youngsters called to us, and we stopped by the fence for a few moments and talked to them. It was fun to stop and talk with the young children. They had a lot of questions for us to answer, and we enjoyed taking the time to talk to them.

For this short time on our walk, I felt freed from all my duties, my concerns, and my thoughts of the future. It was such a pleasure to be strolling down this road with my friends. As we walked on, we continued to sing such songs as "Six Pence" and "One Keg of Beer." Everyone could hear us coming down the road. Some people came out of their houses and offered us glasses of milk or a drink of cold water from their well. They smiled at us and welcomed us, and we cheerily smiled back.

Farther down the road, the owners of a small but charming house came outside and invited us to come in and see their home. The owner's four children were waiting inside to greet us. This house was so different from my house back in Massachusetts. The thatched roofs still intrigued me, and I asked the husband if it kept the rain out. He assured us that their thatched roof was very strong and it certainly did keep the rain out. The floors were hard-packed dirt that seemed to be as hard as a slate floor. The interior of the home was spotlessly clean. The children's mother offered each of us a glass of cold milk, which we thankfully accepted. The milk tasted more like a light cream. It was delicious. I personally would have liked to stay a little longer and learn more about Ireland and the people, but some of the crewmembers were ready to move on. We had a limited time, and wanted to get to Belfast. On the way out of the house we gave the four children some of our British coins.

This walk was one of the most pleasurable times in my life. I knew I would always hold the memory of this walk and these people in my thoughts. How could I ever forget the beauty of Ireland and the warmth of its people? I was really glad that we had decided to walk instead of waiting for the bus.

When we finally arrived in Belfast, I was surprised that it was such a big, crowded city. I thought it would be like a small town. We walked around the downtown area until it was lunchtime. We stopped at one of the storefront vendors to buy some fish and chips to "take away" as the Irish called it. Back home we called it "take out." The deep-fried fish was excellent and the chips were just like our french fries back home. It was fascinating to watch the way the vendor served the fish and chips to us. The cook at the deep fryer took some pieces of an old newspaper and rolled the paper in such a way that it made a cone-shaped container. He put our fish and chips into separate containers, one for each of us, and we walked along the sidewalk eating. I was a little concerned about the newspaper wrapping. It seemed to be reasonably clean, but newspapers were not always the cleanest things to wrap food in. Nevertheless, I thoroughly enjoyed eating my fish and chips as I walked around in Belfast.

We finished eating, threw our cone-shaped newspapers into the trash barrel, and continued walking around, taking in all the wonderful sights. It felt good to be away from the base for a while. I was beginning to feel almost

Front cover of booklet about Britain and how the American airmen should behave in England.

like a tourist on vacation. Belfast was a beautiful city, and we enjoyed the leisurely freedom of wandering around seeing the sights. We only had one day to visit Belfast so we made the most of the time. It was a pleasure to see the charm of the old buildings and churches and to feel the friendliness and warmth of the people.

The one-day pass and the chance to go sightseeing and meet so many wonderful people seemed to cast a magic spell on us. For one day, at least, there was no war, no orientation sessions, and no planes flying around us. It was great. But now the day was almost over and it was time to go back. We took the bus back so we would not be late returning to the base.

The next day the lectures and orientation sessions began, and they were continued every day until it was time for us to leave. In one of the lectures, an officer told us how we were expected to behave with our British Allies when we got to England. We were reminded that we were guests of the British people and their government. We were to show respect for British military personnel and civilians at all times. Then we were warned to be very careful not to do anything that would embarrass our government. I guessed, from these strong warnings, that there had been problems with some of our military personnel who had been here before us. I certainly had no intention of creating any problems. I just wanted to get on with our trip to England, and prepare for our combat missions. We did not get any information about flying combat missions while we were at the Nuts Corner Air Base. Evidently that training would take place at our new base in England.

We were at the air base for four days when our orders to move out finally came. An officer notified us that we were going to travel by train to southern Ireland, where a ferry would be waiting to transfer us to England. "Why a train?" I wondered. What about the B-17G that we had flown over here? I thought that was going to be our combat plane, but I was wrong. We did not know it at the time, but we had been assigned only to fly the B-17G to the Nuts Corner Air Base. The B-17G would remain at the air base, where it would be completely outfitted for combat. Another crew would take it to England.

The train ride from the air base to the ferry took about one and a half hours. The ferry was at the dock waiting for us, and we began boarding. There were about two hundred and fifty to three hundred men going aboard, which made the ferry very crowded. All the men were airmen being sent as replacement crews. Since there were always ten men to a crew, these two hundred and fifty to three hundred men represented twenty-five to thirty new crews. I hoped that our new base had thirty planes ready for us. It had been a long time for me between signing up for military service in January 1943 to being on this ferry now in February 1944. Sometimes I felt that we would never get to our combat base. Naturally I realized that all the training we had completed so far was necessary, but now I was anxious to get to our destination and join in the combat missions. I really wanted to get our plane and begin flying combat missions. The desire to serve my country and help to protect it from the Germans far outweighed any feelings of fear I might feel from time to time.

During the ferry ride, our crew chatted with each other to pass the time. They must have felt the same way I did about getting a plane. We began to think about a name for our plane even though we did not have it yet. When we began to discuss naming the plane, Lieutenant McFall said that we should wait until we got to the base. Then each one of us could write down his choice for a name, and we could check the names and vote on which one to choose. This sounded good to me. I had heard rumors that the pilot would be the one to name the plane, but I liked McFall's idea better.

The ferry arrived in England, and we disembarked. It was the last week in February. There were trucks and buses waiting for us. After putting our bags and equipment in the trucks, we boarded the buses that were taking crews to different bases to join their bomb group. My bomb group was the 388th Bomb Group, 563rd Bomb Squadron. The 388th Bomb Group Airfield was one of some sixty airfields scattered over the British countryside. The base was located at Knettishall, about 90 kilometers from London, and I wondered if I would ever get a chance to see London.

It didn't take long to reach Knettishall, and as I got off the bus I took a few minutes to look out over the field. The control tower was located at the edge of the runways so that the controllers were able to direct takeoffs and landings. The crash crew, the fire apparatus, and the ambulances were located together in a special area on the field. It was important for them to be placed on the field in order to reach the planes quickly. After every mission there were always some planes damaged and some men wounded. The crash crew needed to be nearby when the planes returned from a mission; it was their duty to be ready when the planes landed. They were the rescue team, ready to put out fires on damaged planes, to rescue the wounded airmen, and to take care of the wounded until the medical team arrived. The doctors and orderlies from the hospital were also ready for any emergencies.

There was a small chapel on the base. The chapel was used a lot, especially before missions. The hardstands, sometimes called the revetments, were scattered on the outer perimeter of the airfield. Every crew had a designated area where their aircraft was parked. These hardstands were purposely

British Nissen hut.

spread out so that when German aircraft came over to bomb or strafe the field, our aircraft wouldn't be grouped together as an easy target. The base only had a few hangars, and these were reserved for planes needing major repairs. Most of the repairs were made at the hardstand site by the ground crew.

As was customary at most bases, we were assigned to a barracks right away. Our officers were assigned to officers' quarters, and we were assigned to the noncoms' barracks. These barracks were not like our wooden barracks. They were British Nissen huts, which were prefabricated buildings made of corrugated steel, similar to our American Quonset huts. Our Nissen hut was a huge room that we shared with two other combat crews who were already there. That made a total of 18 men in the one Nissen hut. But we were not too overcrowded. It was a very large room.

The accommodations were pretty good. There were six empty bunks, three on one side of the room, and three on the other side. The two crews already there had the other twelve bunks. Some members of the other two crews were in the room when we arrived, and they made us feel welcome. The coal-burning stove in the center of the room kept the Nissen hut nice and warm. The warmth felt good after walking through the cold, damp weather from the bus to the hut. Not that I really minded the cold, damp weather outside. Compared to the cold in Goose Bay, Labrador, this was like being in the tropics.

Empty footlockers were at the end of our bunks, and we quickly filled them with our gear. In back of each bunk there was a small shelf to put shaving cream, soap, and other small items on. A bar was attached underneath the shelf to hang our clothes on. As I began hanging some of my extra clothes up and putting other gear in the footlocker, I couldn't help wondering what might have happened to the men who had been here before. Had they finished their missions and gone back to the states on furlough, or had they gone out on a mission and never come back? No matter how hard you try to avoid thinking of things like this, the thoughts find their way into your head, and you have to shake them off.

By the time we finished putting all our gear away, the men in the hut told us it was time for dinner. They offered to show us the way to the mess hall. We were all trying to be cheerful and friendly. It was a good feeling to finally be settled in someplace.

The mess hall was filled with many crews who, like our crew, stayed pretty much together. Some of these crews had flown on combat missions already, and some were new like us. Some of the men were quiet and somber. It was hard to tell what was on their minds. Had they been on missions and lost crew members, or were they getting ready for their first mission? I already knew enough not to ask too many questions. Some crewmembers were loudly describing what it was like as enemy aircraft were attacking their formations. Others described what it was like to see our American aircraft get shot down.

After our meal, as we walked back to our barracks, there was not much in the way of small talk. The war had just come closer to us. I was feeling a little somber myself after hearing the stories of combat from those who had been on missions. It was late, and I was tired from our trip from Ireland to England and then the added bus ride from the ferry. I dropped on my bunk and fell asleep from pure exhaustion.

The next day, after a good night's sleep, I felt much more cheerful and ready to face the day. Today was the big day to name our plane, even though we did not have one yet. Before we split up, with us non-coms in one Nissen hut and the officers in another, we had agreed to meet with our officers later at the day room to discuss the naming of our plane. We were looking forward to getting our plane, and we wanted to be ready with the name when one was assigned to us.

At our meeting, Lieutenant McFall repeated what he had said on the ferry. He told us to write our suggestions on a piece of paper, and then he would read the ten names. McFall handed each of us a small piece of paper on which to write the suggested name. I had thought of a name for the plane while I was still in Grand Island, Nebraska. I had not mentioned it to anyone because we were not yet near to being assigned a plane. I took the small piece of paper from McFall, and wrote the words "Heaven Can Wait" on it. I had thought of this particular name because of what it represented to me. I hoped that on our missions "heaven can wait" before taking any of us. It's difficult to explain, but I just felt that it would be a good name for our plane.

Each crewmember wrote down his choice of a name and put the slip of paper in McFall's hat. We did not mention the names out loud. The hat was passed around and then returned to McFall. He picked out the papers one at a time, and read the names out loud. Out of the ten slips of paper, two crewmen had chosen the same name, "Heaven Can Wait," without knowing that the other person had also chosen it. I was very surprised that someone had thought of the same name that I had. I asked who else wrote that name, "Heaven Can Wait"? Our tail gunner, Walt Pawlesh, said he wrote it. I asked him why he chose that name? He shrugged his shoulders and said, "It just seemed like a good idea." McFall said that it seemed like a good omen to have two men come up with the same name. The crew agreed, and the vote was unanimous for our plane to be called Heaven Can Wait. We returned to our quarters with a feeling of satisfaction for having agreed on our plane's new name.

At 2:30 the next morning, the "wake up" sergeant came into our Nissen hut to wake the other two crews for their combat mission. One of the crews had already flown three combat missions, but the other crew, led by Lieutenant Amann, was going on their first mission. Because of the close quarters, our crew woke up also. There was very little talking among my crew as we watched the other men prepare for their combat mission. We did not know where they were going, and they probably didn't know yet. They would go to breakfast first and then at their briefing they would learn the target. It was a somber moment for us. It was the first time we had seen men prepare for their mission, and I said nothing to anyone. I was wondering how I would feel when the call came for my first combat mission.

Later that morning, we learned that Lieutenant Amann's first combat mission was scheduled for Berlin. The squadrons were on the way to complete the mission when they were forced to abort because of adverse weather conditions. They returned to the base. It was not until they landed that Amann's crew discovered that there was a death on the plane. Sergeant Lutes, the right waist gunner, had died from anoxia as the result of his face mask freezing up on him.

We had only known Sergeant Lutes for the one day when we moved into the same Nissen hut, but that did not make it any less difficult to watch the remaining five enlisted men from his crew return to our Nissen hut. You could tell that they were agonizing over the death of one of their crew. Lutes' death alerted us to the stark, grim reality of flying combat, and taught us an important lesson. We were already in combat from the moment our plane took off from the airfield. We did not have to fly over enemy territory to die. Lute's death reminded us that we were vulnerable from the moment we took off until the final moment when we landed back on the base.

During training we had seen a couple of accidents resulting in deaths and injuries, but they were occasional occurrences, usually due to equipment failure or bad weather. But in combat our planes went up day after day to bomb the Germans. It did not take us long to realize that the odds of everyone returning safely were not too good.

Sergeant Lutes' death made us remember one of the classes that we had during our training. The class was designed to teach us the effect high-altitude flying had on our body. The instructor told us how the lack of oxygen at high altitudes could cause anoxia, which would result in a crewman's passing out within fifteen seconds. Death would occur a few minutes later. Sergeant Lutes' death brought that lesson home to us very emphatically.

Lieutenant McFall, our pilot, was very concerned about Lutes' death, and he was determined to make sure that none of us died in that way. He called all of us together and told us that one of our responsibilities was to make frequent checks on the oxygen and on each other. Bombardier Roy Eggman and Navigator Ed Brazies were located close together in the nose of the plane, and McFall told them to watch out for each other. McFall, as pilot, Irizzary, as copilot, and the engineer, Sergeant William Kemp, were within touching distance of each other, and they were told to check on each other periodically. The radio operator, Sergeant Ernest Alcorn, was close enough to Sergeant Willy Krupitsch, the ball turret gunner, for each of them to keep an eye on the other. Sergeant Alan "Pop" Grimshaw, the left waist gunner, and me, the right waist gunner, were so close that we were always bumping into each other. We were to watch out for each other, and also we were in a position where we could help Ernie keep an eye on Willy, the ball turret gunner. Sergeant Walter Pawlesh's isolated position in the tail made it difficult for him to keep an eye on anybody, so Walt and I reaffirmed our agreement to keep an eye on each other and check each other more often. Little did I know that these extra precautions would pay off later.

Another unsettling incident occurred one night in our Nissen hut. We had not as yet been assigned a mission and I was becoming a little anxious to get moving and have our crew assigned to a mission. When the assignments were announced that night, we still were not given a mission. One of the other crews in our hut was assigned to the mission. Once again we would just have to wait. I was trying to relax at my bunk, when I noticed that one of the airmen was sitting on his bunk with a bottle of liquor in his hand. He was drinking from the bottle. I hoped he wasn't one of the men going on the mission the next morning. Just then another airman entered the hut, and he became furious when he saw the man drinking. He rushed over to the crewmember who was drinking, and grabbed the bottle out of his hand. He carried the bottle over to the potbelly stove, opened the top of the stove, and poured the liquor in. When the liquor hit the fire, flames shot up into the air, and nearly burned his hands. He was really upset with the man who had been drinking and he let him know it in no uncertain terms. Both of these men were members of the crew that was scheduled to fly the mission the next morning. Fortunately, the airman who had been caught drinking was stopped in time. He was able to fly the mission the next morning with his crew. Alcoholic beverages the night before a mission were clearly against the rules, and anyone breaking the rule created a dangerous situation for the other men who would be flying with him.

The weather in February was not the best for flying in jolly old England. For the first week at the Knettishall Base we had been scheduled for orientation sessions. At our first meeting, the captain who was in charge of meeting new crews instructed us on how to behave when meeting the local people. He even gave us pamphlets with instructions printed in them as a reminder in case we received a pass to go to London or to the town of Knettishall. We never did get a chance to go to London. We not only had to become familiar with the location of the various buildings and areas of the air base, but we were kept busy attending many orientation sessions to learn more about our future combat assignments. Some of these meetings included showing films of actual combat missions.

Watching the combat films made me more anxious to get into combat. Fear seemed to be replaced by the excitement of getting into the fight even though it meant facing the unknown. I knew that the entire crew was also eager to start our missions because we had discussed being combat ready after watching the films. Waiting was sometimes harder than just going on the missions. We were anxious to get a plane assigned to us so we could have the ground crew paint the name "Heaven Can Wait" on it.

One day, after yet another lecture was over, the captain called Lieutenant McFall aside and said to him, "You've been assigned your plane. It's out on the revetment waiting for you and your crew." McFall told us that we had our plane and he would notify the crew chief for our plane to have "Heaven Can Wait" painted on it. The men who painted the names on the planes knew what to do, and they would take care of it. We were excited. At last we had a plane and were closer to doing what we had been trained to do, fly combat missions. It may seem strange to some that we were eager to fly combat missions and maybe get killed, and sometimes it is difficult to explain. But I felt a certain satisfaction and pride in finally getting our own plane that we had personally named. I sincerely hoped that the name "Heaven Can Wait" was going to be lucky for us.

CHAPTER FOUR

The Missions

Our mission #1 (388th Bomb Group Mission #78)
March 9, 1944   Target: Berlin

It was March 8, 1944. They told us that we were flying a mission the next day and would be awakened at 0230. (2:30 A.M.). The NCO Club (the Noncommissioned officers' club) was usually open until 10 P.M., but it was always closed at 7 P.M. on the night before a posted mission. Nobody wanted the men to have a hangover or be sick the next morning. Closing the NCO club early did not bother me at all because I planned to go to bed early to be rested for the wake-up call. I did go to bed early, but going to bed was the easy part. Getting to sleep was easier said than done. Just thinking about our first mission was enough to keep me awake. I had no idea what would happen to us on this mission, but after listening to some of the combat experiences from the crews of other planes, I began to think about the length of the mission and the flak we would get. I could almost picture hundreds of German fighter planes attacking us.

Eventually I was tired enough to fall asleep, but it seemed like I had no sooner fallen asleep than it was 2:30 A.M., and the sergeant was calling for us to get up. He came stomping into the hut, and began yelling, "It's time to get up. Let's go. Let's go. Everybody up. It's time to get ready for your mission."

It was so dark and cold outside that it didn't seem like it could be morning already. I dragged myself out of my bunk and went out into the cold to the Nissen hut next to our hut. This hut served as a latrine and as the only place to shower and shave. I wore the shorts that I had slept in, and carried clean shorts along with my towel, soap, shaving cream, and razor. Some of the men who had been here much longer than me had bathrobes with them. They were prepared for the cold walk between Nissen

388th Bomb Group, B-17.

huts. I did not have a robe, and had to suffer the cold going back and forth to the showers.

I had already been warned that shaving was a must before we left for a mission. If any of the men allowed a beard to grow, no matter how slight, they would soon find out that wearing an oxygen mask for five or six hours during the flight could result in itchy, irritated skin. At 23,000 feet you could not take off the oxygen mask. You would just have to suffer. I had just turned twenty years old in December and did not have much of a beard, but there was a little fuzz on my face. I decided to shave the fuzz off and not take any chances with skin irritation. Strangely enough, rather than worrying about the mission, it made me feel good to be shaving along with the other men.

I showered, put on my clean shorts, shaved, and returned to my own Nissen hut. I put on my flight clothing, and was ready to go to breakfast. It was too early to put on our high-altitude flying equipment yet. We would do that after breakfast. While we were dressing, we laughed and joked with each other. Our crewmembers were not silent like we had been a couple of days ago when we watched one of the other crews get ready for their mission. Maybe our joking and laughing seemed like callousness or bravado. It might even have seemed like boasting, but it really was to ease our own tension. Others had told us that the first mission was the hardest to adjust to, and maybe it was. I know that deep down I was scared of what might happen, and yet I was not afraid to join with my crew on the mission.

When we left the barracks, a truck was waiting outside to take us to the mess hall. Some of the crews had already finished breakfast and were leaving just as we were going in. A normal morning's breakfast was powdered eggs, toast, and bacon, with ham once in awhile. But going to breakfast this early on a mission day was special. We could have bacon, ham or corned beef hash, hash brown potatoes, and real eggs cooked any way we wanted. There was plenty of hot coffee, but we had to be careful not to drink too much of the coffee. No one wanted to have to relieve themselves by using the relief tubes located in various positions on the aircraft. In an aircraft at 24,000 feet with an inside temperature at 35 degrees below zero, it was not a very pleasant experience. And it could be dangerous because your skin could freeze to the metal relief tube. Also, you could not leave your position during combat. So I only had one cup of coffee, and I noticed that most of my crewmembers did not drink too much coffee.

The smell of the bacon and eggs filled the room. The noisy clatter of the aluminum food trays, and the chatter of nearly one hundred men as they ate breakfast together, echoed throughout the mess hall. By the time we got to the mess hall, many of the men had already finished their breakfast and had lighted up their cigarettes.

We had only been at Knettishall for a few days, so we did not know all of the crews. But, for me, sitting here with all of the men, especially with my own crew, was a calming experience. I knew that the odds of every single plane and every single man returning safely were too high for me to even contemplate. It was still exciting to be going out on our first mission, and, once again, I put my trust in God and my fellow crewmembers.

After we finished breakfast, we went to the briefing hut, where we sat up back with the noncoms. Our four officers, McFall, Irizarry, Brazies, and Eggman, sat down front with the other officers. The briefing room was filled with long benches and some folding chairs. A small foot-high stage was located at the front of the room. A four-by-six-foot easel on the stage platform was covered with a white sheet. As men began to enter the room, the murmur of voices got louder and louder. They were all talking to each other and guessing what our target would be.

The intelligence officer, a captain, was already standing on the platform when we entered. When the CO (commanding officer) entered the room, someone yelled, "Ten-shun!" Everybody rose and snapped to attention. All conversation ceased. In the past year, I had been called to attention many times, but this time, it was very special to me. It was in preparation for my first mission. I wanted to pay close attention so I could hear and understand everything that was said.

The CO said, "Be seated, gentlemen." He then nodded to the intelligence officer to continue. The captain removed the white sheet from the easel. I could see then that there was a map of the continent on the easel. A piece of red yarn was attached to the map with pins. The red yarn curved from England across the North Sea to the continent and then to our target, Berlin. The red yarn showed us the route to be taken to get to Berlin. It was not a straight route. We could never fly a straight route to the target because we did not want the Germans to know exactly where we were going.

When Berlin was revealed as the target, a collective groan came from some of the experienced crews who had been on previous missions. Berlin had been bombed before, but not often, and the crews knew that the city was one target that was sure to be protected by extra-heavy flak and a lot of fighters.

The captain waited a moment until the groans died down, and then he proceeded to brief us on the route to Berlin and back to the base. He told us we could expect very heavy flak and many German fighters, and he indicated on the map where we could expect flak and fighters. Then he pointed again to Berlin on the map, and said, "Ordinarily there would be ninety 80mm cannons shooting at you."

"But," he continued, "early this morning three of the cannons were reported as out of action, so there are only eighty-seven cannons operational."

I heard some snickers from the men, but I just stared at the captain. I didn't know whether to laugh or groan. If it was the captain's attempt at humor, I did not see the humor in it.

The captain continued his briefing. "The Germans have seventy-five Me-109 fighter planes at the airfield. But we have received information that three of the fighters were being repaired, so only seventy-two German fighters can come up to challenge you."

Maybe the intelligence officer thought that adding a little humor would take some of the apprehension away from us. The captain's humor was about as funny to me as a broken leg would be. As soon as the briefing was over, we left the briefing hut. There was always a chaplain available when a combat mission was getting ready to take off. Some of the crewmembers would spend a few minutes with the chaplain for prayer.

After the main briefing was over, the navigators had a special meeting while the bombardiers and radio operators stopped to gather other information. The copilot received ten escape kits to hand out to the crew later. The rest of our crew went on ahead to a special area to get our high-altitude suits and other flying gear such as our flak suits, parachutes, Mae West life preserver jackets, and our 45 automatic pistols. When we reached our plane, Irizarry gave us our escape kits. These kits could be helpful if we were shot down. They contained German and French money, matches, chocolate bars, a compass and knife, and a map of the continent. The map was made on silk instead of paper. Silk was very light and much easier to fold than paper. This made the map easier to fold and put into the escape kits. I hoped I never had to use one of the escape kits.

Our officers were with us as our truck pulled up to the revetment, where we saw our plane for the first time. Two spotlights on the ground lighted the plane. We could see that we were not lucky enough to get one of the new silver B-17Gs like the one we had flown to England. But when we looked closer at the plane, we could see the insignia painted on the ship. The insignia looked fantastic. It was a portrait of a beautiful blue sky with a white cloud formation. Heaven Can Wait was painted in the middle of the blue sky and cloud formation. We stood for a moment and just enjoyed looking at our aircraft. Nobody said anything. This was our plane. We had finally reached the time when we were ready to do what we had been trained for. In a few minutes we would be flying off the base for our first mission.

The ordinance and armament crew had cleaned and oiled all the .50-caliber machine guns and placed five hundred rounds of ammunition at each gun position. The bombs had been loaded while we slept. It was time for our preflight check. Every member of the crew had preflight duties to perform while our plane was still at the hardstand. My job was to check my right waist gun position to make sure the correct amount of ammunition was there, to check the oxygen outlet and to plug in my oxygen mask, as well as to check my radio headset and throat mike.

I was the second engineer, and after the crew completed all the preflight duties in the plane, I had to go out on the hardstand and meet with our pilot, George McFall and our first engineer, Bill Kemp. The three of us would go around the plane making a visual inspection of all the outer parts of the aircraft, checking everything including engines, flaps, and landing gear. As the second engineer, I had been through flight engineer training. I knew as much about the functions of the aircraft as the first flight engineer. If something happened to the first flight engineer on our mission, I would have to take over.

After we finished the preflight checks and the visual check of the exterior of the plane, we had to wait in line for five to ten minutes before the green flare went up from the control tower. The green flare was the signal for takeoff. Up to the time of takeoff our whole crew had been busy with preflight checks, but now we all were at our assigned places in the plane with the engines running. Waiting for the green flare to go up was one of the most difficult times for me. No one spoke. We just watched and waited to see the green flare so we could begin our mission. Those few minutes we waited for takeoff were stressful, and sometimes the wait made crewmembers a little anxious. I actually began to relax when the green flare went up. It meant we were on our way at last. Instead of being apprehensive, I was very excited.

As plane after plane took off from the field, McFall moved our plane closer to takeoff. I knew there were always problems that could occur during takeoff, problems like fire in the engine or collisions with another aircraft in bad weather, but I had confidence in McFall and the rest of my crew, and tried not to think of all the things that could go wrong. We knew there would be flak and enemy fighters. We knew that we might die this day, but as we joined our airborne squadron we were prepared and ready to face the enemy.

Twenty-one planes were in our squadron plus three additional planes designated as spares. Each of the other two squadrons also had three spares. Our complete formation consisted of three squadrons and nine spares for a total of 72 planes. The spares were backups ready to take the place of any plane in the formation that had to abort for any reason. When a plane had to abort the mission and head back to the base, one of the spares moved up to replace that aircraft in the formation. When the formation reached a certain designated point, the pilots of the spare planes not needed were notified by radio that it was all right for them to turn back to base. The designated point was either over the English Channel or the middle of the North Sea. This mission was to Berlin, so the turnback point was the North Sea. At the briefing our plane had been designated as one of the three spares. But that did not make us feel any easier. Quite often the spares were called upon to move up into the formation and complete the bombing run. So, even though we were one of the three spares, we prepared carefully, checked all our equipment, loaded our .45 automatics and took off for Berlin.

Later, as our bombing group, escorted by fighter planes, flew over the North Sea, all nine spares, including us, were ordered back to base along with some of the fighters. None of the planes in the formation had to abort, and we had reached the designated turnback point. Our bombs were not yet armed, so we did not have to jettison them somewhere. Once the bombs were armed, we would be unable to land back at the base because they might explode when landing. Some of our fighters returned to the base with us as protection in case German fighters attacked us. The rest of the fighter planes stayed with the bomber formation. When they got low on fuel they would have to leave the bombers and turn back to the base. The bomber squadrons heading for Berlin would no longer have fighter cover for protection.

When we headed back to the base, I felt somewhat disappointed that we had to turn back. Nobody wants to die, but I had prepared myself mentally to face a completed mission. Even though we were a spare, I was hoping to be able to complete the mission over Berlin. Flying combat with the other nine members of my crew made me feel safe and free from doubt. My fear was somewhat abated by my confidence in my training and in the expertise of my crew. I believed that the whole crew felt the same way, and this made it easier to face the challenge of combat.

Twenty-five completed missions were necessary before we could get rotated home. Unfortunately, aborted missions, and missions where spares were not used in the actual raid, did not count toward our twenty-five missions. Nevertheless, for each bombing mission, whether designated as a "spare" or not, we never knew whether we would get called back or have to abort. We never knew if we would get shot down, or if we would complete the mission and return safely. So each time we took off from the airfield for a bombing raid over Germany, I was ready mentally and physically to face the enemy.

Our mission #2   (388th Bomb Group Mission #79)
March 15, 1944   Target: Brunswick

It was now March 14, 1944. Our first mission had been five days ago, on March 9. We never completed that one because we were a spare and had not been needed. We were bored during the five days of waiting for another mission. Some days the flying weather was so bad that no planes could take off at all. Sometimes it seemed like the English weather consisted of nothing but fog, fog, and more fog. During the wait for our next mission we tried to keep busy. We played cards, wrote letters home, and saw some movies on the base, mostly John Wayne movies. Sometimes we had a few beers at the Noncoms' Club. We even had bicycles available to ride around the base. There were a lot of bicycles around the Nissen huts, and I asked someone why there were so many available. He said that the men bought bicycles, and then some of those men were shot down on a later mission. Their bicycles were left with all the others. This story did not exactly cheer me up. The thought of the bicycles' owners now being dead or captured did nothing to motivate me toward bicycle riding, and, in fact, the story was a little disturbing. But I always tried to think positive, and, along with my crewmembers, I continued to believe that we could make it through this war.

All the crews were always on standby. We never knew when our next mission would be assigned until the day before. Because we all were on standby, no passes were issued. Passes were only given out after a crew had completed five missions. Then they could get a four- or five-day pass. A five-day pass was the best. Five days was long enough for a quick trip to London and back.

We got the word later in the day that we were going on a mission the next morning, March 15, 1944. We were no longer bored. We were going out on our second mission. We went to bed early to get some sleep before the early-morning wake-up call. The next morning we did all the usual things to prepare for the mission. We ate our breakfast, prepared our gear, and went to the morning briefing. At the briefing we found out that our target was Brunswick, but we also found out that we were once again designated as one of the three spares. Unless something happened and the spares were needed, we would not be completing the mission. It was a little disappointing because we really wanted to complete a mission. But we still had a chance. No one could predict when a spare would be needed.

After the briefing we went to our plane, Heaven Can Wait, and took off to join our squadron in the air. We had been in the air about two and a half hours when one of our inboard engines began to heat up. McFall had to shut the engine down. If we had kept going, the engine might have caught fire, and we could crash. Standard procedure in a situation like this was to turn back to the base for the safety of both the plane and the crew. The mission to Brunswick took us over the North Sea. If our plane went down it would be into the sea, and rescue was impossible. McFall used his radio and notified the base and the 388th Group leader that he had to return to base because of engine trouble.

I was not afraid of crashing because I had complete faith in McFall's ability to get us back to the base safely. So far we were two for two in uncompleted missions. The first mission was not completed because we were a spare and were not needed. On our second mission we started out as a spare, but had to abort because of engine trouble. When we took off from the airfield that morning, we had all of the same anxieties and tension in preparation for this mission as we had for our first one. And even though we were a spare, we still were prepared if we were called upon to replace a returning aircraft. Unfortunately, we were the returning aircraft. Even though it was right to return to the air base for safety precautions, it was still a letdown to have to abort.

After landing at the base, McFall told the ground crew the problems he had with the engine. They would check it out, and fix it as quickly as they could. Since we had nothing to report about a completed mission, we did not have to attend a debriefing. We were a disappointed crew heading back to the barracks. Maybe on the next assigned mission we would have better luck and could complete the mission.

Our Mission #3   (388th Bomb Group Mission #80)
March 16, 1944   Target: Augsburg

This was my first mission actually flying into enemy territory. This time our plane was not assigned as a spare. We were in our 563rd Squadron's regular formation of twenty-one planes and joined with the other squadrons of the 388th Bomb Group. One of the aircraft from our squadron aborted within the first hour because of mechanical problems. One of the spares took its place. The other two spares were ordered back to base as we approached enemy territory. As we flew over occupied France, three more planes in our 563rd formation had to abort. The other two spares had already been ordered back to base, so we had to continue the mission with only eighteen planes left in our squadron. I couldn't count how many were left in the other two squadrons, but they seemed to be all right.

The planes that had aborted over France had to jettison their bombs over wooded areas in that country. The crew did not want to drop them on civilians, but they could not return to the base with the armed bombs still in the plane. The bombs had been armed as soon as the planes were over enemy territory and there was a possibility that the bombs might explode when the planes landed back at the base. Dropping them from the aircraft was much safer, and crews did their best not to drop them in populated areas. Our fighter cover had also returned to base, and we would have to face the German fighters alone.

Augsburg was our primary target, but heavy clouds covered the area, and we had to turn to our secondary target on the outskirts of Augsburg. As we got nearer to the target, we were being hit by moderate flak that did some damage to our plane, but not enough to abort the mission. Clouds also covered the secondary target, so we had to rely on our two PFF planes to lead us into the target area. The two lead planes were a part of the Path Finder Force, hence the PFF title. These planes were equipped with a radar dome. By operating the radar instead of using the bombsight, the bombardier could see the target through the cloud cover. Our planes followed the lead of the two PFF aircraft. When they dropped their bombs, our planes followed right behind them to drop our bombs on the target.

At first the enemy fighters attacked us in force at the IP (the Initial Point at the beginning of the bomb run). But when we began our bomb run, the German fighters had to back off. They did not dare to follow us because the flak aimed at us might hit them. We were at 23,000 feet and began to drop our bombs. The flak was very heavy, resulting in damage to our plane from the closeness of the bursts. We did not suffer a direct hit, but the heavy flak was creating holes in the plane.

This was my first mission actually reaching enemy territory, and it was my first experience of being on oxygen for five to six hours. The temperature inside the plane ranged from thirty to forty degrees below zero. Even though we had electrically heated suits, heated felt booties, and heated gloves under our heavy leather gloves, the freezing cold was extremely uncomfortable. When we breathed in and then exhaled, small frost crystals came out of our masks and covered the floor around Pop and me. The waist windows were wide open so that we could shoot at the German fighters again when we finished the bombing. The outside air rushing through our gun positions made us feel like it was closer to sixty degrees below zero rather than forty below.

When we finished the bomb run and turned back toward home base, the fighters began attacking us again. They attacked us over and over again, lobbing rockets into our formation. We were surprised that some of the German fighters had rockets under their wings. Quite a few of our aircraft were damaged and one Me-110 with rockets came too close to one of our airplanes and got shot down. I was too busy shooting my .50-caliber machine gun to tell how many other German planes were shot down. The rest of the German fighters had to break off because they were out of ammunition.

As we headed for home, ground fire from artillery batteries at different sites harassed us. These smaller flak barrages weren't close enough to hit us, but we had to watch out for enemy aircraft. When we reached the English Channel and saw the White Cliffs of Dover, I gave a deep sigh of relief. I was exhausted, and it was great to be over friendly territory again. McFall announced over the intercom, "We're down to 10,000 feet, so you can come off oxygen now." This resulted in my second great sigh of relief. After wearing the uncomfortable oxygen mask for over five hours, it was a terrific feeling to get it off.

As we took off our oxygen masks, Pop and I looked around our area of the plane. We could see the holes made by the guns of the German fighters and by the flak from the ground fire. The flak had punched quite a few good-sized holes in our plane. We picked up pieces of the 80mm shrapnel inside the plane. Some of the shrapnel pieces were almost as big as a person's thumb.

As our planes approached the airfield, we saw that double red flares were being fired from some of our squadron's aircraft. Double red flares indicated wounded on board. A single red flare indicated that the plane was either damaged or low on fuel, or both. Planes with a double red flare were given top priority for landing, and single red flare planes were the next planes allowed to land. Our plane was damaged by flak, but the damage did not imperil our ability to land. We were dangerously low on fuel, however, and had to shoot up a single red flare. We managed to land safely.

I was very glad this mission was over. It was my first time coming under enemy fire. I felt good that I had done everything I was supposed to do during the attack. Sometimes there is a fear that you may not do well in combat, that you may let your buddies down, or that you may freeze up in battle and not fulfill your duties. This did not happen to me. I had now been in combat. I did not freeze up, and I did all the things I was trained to do. I think the first time an airman faces combat is something he will never forget. I know I will always remember it.

We started out with 21 planes in our squadron. Three of our squadron's planes had aborted after the spares had been called back, so our squadron actually took eighteen planes into combat and all eighteen returned safely even though most of the planes were damaged. I didn't know how the other squadrons made out.

We had been in the air just over nine hours. We were exhausted and would be glad to get out of our flying gear. As we got out of our aircraft, we inspected the damage to the plane, and I looked at the name, *Heaven Can Wait*. I guess heaven could wait for us a little longer. There were so many holes in our plane that I didn't bother to count them. We were amazed that none of us had been hit, and we were lucky that none of the vital parts of our plane had been hit. The ground crew chief told McFall that the plane would be repaired and ready for the next mission.

There was a truck waiting to take us to the debriefing hut. At the debriefing we were asked to tell more about the German rockets, and to describe them. These German Me-110s were twin-engine planes carrying rockets attached under their wings. The pilots said they had never had rockets shot at them before, and they had never seen this type of German plane.

After the debriefing, I just wanted to rest. We were flying almost every other day now, and were not allowed to leave the base. That didn't matter. After this mission and the debriefing, I was so exhausted I just went back to the barracks to rest.

Our Mission #4   (388th Bomb Group Mission #81)
March 18, 1944   Target: Munich

With only one day's rest from our last mission over Augsburg, we were told at the briefing that we were going to Augsburg again. Later, as we were in flight on our way to Augsburg, McFall received a communication from the leader of our 388th Bomb Group that our destination had been changed to Munich. No explanation was given. McFall made the announcement to us over the intercom that Munich was our target instead of Augsburg. McFall also warned us that this mission would be the longest one we had ever taken. It would be about a ten-hour mission, and we would be very short of fuel on our way back.

I was a little bit surprised about the sudden change of targets while we were already in the air, but I tried not to dwell on the length of the flight or the fact that we might run out of fuel on the way back. It would take almost six hours to reach the target because we had to follow the evasive route planned for us. We didn't want the Germans to determine our target in advance. The way back would be shorter, about four hours instead of six, because we could head straight back to the base after the bombing run.

As we were flying toward our target, our navigator, Ed Brazies, told us over the intercom that if we looked to our right we could see the Swiss Alps. I looked out my right waist gunner's window, and I was able to see the beautiful, majestic Swiss Alps. The picturesque view of the mountain peaks covered with snow was awesome. It was such a peaceful view that, for a few moments, the war ceased to exist for me. If we had gone to our original target of Augsburg, we would have missed seeing these beautiful mountains. The whole crew managed to get a glimpse of the Alps. But then we all had to get back to our own gunnery positions, and the war became a reality again.

We were approaching Munich when McFall notified us that we were close to the start of our bomb run. After McFall's announcement that we were approaching the bombing run, flak was more of a concern to us than German fighter planes. We were always on the alert for any German fighters that might attack us, but we knew that the fighters would not attack during the bombing run for fear of getting hit by the flak.

The squadron ahead of us began the bombing run, and our squadron, the 563rd, was right behind them. The first squadron encountered very heavy flak. I watched them going through the flak barrage. Suddenly one of their planes got hit and exploded. I saw it get hit, and the violent explosion of the plane was so powerful that it took a second plane down with it. Both aircraft exploded into pieces, and I watched as the pieces of the plane were falling to the ground. I could not see any parachutes opening. Then a third plane was hit. Its left wing came off, and the plane spiraled towards the ground. As this plane went down, I saw seven parachutes open one by one. The other three men either went down with the plane or their parachutes did not open. The first squadron finished its bombing run. In addition to the three planes I saw go down, the squadron also lost a couple of other planes that I did not see get hit, but I heard the words as someone in our plane yelled, "There goes another one down."

I heard that two different times, and then our squadron followed the lead squadron right into the middle of the flak as we began our bombing run. The flak was getting thicker all the time. In fact, it was so thick that our plane was bouncing all over the sky from the effects of the flak bursts. The flak was so bad that I wondered how McFall and the other pilots held their position in the formation.

In our debriefing sessions, this type of heavy flak was often described as, "The flak was so thick and heavy that you could walk on it." That's exactly what it was like now. The bursts were so close that I could hear the exploding shells just outside our aircraft. The pieces of shrapnel hitting our aircraft sounded like giant hailstones and some of the shrapnel broke right through the metal into the aircraft. This flak was the heaviest I had ever seen or heard. By the time we finished the bomb run, there were so many holes in our plane that it was a miracle our gas tanks had not been hit.

We dropped our bombs on the target and got away as quickly as we could. As soon as we were clear of the flak area, we were attacked head-on by Me-109s. The German fighter planes were swarming all over us. Over and over they attacked our planes, firing their guns. Now we had bullet holes in our plane as well as the many holes caused by the flak. I was amazed that we were still in the air; but, thank God, we were still flying. Eventually we outdistanced the German fighters and continued on our way back to the base.

This was the most terrifying and exhausting mission I had been on so far. I knew I would never forget that day, March 18, 1944. Our 388th Bomb Group suffered more damage to our planes and more wounded personnel than on any of the previous missions I had been on.

When we approached the airfield at Knettishall, double red flares were shooting up from almost all of the 388th Bomb Group's aircraft. The planes with the double red flares lighting up the sky were given first priority to land because they had wounded men on board. The other planes, like mine, shot single red flares out the window to show that they were low on fuel. After we landed and parked our aircraft, the ground crew chief jumped up on the wing to check our fuel tanks. As we were getting into the trucks to go to the debriefing hut, the crew chief yelled down to McFall, "Lieutenant, your tanks are completely empty. There isn't enough fuel left to fill a cigarette lighter." We all looked at each other and smiled. All of us were thinking the same thing. It wasn't our time yet, and we looked up knowingly at the name on our plane, *Heaven Can Wait*.

On the way to the debriefing hut, our trucks passed a badly damaged plane riddled with holes from the flak. Two ambulances were beside the plane. Doctors and corpsmen were removing the wounded men from the damaged B-17. I saw a man beside a water tank truck washing the inside and outside of the damaged tail-gun position. I did not know if the gunner had survived or not.

During the debriefing, we asked about that damaged plane, and an officer explained what had happened. The plane's tail gunner was blown to pieces by a direct 80mm flak explosion. The medics had picked up all that remained of the tail gunner's body. What we had seen on the airfield were the men washing the blood out of the tail-gun position.

This kind of experience was commonplace in combat. We didn't want to talk about it anymore, even though it concerned all of us. We really felt bad for those who got killed or wounded. We always knew that one day it might be one of us, but we could not let ourselves think about it.

Our Mission #5   (388th Bomb Group Mission #82)
March 20, 1944   Target: Frankfurt

Our 388th Bomb Group was assigned the Heddnbeum Prop Factory near Frankfurt. At the briefing we were told that the target could be bombed visually because the weather would be clear. After takeoff, our squadron assembled in formation without difficulty. Sometimes at the beginning of a mission, especially in bad weather, the sky would be crowded with planes. The 388th had four squadrons in the group. With all four squadrons trying to take off and assemble in formation at the same time, we had to be careful to keep our distance.

At 10,000 feet over the English Channel we went on oxygen. We also test fired our machine guns. The officer at the briefing had told us that the weather would be good and the skies would be clear. Unfortunately, as we approached the continent, we could see that the skies were not clear. However, we were not surprised. The rapid change in weather conditions often occurred in the middle of a mission. And usually, the change was not a good one for us. The clouds now surrounding our planes were so heavy that we had to begin flying on instruments. Most of the other squadrons broke formation because of the thick clouds, but our squadron managed to stay together right up to the bombing run. We could not see the target clearly but dropped our bombs and hoped that we had hit our target. The cloud cover was so thick that we could not see below us. In spite of the heavy clouds hindering their view of our planes, the Germans still fired their artillery up at us. Flak exploded all around us, but fortunately our plane did not get hit. The flak had been moderate compared to what we had faced on other missions. Even though the Germans could not see us clearly, their artillery had been fairly accurate and some of our aircraft had been damaged. We dropped our bombs and got out of the flak areas as fast as we could. The clouds were even thicker now than when we began our bomb run. Our squadron had to break up, just as the other squadrons had already done.

McFall warned us over the intercom that our formation had broken up, and he said that we were now on our own. He told us that he was going to fly in and out of the clouds because there were several layers of clouds and they were very thick. Hopefully, that way we could hide from both the German fighters and the ground fire. McFall told us to keep a sharp eye out for any of our bombers that had been separated from their group. He also warned us to be especially alert for German fighters.

As we came out of a cloud and were in the clear sky, tail gunner Walt Pawlesh yelled for us to look below and to the left of our plane. We saw a crippled B-17. The B-17 had two engines feathered, and the crew was dumping guns and ammunition, and anything else that was loose in the plane. They were trying to make the plane lighter in hopes that they could make landfall. We were watching the aircraft as it was heading toward Switzerland. Walt used the intercom to tell McFall about the damaged plane. We were really getting low on fuel, so Walt suggested to McFall that maybe we, too, should try for Switzerland.

Switzerland was a neutral country, and sometimes if a plane could not get back to its base in England because it was so badly damaged, the pilot would try for Switzerland. If they made it there safely, the crew would be interned for the duration of the war. It was a better choice than a German prisoner of war camp. McFall's answer, however, was very short, "We're going back to England."

We were now flying alone, separated from the rest of our squadron. Brazies, the navigator, was busy trying to get a fix on our exact location along the French coastline. We were now down to just below 10,000 feet, so we could safely get off of oxygen. On the way back to the base, McFall continued flying in and out of the cloud formations to avoid German fighters and any flak that might be shot at us. We were flying low enough to see breaks in the clouds. We could see some trains moving on the ground. I called McFall on the intercom and asked him if we could do some strafing if we saw a military target.

"Absolutely not," he replied. "We need to save our ammunition in case we get attacked by German fighters. Besides," he continued, "we will be lucky to get back to the base with what little fuel we have left."

That message certainly made us more aware of the dangerous position we were in. We were all alone in the air, were wide open to attacks by German fighters, and were extremely low on fuel. We prayed that we didn't encounter enemy fighters. As we flew on toward the base, time seemed to stop. I felt as if this flight would never end. My eyes were strained from watching the sky for enemy planes. I could practically visualize the empty fuel tanks, and was waiting to hear the sputter of the engines. But just when I thought our fuel tanks must be empty, Brazies announced over the intercom that the English Channel was dead-ahead. Within an hour we would be back at the base if the fuel held out. This announcement cheered me up considerably. I stretched as far as I could to look out the right waist window. I was somewhat reassured when I looked down and saw the end of the northern coast of France and the beginning of the English Channel.

We were not yet safe from the German planes, but the sky ahead was clear. We were leaving the cloud cover behind us, and even though we were getting closer to our base, we still had to be very alert for German fighters. Other B-17s were straggling back just as we were. We saw three damaged B-17s that did not make it back to the base. They were too badly damaged from the flak and were forced to ditch in the English Channel. Hopefully, the British Sea Rescue men, who were always standing by for such emergencies, would pick up the crews. Fifteen minutes was the longest amount of time you could survive in the frigid waters of the English Channel.

We were over the English Channel when Walt saw a B-17 approaching on the left side of our plane. Something about the plane did not look right to Walt. Every bomb group had a different identifying marker on the tail of each aircraft in its group. Our 388th Bomb Group had a large square with an H in the middle as its identification. We knew the markings identification of our 388th Bomb Group and the other two bomb groups that had been with us. The identifying marker on the approaching B-17 did not match any of our group's markings.

Walt told us over the intercom that the B-17 coming up beside us was an imposter, and he immediately began firing at it. We couldn't tell if Walt hit the plane or not. Once Walt started shooting at the Germans, they flew away from us. The imposter plane disappeared so fast that no one else had a chance to shoot at it.

Sometimes the Germans were able to reconstruct a B-17 that had been shot down over their territory. They used the parts from other damaged B-17s that had been shot down. The Germans would then man the plane and try to get in with our B-17s to shoot us down. The Germans were unable to get ammunition for the B-17s' .50-caliber machine guns, so they inserted hidden 20mm cannons behind the .50-calibers in the gun turrets. That way it would still appear to be one of our own B-17s. The 20mm weapons stayed hidden until the Germans were ready to shoot at the American B-17s. Walt was right on the ball in noticing that this plane was an imposter. He saved us from being shot down.

At last we were nearing our airfield. Most of our planes were nearly out of fuel as we approached the field. The single red flares were shooting up everywhere. Twenty planes, out of the twenty-one in my squadron, eventually made it back to the field. Seven of our planes had to land at other airfields, but five of those seven refueled at the other airfields and returned to our base later the same day. Two planes had to stay at the other base for repairs and were able to return to us a couple of days later. One of our planes never returned to the base, and nobody knew what happened to it. The planes were so widely scattered while they were trying to get back to the base that it was impossible to keep track of everyone. We didn't even know that we had lost a plane until we got back to the base. I did not know any of the airmen on the crew of the lost plane, but I mourned for them as all fliers mourned when a fellow airman was missing in action, captured, or killed.

The orientations, procedures, and lectures during the first few days that we were at Knettishall kept us so busy that we did not have a chance to get to know many of the crews. And then when we began to fly our own missions, we really did not have much free time to get to know the other crews who were also flying missions. Planes flew in and out so often that we didn't get a chance to know many of the airmen. We were flying almost every other day. That did not give us much time for socializing. By the time we got back from a mission we were exhausted and just wanted to go back to our Nissen huts and rest.

Our Mission #6   (388th Bomb Group Mission #83)
March 21, 1944   Target: Berlin

On my first mission, March 9, 1944, the target had been Berlin, and our plane had been designated as a spare. On that mission, just as we reached the designated point of no return, we were informed that all the planes in the formation were going forward. Our plane and the other two spares were recalled. Even though I had never completed a mission over Berlin, I knew from our first briefing what a tough assignment it was. I knew that the target would be covered by a lot of German fighters and that we would receive extra-heavy flak on our bombing run. For this mission our target was Berlin, and I was very eager to participate. We were not a spare plane this time.

After we had breakfast and finished our briefing, we took off and began our evasive route toward Berlin. Our plane had been badly damaged in previous missions, and had been repaired every time we returned to the base. But, in spite of the dedicated work of the ground crew to make repairs and to keep us flying safely, the planes sometimes just broke down anyhow. We went on missions almost every other day, and the planes took a beating.

We were just about two hours into the flight when mechanical trouble began to plague us. The plane was not responding properly to the pilot's instruments. McFall was sure that the previous damage to the plane was affecting the controls. Any attempt to continue the mission with mechanical problems would jeopardize the plane and the safety of the crew. McFall notified the base and was given the OK to abort.

We were over the English Channel when we left the formation. I could see one of the spares moving up to take our place. Obviously I did not want to go into combat with a damaged plane that was not functioning properly, but somehow, I was very disappointed not to be completing this mission over Berlin. Berlin seemed to me to represent the heart of the Nazi regime, and I wanted to be with the rest of my squadron on the bombing run. But we can't always get what we want, I thought to myself as our plane turned back to the base.

Our Mission #7   (388th Bomb Group Mission #84)
March 23, 1944   Target: Brunswick

March 23, 1944, was a day like any other mission day, with an early wake-up call, dressing and going to breakfast, then going to the briefing hut to learn about the day's mission. As we walked to the briefing hut, I couldn't help but think of all the men who walked this same path before me, just as I had walked it six previous times. I discovered that I could not remember the names or faces of many of the men who had gone before me and had never come back. These thoughts made a person pause for a while and think about the future, or even if there would be a future. I forced myself to put these thoughts aside as I walked along with my crewmembers, talking and joking.

The briefing officer told us our mission was to Brunswick. He also said that we were going to get fighter support. That announcement made us feel much better about the mission. Having our fighters there to battle the German fighters helped to get us nearer to the target. Once we approached the target area, we knew our fighters would have to back off. They could not help us while we flew through the flak that was exploding all around us. We remembered the saying, "The flak was so thick you could walk on it." But it was still comforting to know that our fighters were there to protect us as much as they could.

It was dawn when the briefing was finished and we hurried to our planes for takeoff. We were not flying our plane today. On March 20, 1944, we had gone on a mission to Frankfurt, and our plane, *Heaven Can Wait* was heavily damaged by flak. The ground crew repaired the damage as best they could, and on March 21 we took *Heaven Can Wait* on a mission to Berlin. We had mechanical trouble and had to abort. Evidently our plane was still in bad shape from the flak pounding over Frankfurt. For the March 23 mission to Brunswick, *Heaven Can Wait* was still being repaired and we were assigned another plane. At first I was a little apprehensive about not flying in our own plane. We had felt that the name of our plane had been lucky for us, and I would have preferred to be on it now for this mission. But the plane was not yet repaired and we had to take what was available. I liked flying in *Heaven Can Wait* with my crew, but I was not worried about flying another plane on this mission because I was still flying with my crew, and I trusted them.

Our 563rd Squadron rendezvoused over the clouds, and then joined the rest of the 388th Bomb Group. We chattered a bit over the intercom, and I guessed that the other crews might be doing the same thing. This helped to relieve some of the tension we were feeling. As soon as we reached 10,000 feet, and went on oxygen, the word came from McFall: "No more chatting on the intercom." We understood why. We were heading for our target in Germany, and from here on until the end of our mission the intercom was used only when a crewmember had something important to say to the crew concerning the mission.

We were flying over the North Sea when McFall ordered us to check our guns. The belt of .50-calibers was already hooked into our machine guns, but we had not put a shell into the chamber yet. For safety purposes, we never put a shell into the chamber while the plane was on the ground. When McFall gave the order to check our guns, we pulled the charging handle that loaded the shell into the chamber. As each of us gave a short burst at random from our weapons and checked in from our stations, we could feel the plane vibrate from the shooting. Like our previous chatter on the intercom, test firing our guns helped to ease the tension as we drew nearer to our target.

As we approached Holland and flew over the Zuider Zee, we watched for our fighter cover. So far, we could not see any sign of them. Our navigator told us we were fifteen minutes early. The fighters were not here yet. We were disappointed to miss the fighter cover, but we could not just fly around the sky for the next fifteen minutes. We had to go forward to the target.

The picture of planes going down is in my log book, drawn while I was in the POW camp. The picture represents my memories of my last mission when we were shot down in a furious battle over Brunswick, Germany.

We were now flying over enemy territory without fighter cover. I wished our fighter planes would hurry up and arrive. Suddenly I heard a call over the intercom, "Fighters at 10 o'clock." They weren't our fighters. They were German FW-190s coming in at us at 10 o'clock high. Pop Grimshaw was aiming his .50-caliber machine gun and was ready to fire when they got close enough. I could see out over his gunsight. The German planes were so far away that they looked like a swarm of little black bees.

I watched the fighters approach with their guns blazing, but I couldn't do anything. I had to wait until they passed to my side of the plane and were in my line of fire. Pop was firing away at them as they approached his side. Ernie had already shot down one German fighter, and shortly after that, Walt shot down another one. The German planes continued to swarm in on us, with their pilots firing steadily at our airplanes. I saw four of our planes hit and going down. I couldn't see all our planes, but I knew that others must have been hit. There were just too many German fighters and we had no fighter protection.

Some of the German planes were now at about 4 o'clock, going away. As I turned my guns on them, ready to shoot, a loud explosion from behind knocked me to the floor, and I lost consciousness. The next thing I remember was trying to push Pop off me. I realized that I had been thrown to the floor of the plane by the force of the explosion and Pop had landed on top of me. My throat mike and oxygen mask had been knocked off, and before I could help Pop, I passed out.

When I regained consciousness, I saw Ernie Alcorn, our radio operator, bending over me. He had his oxygen mask on and was holding my oxygen mask up to my face. I was too weak and groggy to hold it. As soon the mask was put on my face, I began to breath easier with the fresh oxygen coming into my lungs. Ernie held the oxygen mask against my face until we got below ten thousand feet. We could breathe normally at that height, and he removed his mask and mine.

"Where are you hurt?" Ernie asked.

"There's something wrong with my legs," I said. "They hurt real bad."

Ernie propped me up against the side of the aircraft and took my boots off, but left my heated booties on. Then he cut the legs of my flying suit so he could check my injuries. "You got hit in the legs," he said. "Both legs are really hurt. I've got to stop the bleeding." He made tourniquets and tied them around my thighs on both legs.

"Loosen those tourniquets every so often," Ernie told me as he turned around to take care of Pop. The same explosion that got me injured Pop also. Ernie took care of Pop as best he could, and then he came back to me and handed me my parachute. "Put it on," he said. My parachute was beside my gun position, but, because of my injuries, I was unable to reach it myself. After Ernie handed it to me, I was able to snap it onto my harness. Then Ernie said the words that I had dreaded for so long. "The plane's on fire," he said. "Be prepared. We may have to bail out."

There was still hope, I thought. We haven't been ordered to bail out yet. Maybe we can make it back. In spite of the pain in both my legs, I crawled to the right waist window to see for myself. It didn't look good. Flames were coming out of the wing between the two engines and one of the engines had stopped. I knew then that we didn't have any chance of making it back to the base.

The intercom had been shot out and was useless, so we had no communication with McFall. It was Ernie who soon confirmed my fears. "The wings are on fire. It's time to bail out," he announced. If I said I was only afraid, I would be lying. I was scared shitless.

I crawled to the rear door and had just pulled the red handle that jettisoned the door when I heard gunfire from Walt's tail-gun position. He was still shooting at the Germans. I was afraid that he did not know that we had been told to bail out. I crawled back almost to the rear wheel well so that I could see Walt. I hollered to Walt that we were bailing out. He didn't hear me because of the noise of his guns firing. I picked up two spent

.50-caliber shells and threw them at him. They hit him on the back, and he turned around. I was stunned when I saw his face. He had been wounded in the head, and there was blood all over his face. But he still kept firing at the German fighters. When he looked at me, I yelled to him that we were bailing out. He acknowledged that he understood.

The pain in my legs was getting worse, but I managed to crawl back to the rear door frame and put my hands on each side of the opening. Leaning forward, I put my head out into the wind and prepared to dive downward. But the powerful forces of the slipstream made me pull my head in very quickly. I was a little nervous about the strong wind. I did not want to hit the leading edge of the tail section. I had already seen the engines on the right in flames. Now, as I looked back and out through the left waist window, I saw flames shooting out between the left engines also. I had never bailed out of a plane before. We never had the opportunity to practice bailing out of a plane, but now, without any more hesitation, I dived out of the aircraft! After counting six seconds as we had been trained to do, I pulled the ripcord.

What a relief it was when I felt the tug as my chute billowed open. When my chute snapped open, it made the same sound that a bedsheet made when two people snapped a sheet up and down as they made the bed. It was a wonderful sound to me because it meant that my chute had opened. I turned my head and looked up to my left and watched my flaming B-17 pulling away from me. It was still on a level course even though flames and heavy black smoke were coming from the plane.

Suddenly I was shaken up by the thought, what if they got back to the base OK in spite of the damage to the plane? The plane was still flying on a level course. I had not seen their parachutes so maybe the other men were still on the plane. Maybe they got the ship under control and will keep on going toward the base. Maybe I bailed out too soon. And now here I was, floating all alone in the sky. I silently wished the members of my crew who were still on the plane a safe journey home. I was grateful to still be alive and floating safely toward the ground. Safe, yes, but I was very concerned about what awaited me on the ground. It's not a good feeling to suddenly find yourself alone in enemy territory.

Even as I floated to the ground, in pain from my injuries, and worried about where I was, I thought about my mother and father. How would I let them know I was alive? How was I to even know if I would survive and stay alive? As I got nearer to the ground I saw a large windmill below me on the left. Maybe I was still over Holland. I certainly hoped so. In Holland there was a chance that the underground would find me before the Germans did. I knew I would need medical attention soon, because my legs were beginning to get numb. Resistance fighters would help me and get me needed medical assistance. I realized that I was too weak to fight my way out of enemy territory. Just before I hit the ground, I threw my .45-caliber automatic away. If the Germans were waiting for me, I did not want to be shot. We had been told in orientation meetings that being armed would be an excuse for the Germans to shoot us.

All of those thoughts were racing through my mind as I was floating down. I was very close to landing now, and carefully surveyed the land below me. I did not want to end up in a tree if I could avoid it. The land below looked like a section of farmland surrounded by trees. The land seemed to have just been plowed so the ground should be soft. I was trying to look on the bright side. When I hit the ground, the impact sent terrible pains through my legs. I tried to stand, but my legs would not hold me up. I had to gather up my parachute. We had been taught that the first thing to do after your parachute landing was to hide the parachute so the Germans would not know where you landed. Since I could not stand, I had to gather up my parachute while on my knees. But I got it done. My first thought was to hide my parachute by burying it, but I did not have the strength to do it. Anyhow, it was too late. Two people were running across the field toward me already.

I looked around to get my bearings, not that it mattered. I could not walk well enough to go anywhere. No Germans were in sight. The two people coming toward me were civilians, an older man and woman. I still hoped that I was in Holland and that these people were Dutch. Then they might hide me and get me medical attention. It was probably wishful thinking, but I still had hope.

The couple stopped a few feet in front of me. I put up my hands and yelled, "American. American." The old man was agitated, and waved his hand, repeatedly yelling, "Pistol. Pistol." They appeared to be afraid of me and would not come near me at first. I showed them my empty holster. Then they made motions for me to follow them, but they did not offer to come near me or help me walk. I had to crawl on my hands and knees to their farmhouse. The old woman opened the door, and I had to crawl into the kitchen. I was trying to explain to them that I was an American and wanted them to hide me. I pulled myself onto a chair next to the window, and again tried to get them to help me. But they did nothing except keep their distance and stare at me. I turned to look out the window, and my heart began pounding. It was all over. I saw German soldiers in cars and on motorcycles driving recklessly into the farmyard. With their rifles ready, they jumped to the ground and made their way to the farmhouse where I sat helpless. This was it — no resistance fighters, no underground, no help at all. I was trapped.

CHAPTER FIVE

Captured

As the Germans approached, I became more fearful. I didn't know what to expect from them, harsh treatment or medical care. I was getting weaker and weaker from the pain in my legs and the loss of blood. I passed out. When I came to, I was no longer sitting in the chair, but was lying on the floor. A German doctor was bending over me, preparing a shot of morphine to ease my pain. I never thought I would be so happy to see a German. In a few minutes the morphine began to work. My pain was gone, and I felt light-headed, as if I was floating in the air.

Two Germans put me on a blanket, lifted me up, and carried me outside the farmhouse. With all this movement, I was very thankful that the pain in my legs had been considerably lessened by the morphine. The two Germans laid me down in the back of a two-wheel ox cart. I had no idea where we were going, and, honestly, thanks to the morphine, I didn't care. I kept slipping in and out of consciousness.

An old man was driving the cart very slowly while two German soldiers walked on each side of the cart as escorts. The ride was very bumpy and uncomfortable. In those moments when I was jarred awake by the rough roads, I realized that we had left the old dirt road near the farmhouse and were on a cobblestone road. I thought this might mean that we were getting close to a town. From time to time, I tried to see where we were going. At one place I saw a small gas station with a Gulf sign over it. Somehow that struck me as funny. Here I was, a prisoner of war in a foreign country, and the first sign I understood was on a station that had sold Gulf gasoline. Because of the war, I doubt if they had any at that moment. I closed my eyes and drifted off to sleep again. Later, I heard people talking and tried again to see where we were. As we passed through the streets, I saw a Coca-Cola sign. I thought for sure that I was hallucinating. I couldn't get a good view of the town because I was lying down in the ox cart. I closed my eyes again and was just drifting off to sleep when the ox cart came to an abrupt stop. I opened my eyes and tried to sit up. We were in the town square, and there was a scaffold just over my head. A rope was hanging down from the scaffold. I was terrified and completely helpless. In my dazed state from the morphine, from my injuries, and from lack of a good night's sleep, I became disoriented and confused. I thought they were going to hang me in the town square. We had heard about the rage of the Germans against Americans and how some American prisoners had been killed.

I thought that this was it. They were going to hang me. I closed my eyes and prayed when I felt some men lifting me out of the ox cart. One of the men said, "Careful," as they lifted me. He spoke the word in English, and I quickly opened my eyes. I nearly cried with relief when I saw the officers from my own crew lifting me out of the cart. McFall, Irizarry, Brazies, and Eggman had crash-landed with the plane. This was the first time I had seen them since I bailed out. The four officers carried me in the blanket past the scaffold into the town hall. When my officers put me down on a stretcher, I saw Pop Grimshaw lying on a nearby stretcher. So now I knew that along with our four officers and myself, Pop had survived.

On the other side of the room I saw Willy Krupitsch, Bill Kemp and Ernie Alcorn and I was glad to see them. Pop Grimshaw, Willy Krupitsch, and Bill Kemp had been unable to bail out, and had crash-landed in the plane with the officers. Now, at least I knew that they had survived. Even though Walt Pawlesh and Ernie Alcorn had been able to bail out with me, Walt Pawlesh was unaccounted for. Nine out of ten of our crewmembers were here, and I was very happy to know that we had all survived.

Now I could find out what had happened to the plane. McFall told me that the plane crash-landed, narrowly missing a farmhouse. The plane had hit the ground, bounced a couple of times, and then broke in two. The crewmembers who crash-landed with the plane were able to crawl out, except for Grimshaw. He had to be rescued and pulled out by McFall and other members of the crew. Pop Grimshaw's left leg was broken in three places. McFall, Irizarry, Eggman, Brazies, Krupitsch, and Kemp were very lucky to survive the crash with only minor injuries.

After parachuting from the plane, I had watched the flaming aircraft continue to fly. There were no other parachutes in sight. Even though I had been scared to be left in enemy territory alone, I had hoped they would make it back to the base. Now, after hearing McFall's story of the crash, I was truly sorry that they had not made it back. But at the same time, I was really happy to see them and to know that they were all right. It was a good thing that Ernie told Walt and me to bail out. Otherwise, we would have been in the plane when it crashed, and we might have been killed.

We had been carefully whispering our information to each other because Lieutenant McFall warned us not to talk about our mission or the crash-landing. Two German guards entered the room, and we stopped talking. McFall had also told us not to talk about Walt, our missing crewmember. We were not sure if Walt was dead or alive, but there was a chance that he was alive and had escaped being captured by the Germans. We did not want them to go out searching for him, so we kept quiet.

When the police arrived to talk to us, Lieutenant McFall was the first to be questioned. The policemen did not speak English, but they had a fifteen-year-old local youth with them. The young boy spoke fairly good English. With the boy acting as interpreter, the police began asking McFall questions about his mission, what airfield he had taken off from, how many planes were in the attack, and other questions about military planning. McFall steadfastly refused to answer all questions. After each question he gave them his name, rank, and serial number. When it was our turn to be questioned, we answered in the same way: name, rank, and serial number.

Later in the afternoon, four German Luftwaffe soldiers came into the cellar. They picked up Pop Grimshaw and me and carried us out of the cellar on stretchers. We could tell that they were Luftwaffe soldiers by the uniforms they wore. Everything the Germans did to us, or for us, was done without warning and without any explanation. We had no idea what was awaiting us outside this building. As it turned out, a military ambulance was outside. I felt much better when I saw the ambulance instead of a crowd of angry civilians preparing to attack us, or some German soldiers ready to shoot us. Pop and I were carried to the ambulance and lifted inside. Two of the guards entered the ambulance and sat near us. Pop and I were lying on stretchers beside each other, but we did not talk. We weren't sure if the two guards could understand English or not. McFall, Irizarry, Brazies, Eggman, Willy Krupitsch, Bill Kemp, and Ernie Alcorn were not moved out with us. Pop and I did not even get a chance to say goodbye to them.

The ambulance ride was very bumpy and my wounds began to hurt even worse than before. Because Pop and I were afraid to talk in front of the German guards, we were silent in the ambulance. Unfortunately, this gave me time to think. And my thoughts were not cheerful ones. As much as I tried to remain confident and upbeat, a sense of impending doom sometimes invaded my thoughts. Right now, I was being bounced around on my stretcher because of the bumpy ride. The rough ride was hurting my wounded legs. The morphine was wearing off, and once again I felt increased pain from my wounds. I could not talk to Pop to alleviate my fears, nor could he talk to me. In case one of the Germans understood English, we did not want them to overhear what we said. At first I had been relieved to see the ambulance waiting for us, but now I was not so sure about our destination or our fate. We still did not know where we were going or how we would be treated. Inside, my fear and anxieties were rising to a very high level, but on the outside I pretended to be calm and not afraid of anything.

The ambulance only had one window, in the rear door, and we were unable to see out of the vehicle. The ride to a nearby military hospital took about twenty minutes. When the ambulance stopped at the hospital, German soldiers carried us into the building. The room where we were taken had six beds. Four of the beds were already taken by American fliers who had been shot down and wounded. There were two empty beds. I was put in one of the beds and Pop was put in the other, beside me. We knew that we were in a Luftwaffe hospital at a German fighter base because we could hear the planes taking off from the base and other planes landing. We could tell by the sounds of the engines that they were German Me-109s and FW-190s. We had heard the sounds often enough when they attacked us on our missions.

Two doctors and two nurses came in to examine us for treatment. We were fortunate that one of the doctors and a nurse spoke fairly good English. Pop was more seriously wounded than I was. He had been hit by the 20mm shrapnel during the bombing run and was unable to bail out of the plane. The force of the plane crash broke his left leg in three places. The doctors took Pop out of the room to be treated. When they brought him back into the room, he had a cast on his left leg.

When the doctor looked me over, he discovered that I had nineteen pieces of 20mm shrapnel spread out in my legs, in my right buttock, and in my right arm at the elbow. There were also smaller pieces of shrapnel embedded in the back of my head. Until now, I had not known how many pieces of shrapnel were inside me. After the examination, the doctor ordered the nurse to treat and bandage the wounds. The doctor made no effort to remove the shrapnel from my body. It seemed to me that this hospital was not set up to do complicated procedures. It was more like a field hospital. I guessed that the surgery and recovery time would take too long, and the Germans were anxious to move us on.

The nurse applied sulfur powder to my wounds. I guessed that it was sulfur powder that she used. I was not in any condition to ask what she was doing. By this time I was in a lot of pain and was not always aware of what was going on. Even though I was in such bad shape, I was surprised when she bandaged my wounds with paper bandages. I had never seen paper bandages before. The Germans were getting short on medical supplies, especially bandages. These paper bandages were specially prepared to take the place of regular bandages, and I was glad to have them rather than to go without them.

While the doctors and nurses were caring for us, I got the feeling that, because we were American Air Corps fliers being treated at a German Air Force fliers' base, we received a certain amount of respect. We were not mistreated and received better care from the Luftwaffe hospital doctors and staff than we had expected.

Three days passed, and Pop and I were wondering what was going to happen to us when we left there. We tried to stay calm and think positive. I will have to admit that it was not very relaxing to be lying on a bed, suffering with painful wounds, and wondering what will happen next. The fear of death always stayed with us. We had no idea what was going on around us, where we would be sent, or how the war was going. Every once in a while a doctor or a nurse came into the room. They treated us all right, but they were not overly friendly.

One day, a tall, blond-haired German soldier using crutches appeared in the doorway of our room. His left leg was missing just below the knee. He stood there for a moment glaring at each of us in the room. He made me kind of nervous. It seemed as if he wanted to get into the room and start swinging a crutch at us. We were helpless to defend ourselves. After a minute or two, he pointed to the remaining part of his leg and said, without animosity, "B-17," and then he turned and went away. At least, he did not take out his feelings on us as he left. I have no idea why he took the time to stand in our doorway to let us know that his war wound was caused by a B-17. I guessed that it was probably because we were B-17 crewmen. Later we told the English-speaking nurse about the German pilot who had come to our door. She told us he was an Me-109 fighter pilot from that base who was shot down by gunners from a B-17. His leg was badly shattered and had to be amputated.

We had been in the Luftwaffe hospital for four days when one of the airmen in a nearby bed called for the nurse. He told me that his bowels had not moved since he was shot down. He was constipated and terribly uncomfortable. The nurse came in and asked him what was wrong. He explained his problem and she gave him a glass of water and some pills to swallow. I stayed with him, talking and trying to cheer him up. After an hour had gone by, he said he felt an urge to have a movement. We called for the nurse to bring him a bedpan. Because the wounded airman had a cast on his left leg from his foot up to the top of his leg, he was unable to get out of bed and needed help using the bedpan. Two nurses came in and helped to position the bedpan under him.

Unfortunately, as hard as he tried to make use of the bedpan, the attempt to do so increased his pain, and he was extremely uncomfortable. He was unable to stand the bedpan under his body. We called for the nurse again, and he asked her to remove the bedpan because it hurt him so much. She did not seem to be very happy to be called again, but she removed the bedpan and then gave him some liquid that she said would help him.

A few minutes later he began groaning again as his pain increased. One of the airmen called out for the nurse to come and help. She came, looked in the door, and said she would be back. She didn't return. About twenty minutes later, the suffering airman felt the urge for a bowel movement again because of the pill, the liquid, and whatever else the nurse had given him. He told us he felt sure he was ready to relieve himself.

We called again for the nurse, but she never answered us. The wounded airman was now in agony and could not hold it any longer. He was lying on the bed, groaning and clutching his stomach. He raised his right leg as high as he could, and suddenly he had his bowel movement. Brown, watery feces shot out of his body, sailed across the room and hit another bed that was nearly ten feet away. The brown, watery substance hurtling across the room had the force of a surge of water coming from a fire hose in full operation.

We didn't think that this watery stream was ever going to stop. The smell itself was enough to choke us, and the mess made in the room as the substance landed horrified us. It was all over the middle of the room. We were chattering among ourselves, and didn't know what to do. Evidently the commotion we were making was loud because a nurse and an orderly came running into the room before we even had time to call for help. When they saw what had happened, they were really pissed off. They took a look around and glared at each one of us as if all this trouble was our fault. If looks could kill, we would have been dead that day. Then they both left the room saying they would send someone to clean up the mess.

We hoped that there would not be any kind of punishment for what happened. We never knew what the Germans would do. We were truly sorry for our buddy's pain and suffering, but we all agreed that had this been under different circumstances, without the pain and suffering, the last few minutes of the airman's relief would have been hilariously funny.

After six days at the Luftwaffe hospital, one of the nurses told me I was going to be moved. Pop was not being transferred with me. He could not be moved yet because he was still in a cast. I was being transferred to the Dulag Luft Interrogation Center in Oberursel, a small town located near Frankfurt. The words "interrogation center" were enough to send a chill up and down my spine. I had heard rumors about how badly American airmen were treated at the German interrogation centers. At least I would have some help on the way there. Two other American fliers were going to be traveling with me. They had just been released from the cells where they had been detained in the base stockade. They were not injured, and both of them were allowed to come into the room and help me up. I had to put my arms around the two American airmen's necks so I could hobble between them. I could not walk without assistance. Even with their help, I was having a very difficult time trying to walk.

The three of us were in bad shape. I had no shoes on, just the felt heated-element inserts that I had been wearing when the plane crashed. The pants underneath my flight suit had been cut up to my knees for the wounds to be treated. Dried blood covered my torn pant legs. The other two airmen still had most of their flight gear with them. They were fortunate not to have incurred any serious injuries. But, like me, they were hungry, dirty, exhausted, and badly in need of a shave.

We were put into an army truck and driven from the Luftwaffe hospital to the railroad station in Oldenburg. We reached the train station and with two German soldiers guarding us, we made our way to the station platform, filled with German civilians. Only the two guards stood between the people and us as we were hurried through the station.

The German people in the train station glared at us. Their anger and hatred was plainly expressed in their faces as they pushed and shoved their way toward us. We were still afraid of rough treatment from the German civilians. We thought they were going to attack us as we walked through the station. I was glad to get on the train and away from the people. It was a great relief to be able to sit down inside the train car and rest my legs. The looks and the threatening gestures the civilians gave us were enough to make us thankful for the German guards. We now realized that the two German guards had a dual role. They had to stop us from escaping, and at the same time, protect us from the German people.

It was only a short train ride from Oldenburg to the next city. As we approached the city limits, we could see from the train windows that our bombings had devastated this German city and the surrounding area. I did not know the name of this city or why it had been a target for our bombers. And while I could understand the people being angry at us, I was sure there must have been a military target in the area. We always had specific instructions to avoid hitting civilians whenever possible on our bombing missions. I felt sorry for their loss, but we did what we had to do to protect our country and our soldiers. We did not start the war, and I would have been much happier at home going to school, but we had a job to do, and I was proud to be in the U.S. Army Air Corps.

When the train stopped at the next station, the guards motioned for us to get up, and they escorted us off the train. We were being taken to a second train to continue our journey. The guards pushed us up against the wall of the station, and we had to stand there waiting for the other train to arrive. I noticed an older man with a cane walking closer. He stopped in front of us and reached into his coat pocket. I was fearful that he might be reaching for a gun. Instead he pulled out a large leather billfold, opened it, waved a picture, and shouted at us, "Frau und Kinder." While he was shouting, he was wildly waving his cane in the air. The other two prisoners ducked in time to avoid being hit, but I received a couple of blows on my head and shoulder. The shouting attracted other people toward us, and more German civilians began to move closer. We were still backed up against the wall. There was no way for us to escape the crowd approaching us. The two guards quickly responded to this attack and moved to protect us. They tightened their grip on their rifles and stood in front of us while at the same time ordering the people to get back. The crowd stopped moving, and then slowly, but reluctantly, began to move away from us. After things had calmed down, one of the guards who spoke a little English explained to us that the old man had held up a picture of his wife, daughter, and two grandchildren. They had all been killed in a bombing raid. I wondered what would have happened if the crowd had continued to surge forward to get at us. Would the German soldiers have shot at their own people to protect American prisoners of war? I was glad we did not have to find out.

Finally our train arrived. There were no more incidents when we boarded the train but we continued to get hostile stares and unfriendly comments from the Germans on board the train. Even though the civilians spoke to us in German, we knew it wasn't the welcome wagon greeting us. The train ride was very uncomfortable. Not only was I in pain, but also we had to stand because the train was overcrowded with passengers. The guards tried to keep the three of us in a corner of the train car to protect us from possible harm from the angry civilians. I have often thought about the two American airmen who helped me walk from station to station. I could never have made it without their help. We were separated later, and I never found out if they survived. But I know how grateful I was to them for helping to save my life. I have to admit that, in spite of being a prisoner of war, I was also thankful to the two German guards who saved the three of us from being attacked by the German civilians.

At the next station, we had to get out and change trains again. While we were walking through this train station, we saw the damage to the station and the surrounding area. There had evidently been a recent bombing raid to hit the railroad yard. It was necessary to knock out the Germans' means of transportation so that soldiers and military equipment could not be transported. That was also one of the reasons it took us so long to reach any given destination. In many areas, the tracks and trains were destroyed. We had to switch trains so often and suffered so many delays that I felt it would be a miracle if we reached our destination safely.

The guards suddenly stopped us on the station platform and pointed up. We looked up and were horrified to see two dead American airmen. They had been hanged and left outside hanging from a beam for all to see. It was a chilling, frightening sight, and it suddenly made me realize how close we had come to the same treatment at the last railroad station. I hoped that this next train would take us to our destination without any further transfers. My wounds were becoming increasingly painful because of the constant moving about and having to stand most of the time on the trains. I never received any medical treatment on this trip. My paper bandages were falling off, and my legs were sore as hell.

Finally, the train for Frankfurt came into the station and we boarded it. Once again, unfriendly German civilians surrounded us, and again we had to stand, all the way to Frankfurt. Even though I did not know what was awaiting me, I was glad when the train pulled into the Frankfurt station. I had had quite enough train travel, and I wanted to get away from being threatened by angry German civilians. We were exhausted and needed to reach some place where we could hopefully get something to eat and be able to rest. I desperately needed some time to sit down and rest my legs. It was only 250 kilometers from the Luftwaffe hospital to Frankfurt. We had left the Luftwaffe hospital at about 6:30 A.M. and did not arrive at Frankfurt until about 6 P.M. It took us nearly twelve miserable, uncomfortable hours and three different trains to travel that short distance. As I said, transportation in Germany was badly disrupted by the almost daily bombing by the Allies.

When we arrived at the Frankfurt station, I discovered that we still had not reached our destination, the Dulag Luft Interrogation Center. We had to get off the train and walk a short distance to get on a streetcar that would then take us to Oberursel, where the Dulag Luft Interrogation Center was located. When we boarded the streetcar, I almost couldn't believe that I was a prisoner of war. We were riding on a public streetcar filled with civilians. Looking at the armed German guards brought us back to reality. There were no empty seats so we had to stand all the way. Even the guards had to stand, and they stood near us. We were so closely guarded that the civilians did not dare to bother us. Many of the civilians were speaking rather loudly. I couldn't understand what they were saying in

German, but from the looks we got, I assumed that they were not very happy to see us. It seemed a very strange way to transport prisoners of war.

At last we were nearing the interrogation center. The streetcar route was on a main street, and the stop where we had to get off was about half a mile from the Dulag Luft Interrogation Center. We had to walk to Dulag Luft. With all this traveling, walking, and standing, the injuries to my legs were so painful I could hardly walk. As I limped through the open gate of Dulag Luft, a feeling of total helplessness took control of my thoughts. It's a horrible feeling to be pushed around and treated badly, while at the same time suffering from pain and lack of medical help for your wounds. For a brief moment I felt like my life was over, and there was nothing I could do to regain control of my life. Fortunately these thoughts did not always stay with me. But for this brief moment, entering the Dulag Luft Interrogation Center, I was considerably shaken and afraid of what the future might hold.

CHAPTER SIX

Dulag Luft Interrogation Center

Dulag Luft was the largest interrogation center in the area and it was designated especially for captured American and British airmen. The captured airmen were first sent to Dulag Luft to be interrogated before being sent to a permanent prisoner of war camp. The average stay in solitary at the interrogation center was a week to ten days. According to the Geneva Convention, a prisoner could not be kept in solitary confinement for interrogation purposes for more than twenty-eight days. But right now, as I entered the interrogation center, how could I know if the Germans followed the Geneva Convention rules or not. After what I had been through so far, I didn't exactly trust our German enemies.

The Germans brought me to a small cell about six by ten feet. There was only the one small door and no windows. Inside the room was what was supposed to serve as a bed It was not a real bed. It was only a burlap sack filled with straw that was laid on wooden boards. There was no blanket or pillow and no small stove for heat. I would just have to endure the cold. I saw a slop bucket in the corner. That was obviously there for sanitary purposes. The guard pushed me into the room and slammed the door behind me. The grinding sound as the door was locked unnerved me. I felt so helpless and alone. I was in pain, totally exhausted, and very hungry. I tried to get comfortable by lying down on the straw mattress, but I could not get comfortable. The feeling of helplessness and of being alone overwhelmed me.

Suddenly, I heard the door being unlocked. I stood up, ready to face whatever was about to happen to me. A German guard entered the room and put a bowl of watery soup and a piece of black bread on the floor in front of me. The guard quickly backed out of the room and locked the door again. I picked up the bread and the bowl of soup and ate that pathetically meager meal. It was better than nothing. At least now I had something in my stomach. I finished the soup and bread, and flopped back down on the straw mattress. I promptly fell asleep from sheer exhaustion.

If there was any noise that night, or even a bombing raid, I didn't hear it. The next morning a guard rudely awakened me. He didn't speak English, but he pointed to the slop bucket and used hand signals to show that he wanted me to take the slop bucket to be emptied. I went with the guard to the latrine and emptied the bucket. He escorted me back to the room and locked me in. I had no idea what was going to happen next. It was very unsettling to lie back down on the mattress and worry about what would happen the next time the door was opened.

About twenty minutes later the guard returned with a piece of black bread and what looked like porridge, but was really barley. Breakfast was being served. The food didn't taste very good but I was hungry enough to eat anything. I finished eating and sat down to wait for the next German to open the door. I waited for them to begin my interrogation. The thought of being tortured scared me. I was in enough pain already without the Germans adding more. I had nothing to do but wait and think. Uncontrollable bad thoughts raced through my mind.

I imagined that this interrogation center was a place where, if I didn't answer their questions, they would torture me or take me out in the yard and shoot me. I did not want to break down in front of the Germans. I prayed that I would be able to stand up to whatever they did to me. I knew my imagination was running wild, and I felt foolish to have some of these thoughts. But this solitary confinement was one of the most horrendous experiences that I had personally encountered. It was even more stressful to me than being shot down. When I found out later that I was not the only POW to have these terrifying thoughts, I felt better and not so foolish. The worst part of being in solitary was being alone with no one to talk to. I didn't know what the Germans were planning for me, and someone to talk to would have helped ease the tension. While we didn't receive top-notch care at the Luftwaffe hospital, at least we did receive some care when I was first captured, and we had other airmen to talk to. But, here, locked in this small room, I was alone without any medicine or medical care for my injuries, and was facing an unknown future.

A few hours had passed when suddenly the door to my room was unlocked and two guards came into my cell. They took me by the arms and escorted me down the corridor. They practically dragged me up a flight of stairs and into a room at the top of the stairs. When I entered the room, the Luftwaffe officer, a hauptmann (captain), was standing in front of me. I knew this was going to be my first interrogation session. In our orientation lectures in England, we had been told that under the rules of the Geneva Convention we were required to respect all enemy senior officers higher than our own rank. I had no problem with that, and quickly saluted him. I didn't want to get him angry. He returned the salute and told me to sit down. We were also told at our orientation meetings that we were not to give any information to the enemy other than name, rank, and serial number, and I was prepared to stand by that rule.

Now that I was sitting down, the captain sat down in the chair behind his desk. He smiled as he looked at me. I did not smile back. It was as if he was trying to soften me up and get friendly. I was waiting for the hard questions to begin, but when the captain began to talk, instead of threatening me, he told me that he had lived in New Jersey in the early thirties. He said he really liked living in New Jersey, where he had owned a meat market, but when the Fatherland called him back, he had to return because he still had family members in Germany. It was almost as if he was trying to convince me that we had something in common, living in America, and that he was in Germany reluctantly. I couldn't care less why he was there, but I nodded occasionally to show that I was listening.

The captain picked up a manila envelope and emptied its contents onto the desk. I saw my watch fall out, and I knew then that the rest of the contents were mine. My cigarettes and my lighter had also fallen out onto the desk. These things had been confiscated when I was in the Luftwaffe hospital and had been brought here Obviously the captain was using them either to impress me or to intimidate me. So far he had not impressed me nor had he intimidated me. When I saw my own watch and other items spread out on the desk, I was angry, angry that I had been deprived of them, and angry that the captain was using them as if they were his own property. I was careful not to let the captain sense my anger.

He offered me one of my own cigarettes. I accepted it and he lit it with my lighter. I had not had a cigarette for a long time, and it felt good to get a smoke. Evidently the captain assumed that I was completely relaxed now, because as soon as I had taken my first puff on the cigarette, he asked me what bomb group and squadron I flew with.

"Sir," I replied respectfully, "under the rules of the Geneva Convention I only have to give my name, rank, and serial number. My name is Ralph E. Sirianni, Jr., staff sergeant, serial number 31271422."

The captain said he already knew a lot about me. He said that he knew I flew in a B-17F, serial number 42–31745, square H, 388th Bomb Group, 563rd Bomb Squadron. If he already knew that, I wondered why he asked me for the information. Maybe it was just to see how I would respond. The captain continued giving me information. He said, "I know the revetment number where your plane was parked on the west side of the field near Knettishall. And I know that the supply sergeant's name is Smith."

Even though he had some of the information correct, I was assuming he would try to get more specific military information from me, so I repeated my name, rank, and serial number. The German captain did not seem so friendly now. He was beginning to get very annoyed. "Sirianni," he snapped my name out. "That's an Italian name. The Italians are German allies. Aren't you fighting on the wrong side?"

"My parents are American and so am I," I replied.

The captain poured me a cup of ersatz tea and kept firing the questions at me. I was getting a little worried now, waiting for him to threaten me, but I just kept on giving him my name, rank, and serial number. I drank the tea and finished smoking the cigarette while he talked.

Suddenly he switched the conversation to my wounds. He evidently had been briefed on my first week in Germany because he knew I had been wounded and given medical attention. I told him I had been given very good medical treatment at the Luftwaffe hospital. I wasn't about to point out the bad parts of my time there. I irritated the captain enough by not answering his questions, without adding critical comments about their medical treatment. The captain decided that was enough for the day, and he sent me back to solitary confinement. I was taken to the German captain four times in the week that I was there. Other than my name, rank, and serial number, he did not get any information from me.

The cell walls were so thin that by the second day I discovered I could talk through the walls to the man in the next cell. He said he was an English airman. At least I did not feel so lonely now. What a pleasure it was to talk to someone. We only talked small talk, nothing military or personal. I didn't know for sure who he was. He could be a German spy, for all I knew. And even if he wasn't a German spy, the Germans might have our cells bugged. We had been warned about tricks like these for getting information by listening to idle chatter.

My next-door neighbor liked to sing. That's how I learned that the walls were so thin that we could talk to each other. He had been singing since I got there. He sang the same song over and over and over again. I asked him what the name of the song was. He told me it was a well-known British song called "To the Ghost of Anne Boleyn." Anne Boleyn was the second wife of King Henry VIII. In 1536 the king had her beheaded in the Tower of London, and people say that she still haunts the tower. The British airman sang the song so often that I learned the words by heart and found myself singing along with him. It helped to break the monotony of being alone in my cell. But I still was careful what I discussed with him. He might have been a German spy put in the next cell to get information from me.

The song became a very important event in my life at this particular time. Instead of becoming irritated by hearing the same song over and over again, singing this song and keeping in contact with another person helped me to keep my sanity. A person can get some pretty wild thoughts when subjected to solitary confinement. For a very short time I wondered if my next-door cellmate wasn't a German spy and the continual singing of the same song over and over was one of the tortures they used to break a prisoner down. Then I came to my senses and sang along with him. I decided that he was what he said he was, a British airman. But we were both still careful what we talked about. I felt much better being in contact with a friend, and enjoyed singing the song with him. After listening to and singing this song day and night for six consecutive days, the words of the song became embedded in my head, and to this day I can still sing the first two verses from memory.

Late one afternoon I was removed from my solitary cell and taken to a dark, dirty room without windows. The only light came from a small, dim lightbulb. When I entered the room, I gagged and almost threw up. The place smelled like a shithouse. I soon found out that the room not only smelled bad, but it was loaded with lice and bedbugs. There were other men in the room, but because it was so dark and the small room was so crowded, I could not tell how many men were in the room. At least I was not in solitary anymore.

The floor was covered with straw that was saturated with feces and urine. There were no beds or blankets in the room and we had to sleep on the foul-smelling straw. I found a small area where I could sit down without sitting on someone. Two prisoners saw that I was badly wounded and my legs were covered with bandages. They moved around to make some space for me. Later the door was opened and two more men were pushed into the room. The door was quickly slammed shut behind them.

It wasn't long before the door was suddenly opened again. One of the guards yelled for everybody to take off their shoes and tie them together and pass them down to the door to be put outside the room. Someone asked why the Germans took our shoes. One of the airmen said the Germans thought it would be more difficult to escape without shoes. After the shoes were collected and put outside in the hall, the door was slammed shut. Within a few minutes the door to the room was violently pushed open again. Now what? we all wondered. As it turned out, the Germans had discovered that the number of shoes didn't correspond to the number of men in the room. The guard was screaming, half in German, half in broken

English. We managed to figure out that he was upset because there was one pair of shoes missing. Two of the guards came storming into the room with flashlights and looked at everyone's feet.

One of the guards came to me and stared at the felt heated booties on my feet. He was so angry that he hit my wounded legs with the butt of his rifle. Ernie Alcorn had taken off my flying boots on the plane to treat my leg wounds. I had bailed out without the boots and only had the booties on my feet. I didn't consider them shoes so I didn't put them at the door. After the guard slammed me with his rifle, he grabbed the felt booties and left the room, grumbling all the way out. The guards were extremely upset because the wrong count meant they had to walk through the mess on the floor while they were checking everyone's feet. I was even angrier because the butt of the rifle hitting my wounds had caused me some bleeding and a lot of pain.

My first lesson was quickly learned. If you are not sure what the Germans are saying or what orders they are giving, try to find out before you get in trouble. I spent a long, miserable night because of the pain in my legs, and because the lice and bedbugs were crawling in my bed and under my bandages. I was very uncomfortable and was scratching all night. I was also sick from the bad smell in the room. In spite of all the suffering, I still felt better being with American airmen again.

The night dragged on and we did not know if it was daylight yet. Suddenly, without warning, the doors were opened and we were ordered to get up and move out of the room. Our shoes and my booties were on the floor outside the door. Each man grabbed his shoes, and I was able to get my booties. The Germans would not let us stop to put them on, so we tried to get our shoes on while we walked toward the outside door. By the time I got to the yard I had my booties on. Once outside in the yard, we could see that it was morning. What a beautiful sight it was to see the sky again. The yard was crowded with prisoners. Each man was given a slice of black bread and a piece of cheese for breakfast. About one hundred airmen were getting ready to be transported to Stalag Luft I, the prisoner of war camp located in Barth, Germany.

I was glad to be leaving the Dulag Luft Interrogation Center. I hoped that at the camp I could get some medical attention to help heal my wounds. Nobody at the Dulag Luft Interrogation Center bothered to see that I got any treatment for my injuries. They just let me suffer. Maybe at the prisoner of war camp we would get better treatment and some decent food. The bowl of watery soup and the piece of black bread we received once a day at Dulag Luft was barely enough to keep us alive. I tried hard to look on the bright side for things to improve, but so far every move farther into Germany turned out to be worse.

As a civilian, I had always taken my freedom and home comforts for granted. It was not until I became a prisoner of war that I began to realize the devastating effects of the loss of freedom. I was no longer free to go where I wished, to eat whenever I wanted, or even to express an opinion when I wanted. Since the day I had been wounded, shot down, and bailed out of our burning B-17, I knew that my life was out of my control. As I parachuted to earth, I was afraid that even worse things were about to happen to me. My experiences at Dulag Luft proved that I was right. I couldn't help wondering now what was awaiting us at Stalag Luft I.

The guards yelled for us to line up, and then we began our trek down to the railroad station. By this time I could hardly walk, and two airmen held my arms and helped me get to the station, where we boarded the train. The train was filled to capacity with over one hundred prisoners and the guards. We were very quiet as we got on the train. No one felt like talking, and the guards probably would have punished us if we had talked.

The accommodations on this train were almost as bad as the accommodations in our detention room at Dulag Luft. All the seats had been removed from the train. Even with the seats removed, there was not enough room for all of us to sit down on the floor. We took turns, sometimes sitting, sometimes standing. My fellow prisoners allowed me longer periods to sit down because of my wounds. There were no bathroom facilities on the train, just a slop bucket at the end of the car. The Germans did not seem to care about privacy, at least not for us. We had nothing to eat. There were bars on the windows. The car doors were locked and two guards stood outside between the locked doors of each car. I had been concentrating on trying to get my legs in a comfortable position when the sudden movement of the train startled me. It was slowly moving out of the station.

We had been on the train about four hours when American planes came flying overhead on their way to a nearby target. Their target was so close to the train that when the bombs exploded we were afraid of being killed by our own bombers. But we were lucky. The bombs did not hit us and the train kept moving.

Eventually the train arrived near the outskirts of another city. We would be arriving at the next station very shortly. For the second time on our trip we heard bombers overhead. This time the American bombers flew directly over the train station, and we were afraid that the railroad yards were their target. The local air-raid sirens began to blare a warning to the people. Our train came to an abrupt stop. The guards left us locked on the train and ran to the nearest bomb shelter. The train crew was running right behind the guards, seeking shelter. We were left locked in the train with bombs dropping around us. The vibrations caused by the exploding bombs shook the train so badly that I thought this was it. The train would be hit and we would all die. How do you cheer for your fellow airmen for striking at the Germans, while at the same time hoping they miss? Eventually the bombing stopped. Our part of the tracks had not been hit. The guards and the train crew returned, and our train slowly began to move closer to Stalag Luft I.

Later we reached another city, where we had to stop near the marshaling yard just outside the station. I could see through the barred window that some flatbed trains were being loaded with scrap metal. It was not a pleasant sight to see wreckage from our B-17s, and B-24s, and parts of our fighter planes being loaded onto the flatbed trains. The wreckage could only have come from planes that the Germans had shot down. And that meant many of our airmen from those planes had been captured or killed. The Germans were salvaging this material to use in their war effort against us. And that also was not a pleasant thought. As our train continued on its way to the prisoner of war camp, more memories of the past 14 days were racing through my mind. They were memories that made me shiver as I recalled the events.

Compared to what I was going through now, the days in the Luftwaffe hospital hadn't been too bad, except for the pain from my wounds. My wounds were attended to, and I was not mistreated. But we still did not get the full medical treatment that we needed, nor did we receive adequate food. The trip from the Luftwaffe hospital to the Dulag Luft Interrogation Center had been extremely uncomfortable for the three of us Americans aboard a train crowded with German civilians. The threats and attempted attacks by the civilians everywhere we traveled were very unsettling. The German people blamed us for killing members of their families in our air raids. The recurring thoughts of the two American airmen who had been hanged at the railroad station where we changed trains was embedded in my mind. The sight of those two dead airmen hanging from that beam was a traumatic experience, and one I shall never forget. I felt sorrow for the death of the two airmen, and at the same time I feared that soon it might be my fate.

The German civilians that we encountered along the way offered American captives nothing except their glaring expressions, their hatred, and their threats of violence against us. The sights we had seen, the bad treatment we had received, and the fierce attitude of the German people helped to make our trip to the camp a nightmare. I still had no way of knowing whether I would be killed by the civilians, tortured by the German military, or even shot to death. Not knowing what the future held in store continued to make me very apprehensive. But nevertheless, I refused to show any fear or apprehension to my German captors. I had no more time to think of these past events as our train finally pulled into the station at Barth, Germany. We would soon leave the train and be taken to the prisoner of war camp known as Stalag Luft I.

CHAPTER SEVEN

Stalag Luft I: The First Three Months

When the train pulled into the Barth station, the guards hurried to line us up on the station platform. I thought that there would be trucks there to give us a ride to the camp, but the guards ordered us to start walking, and we obeyed. The pain in my infected legs was increasing. The bandages were coming loose. They had not been changed since I left the Luftwaffe hospital eight days ago. Stalag Luft I was about a mile from the train station. That mile seemed more like ten miles to me. I was limping and had great difficulty walking to the camp. But once again, two airmen came to my rescue and helped me walk. With their help, I forced myself to keep moving so the guards would not hit me. Any prisoner who walked too slowly was pushed forward by the guards.

I'll never forget the day I entered Stalag Luft I. It was April 5, 1944. When I saw the barbed-wire fences, the towers with the armed guards on them, and the dirty dilapidated condition of the camp, I knew I would have to make further adjustments to survive. No one could tell when, if ever, we would be rescued. But as the gates closed behind me, I realized that my flying days were over, and I was no longer a free man. This camp was not an improvement over the Dulag Luft Interrogation Center.

I was sure that there would not be any running water, warm clothes, blankets, showers, or clean beds in this camp. We would probably still have to deal with lice, bedbugs, and filth. There would never be enough food. Punishment for the slightest infraction would be swift and painful. I learned all that from the treatment I had already received. The Germans were not noted for their kind treatment of prisoners of war. There were signs printed in English posted all around the camp warning us that prisoners who try to escape would be severely dealt with. The signs also named

Stalag Luft I. My barracks is marked #13.

certain forbidden zones or areas in the camp that were out of bounds to prisoners. Any prisoner entering those forbidden areas would be shot. We soon learned that sometimes the German guards were quick to shoot.

I believed that I could survive the lack of some of the amenities, but could I survive the loss of my freedom? Looking around the prisoner of war camp, it suddenly hit me. Not only was I a prisoner, but also I had no control over whether I lived or died. I swore to myself then and there, that if I ever got out of this German camp, I would never again take my freedom for granted. Losing your dignity is degrading. Losing your freedom is devastating. Sometimes a person has to lose something in order to appreciate it even more.

The only thing that helped me keep my courage up was that I could draw on the strength of the other captured airmen, and we could draw on each others' strength. All of us had learned that the only way to survive this war was to help each other. During our time as crewmembers in our B-17s, we had developed a strong sense of unity. Now, as POWs, we had to maintain that same sense of unity. If we didn't, we would not survive.

Close to a hundred of us had made the trip from Dulag Luft to this camp. We were left standing around in the yard waiting for instructions.

The guards began to move among us to split the prisoners into groups. The groups of prisoners were then moved off to their assigned barracks. I was separated from my fellow prisoners and, along with two other wounded airmen, was taken to the camp infirmary. The wounded were usually taken to the infirmary before being processed any further.

The Germans did not run the camp infirmary. I guess they did not much care if we received medical treatment or not. Two British doctors were in charge of the infirmary. Six British orderlies assisted the doctors. These British prisoners of war had been POWs for nearly four years. They had been captured at Dunkirk in 1940. One of the doctors cleaned my wounds and rebandaged them with clean paper bandages. My wounds already felt a little bit better. But nothing was done to remove the shrapnel from the wounds. The doctor said he was sorry he could not give me better treatment, but the infirmary did not always have the medicine and other supplies that were needed.

The three of us who had been brought to the infirmary to be treated were not there very long. The German guards came and led us to the building where the other airmen were being processed. The airmen were having their hair cut real short. When it was my turn, I sat quietly in the chair while they cut off most of my hair. After that was finished, we had to strip down and put our old clothes in a pile on the floor. Then we were sent into another room for a cold shower and a delousing. After the delousing, we were still standing around naked when the Germans told us to line up to get new clothes.

POW workers were distributing the new clothing under the supervision of the Germans. We lined up at the counter, and the POWs asked each new prisoner what size he took. They tried to give out the closest fit. I got some clean GI clothing and two blankets, courtesy of the Red Cross. We knew it was not from the kindness of the Germans. The Germans even told us it was from the International Red Cross. Even if they hadn't told us, we could see the "International Red Cross" label stamped on all the packages. I also received a new pair of GI shoes. I was very glad to get the shoes because I was still walking around in my felt heated booties. I held onto the clothes, the shoes and the blankets tightly as I moved away from the counter. Finally, the Germans told us to get dressed in our new, clean clothes.

We still wanted to keep our old clothes as spares. We had to search through the piles of clothes on the floor to get our own back. When we were first ordered to strip, we had tried to place our clothes in separate piles to make it easy to find them later. The POW workers had deloused our old clothes by spraying them while they were on the floor. Our old clothes may have been deloused, but there was no way to wash them here. They were just as filthy as they were when we entered the camp. I finished dressing in my clean clothes and gathered my old clothes up from the floor. I decided to keep my felt heated booties in case I had to use them later. All the POWs were gathering up their old clothes. We figured we would be able to find a way to wash them ourselves. We might need them later.

Before we left the building we had to stop and have our picture taken by German photographers. The Germans had identification labels all prepared with each POW's name on it. The label had name, rank and POW number on it. My POW number was 3959. The label also had the letters "KgF.Lg.d.Lw.I" on it. This was an abbreviation for "Kriegesgefanenen," the German word for prisoner of war, along with an abbreviation for the name of the camp where the POW was imprisoned. The label was hung around my neck by a chain so that the photographer could take a photo with the label itself hanging down on the front of my chest. It seemed like the Germans were making it official that I was no longer Sergeant Ralph Sirianni, Jr., of the American Army Air Corps, but was now Sergeant Ralph

This drawing from my log book while I was in the camp shows my corner of the room in barracks #13. I had the lower bunk. I signed all my drawings with my nickname, "Mousie."

Sirianni, Jr., POW # 3959 in the prisoner of war camp named Stalag Luft I. From now on I was under the control of the Germans and they would never let me forget it. Then I stepped aside, and another POW stood before the camera with his name, rank, and POW identification number on the label hanging from his neck. And so it went until all of us were photographed Ten Germans took care of changing the different labels so that they could move the airmen right along. The Germans merely erased the information on each label after the picture was taken, and printed the new information on the label for the next airman.

At last we were finished with their processing system, and we were ordered outside. German guards were waiting to take us to our assigned barracks. The camp was divided into three compounds with seven barracks in each compound. Many of the prisoner of war camps in Germany, including Stalag Luft I, gradually grew larger as more airmen were captured. But when I arrived in April of 1944, there were just the three compounds. Each compound was named according to its location in the camp. There was the South Compound, the West Compound, and the North 1 Compound. I was assigned to North 1 Compound, Barracks #13, Room 2.

My barracks had ten rooms. Each room was 30 feet long and 20 feet wide. There were seven double bunk beds to allow 14 men to sleep in the small, overcrowded room. There were no chairs in the room and there was only one small table, located near the window. The mattress on the bunk bed was a burlap bag filled with wood excelsior, made out of wood savings. The burlap bag was known as a palliasse, which is described as a thin straw mattress used as a pallet. There was no blanket or pillow on the bed. I was glad I had the two blankets from the Red Cross parcel. The room was small, and with fourteen men crowded in it, I felt claustrophobic for a brief moment. It was not easy for any of us to be forced to live in such a small, crowded, uncomfortable room.

Later that night I was startled by loud clanging sounds as the German guards went around the outside of the barracks shuttering and locking all the windows. Then they locked the main door to the barracks so that no prisoners could go outside at night. The sound of the barracks windows and the main door being locked every night bothered me for a long time. It was another daily reminder that we were prisoners. Not that we really needed reminding, because the way we were treated was reminder enough. Every day we faced lack of respect, shortage of food, fear of the armed guards and their vicious dogs, and lack of the proper medical treatment. The month of April was cold, especially at night. I slept with my clothes on and my two thin blankets wrapped around me. I lost count of how many nights I lay awake in that cold room thinking of my home and my family.

The barracks did not have any showers or running water. The washhouse was located in back of the barracks in a separate building. The washhouse had sinks and running water, but no showers. This washhouse was used by the men from the North 1 Compound barracks. With four hundred and twenty men using the same facilities, washing and shaving was often very difficult to do. The building was very cold, and when the men came in, it was very crowded and uncomfortable. We could not take our time because we were punished if we were late for the morning roll call. There were other washhouses scattered around the camp for the other compounds, but they were just as cold and crowded.

The latrine was located in another building, also in back of the barracks.

The latrine, from my log book.

We called it the outside latrine, but it was really inside a building that was outside the barracks. The latrine had seats similar to those in an outhouse. But there was no water and, therefore, no flushing the waste away. A huge cement vault had been built under the building, and the waste from each of the seats was funneled down to that cement vault. The Germans used the Russian prisoners to clean out the mess about every three months. In between times, the smell in the latrine was nauseating. The outside latrine could be used in the daytime, but not at night because we were locked in the barracks at night and were not allowed to use the outside latrine.

Fortunately for us, each barracks had a small inside latrine located at the end of the building. The inside latrine was to be used only at night. No one was allowed to use it in the daytime when the outside latrine was available. The Russians were assigned to come in and clean the inside latrines every day. American airmen were not ordered to do this chore. It seemed that the Germans had no respect for the Russians, and often assigned them the most menial tasks.

As I settled down to meet my 13 roommates, I discovered that I was the only member of my crew in this room. Stalag Luft I was so large and spread out that I didn't know if any of my crewmembers were in the camp. It was a difficult time for the fourteen of us jammed together in this small room. We were strangers to each other, and completely under the control of the Germans. It was something we would have to learn to work out together. We did have two things in common: we were all American airmen and we were all prisoners of war. We had been well trained for war, but we had not been sufficiently prepared for the horrible treatment we would receive as prisoners of war in Germany.

During our combat orientation sessions we were given some instructions about what to do when captured. For example, we were told that if we became prisoners of war, we were to remember that we were still in the military and were to obey our senior officers wherever we were held as POWs, and we were to give no information to the enemy except for name, rank, and serial number. We were also warned not to get too friendly with or trusting of the enemy, who would just be trying to get military information. The instructors also told us to watch out for other tricks of the enemy, like having their doctors and orderlies pretend to be sympathetic and friendly if we were in the hospital. It could be a ruse to get information. Microphones might be hidden in the barracks for the Germans to hear our conversations. The instructors warned us that we should be careful what we say at all times. While we were not directly ordered to escape if captured, the instructions said that we could help defeat the enemy by planning to escape, if possible. All these things and more were explained to us, but nothing really prepared us for confinement in the prison camp. We were not prepared for the brutal treatment that the Germans inflicted on the prisoners of war in their camps.

The horrible conditions and the bad treatment added to the uncertainty of the future. These things were a new challenge for all of us. We had to learn to work together and trust one another. After getting to know one another, we knew that all of us were real American airmen, and no one was a German imposter planted as an American airman. Once that was determined, we faced the uncertainty of the future together.

Three of the men were from Massachusetts. Albert J. Senechal, known as "Red," was from Amesbury, Massachusetts; Matthew R. McGuire, nicknamed "Mickey," was from Gloucester, Massachusetts; and Kenneth D. Simpson, who we called "Sim," was from North Quincy, Massachusetts. Giving nicknames was a favorite pastime in the camp. I was to get a nickname later. Red was thirty, the oldest of the fourteen men in the room. At twenty, I was the youngest. Our bond of solidarity was established from day one, and we agreed to share everything equally, and watch out for each other.

The next day we received our food from the Germans. We only got two loaves of black bread and one bucket of barley soup to feed the fourteen of us. The Germans had given each of us a small, crude metal bowl to put our soup in. Each bowl could hold about two cups of soup. We could see from the way our food was given to us that we needed a system to dole the food out so that each man would receive an equal amount. A. J. "Red" Senechal and I were designated by the men to be in charge of distributing the food. Cooking was a problem. We were given about six blocks of coal a week. The six blocks altogether were equal to the size of a red brick. That was not enough coal to keep the room warm and to cook, too. We only cooked on rare occasions. The rest of the time we ate everything cold. We tried to save as much coal as we could to give us heat in the colder weather.

Red and I distributed the soup and bread among the fourteen of us. We were very hungry, and it was really not enough food to satisfy our hunger. This being our first full day, we did not know when our next food would come. As we were all settling down to eat our meager fare, we were suddenly startled to hear one of the men yelling, "There are maggots in this soup. I can't eat this stuff!"

Everyone checked his own soup, and, pushing it away, looked up in disgust. The words, "There are maggots in my soup, too," echoed around the room. "We can't eat this slop," they cried out.

We had two prisoners from another room visiting us. They had been in the camp for a couple of weeks, and since we were more recent arrivals, they had come to visit us to catch up on the latest news from outside.

"Don't worry," one of our visitors said. "The maggots are well cooked and they are dead."

"Besides that," he added, "they add protein to your diet. Eating them won't kill you or make you sick."

When our two visitors saw the shocked looks on our faces, they got up from the bunk bed they had been sitting on and headed for the door, laughing loudly as they left the room.

Nobody in our room was laughing. We were not reassured by their attempts at humor, and several of the men refused to eat the maggot-laden soup. As time went on I was to learn that this type of humor was prevalent throughout the camp. And I have to admit that sometimes it relieved the tension we all felt.

In a strange way, our visitors had been right. No one got sick or died, and within a week we all ate the soup, maggots or no maggots. The maggots were very big and had two tails. One of the men named them "P-38s." A P-38 was one of our fighter planes with twin tails. We got used to this kind of soup, and no one complained again. In fact, no one even discussed the maggots in the barley soup. Later we learned that the food in the German storehouse was often kept there for so long that the barley became infested with maggots. But this did not prevent the Germans from giving the barley soup to us.

A German cook, with the help of Russian and British prisoners, ran the camp kitchen. The British and Russian prisoners had been in the camp long before we were captured. They volunteered for kitchen duty because they could get extra food from time to time. All our food was prepared in this kitchen and brought to us in our barracks. We soon discovered that there was sawdust in the black bread, supposedly to add bulk to our meager diet. The black bread was baked in the camp kitchen. When the bread was formed into a loaf, it was rolled in sawdust to keep its shape while baking in the oven. It certainly did nothing to enhance the taste of the bread. But after a few days went by, it didn't seem to make much difference if the meal was a good one or a bad one. When you are near to starving, you will eat anything. We ate the soup with maggots in it, the bread with the sawdust, and whatever other horrible concoctions the Germans gave us. I soon learned that my hunger overcame the bad taste of the food. We were just glad to get any food.

Only a couple of weeks had gone by, and I was already cold, hungry, and tired. Getting a good night's sleep was almost impossible while shivering from the cold and with my stomach growling from hunger pangs. I had not been given a nickname yet, and I did not volunteer one. My own name, Ralph, seemed good enough to me. But it seemed as if no one in the camp could get by without a nickname, and I was about to get mine. It was one of the coldest nights of the year, and I was on my bunk wrapped in blankets. There was no heat in the barracks. It was so cold I even had a part of one of my blankets wrapped around my shoulders and my head and face so that only my eyes and nose were visible. One of my buddies saw me on the bunk all bundled up in blankets. He looked at me, and with a smile on his face, he said to everyone, "Gees, Ralph looks just like a mouse." Everyone laughed and from then on I was known as "Mousie." It was not meant in a derogatory manner. It was just the impression given by the quick view of seeing only my eyes and nose showing while I was huddled in my blankets. I accepted my nickname gracefully. After that, when I made entries in my log or drew pictures, I signed them with my nickname, Mousie. The constant noise of the air-raid sirens every other night also made it difficult to sleep. The sirens would go off, and the Germans shut off all the searchlights in the camp. We could hear the drone of the Royal Air Force planes as they passed overhead on the way to their target.

Good news came the next week when we began to receive International Red Cross parcels. We were supposed to get the parcels every week, one parcel for each man. Unfortunately, we did not always get them weekly. The parcels were distributed to us sporadically. We asked the Germans why the Red Cross packages did not come every week. The German guards told us that our planes sometimes bombed the trains carrying the Red Cross packages. That was their explanation, but I did not believe them. It was more likely that they were keeping the Red Cross packages for themselves.

Each Red Cross parcel would barely feed one man for a week. When we did get our packages, we received only seven of them. Instead of a parcel for each man, we had to split the food up among fourteen men. It was not enough food, and we took care to ration it very carefully. Each Red Cross parcel contained variations of food, soap, and cigarettes. For example, each parcel might contain one can of Spam, one can of corned beef, a half pound of cheese, a can of salmon, a box of K-2 biscuits, powdered milk, two chocolate D bars, and one pound of raisins or prunes, plus the soap and cigarettes. The next shipment of Red Cross parcels might contain totally different items.

The Germans continued to give us some food, if you could call it that. Once a day they gave us one bucket of soup and two loaves of black bread. That was not much food to be divided among fourteen hungry airmen. Sometimes the Germans even gave us ersatz tea. Ersatz was a German word for imitation or substitution. In other words, it was not real tea, but we drank it anyhow. It was better than nothing. Once in a great while they gave us a small amount of cheese to be split up among us. The cheese was inside medium-sized tubes that we had to squeeze to get the cheese out. There was French writing on the tubes so we assumed that the cheese came from France, which was occupied by the Germans. Even with the Red Cross food, and with what the Germans gave us, it was barely enough food to keep us alive.

What Red and I had to do was ration out the food from the Red Cross with the slop the Germans gave us in an attempt to stretch the food for the week. We combined all of our canned goods and packaged food and tried to make at least one fairly good meal a day combined with German daily rations. Not everyone in the other rooms combined the food as we did. But we found that this system worked for us.

The Red Cross food was great, but the cigarettes were a real treasure for us. Cigarettes were our medium of currency, with which to barter for anything that was available. I can't remember exactly all the items you could buy with cigarettes, or the number of cigarettes it cost for each item, but I do remember that having cigarettes to barter was very important.

One of our enterprising kriegies started his own bartering system and operated it just like a military base PX (post exchange). Kriegie was our shortened term for the German word kriegsgefangenan, which meant prisoner of war. We got in the habit of using the word kriegies when referring to ourselves. The kriegie who set up his bartering system operated out of his barracks room. We called his room the PX, and when we said we were going to the PX, all the prisoners knew what we meant. The Germans knew about this "PX," and they, too, traded with the kriegie. Fortunately for all of us, there was no rule against this type of bartering, so we did not have to be afraid to openly make these trades.

The kriegie had a list of Red Cross items for sale, just like a PX or grocery store. For example, a can of Spam sold for 20 cigarettes, a bar of soap for 10 cigarettes, and a can of coffee sold for 30 cigarettes. There were many other items available from the Red Cross parcels to be exchanged for cigarettes. The entrepreneur would trade whatever you wanted to trade and he would take a percentage of each sale in cigarettes. When he sold a can of Spam, for example, for thirty cigarettes, he had probably paid twenty-five cigarettes for the Spam. Thus his profit was the extra five cigarettes. Or a POW might sell the entrepreneur his watch for a can of Spam and fifteen cigarettes. The entrepreneur might then sell the watch for any available item or items he wanted and still make a profit. So the guys who were lucky enough to still have their watches or cigarette lighters could exchange them for goods, also.

Cigarettes were also very valuable to the members of the escape committee and to the officers as a way to get information and needed items from the Germans. Our commanding officer had set up a system to get enough cigarettes to be able to barter with the German guards. American cigarettes were such a highly prized medium of exchange that the German guards were eager to get them. They would barter almost anything to get the American cigarettes. Occasionally a POW would try to deal directly with a German guard. Colonel Byerly did not like the American airmen dealing directly with the Germans, and he gave orders not to do so. But some POWs continued to barter with the guards. The escape committee was always allowed to exchange things with the German guards to get materials to help arrange escapes.

Members of the escape committee got the cigarettes from the makeshift PX and used them to barter with the guards. When something was needed, a member of the escape committee would go to the PX and request cigarettes for the committee. The entrepreneur would give him the needed number of cigarettes. This was an outright gift, with no bartering involved. All the men in the camp agreed that this was the right thing to do. They knew that the escape committee would keep us informed, and we all wanted to help in any escape attempts. With these cigarettes, the escape committee was able to get information from the guards, as well as radio parts, cameras, and other items that could be used to help with escapes. Especially needed were wire cutters and paper and ink to be used to make fake identification papers. The committee also traded for maps and railroad time schedules. Parts were desperately needed to keep our radios working. The men who operated the radios made sure to keep us all informed about what was going on with the war effort.

Time in the camp dragged by. It still amazes me how we adapted to life in the camp. In spite of our severe hardships, we continued to help each other cope with life in the POW camp. The English doctors and the male nurses at the small infirmary near the main gate continued to treat me because my wounds were still infected. One of the male nurses, Alex C. "Jock" Nobel, was from Scotland, and the other one, Luther "Taffy" Evans, was from South Wales. They did the best they could to help me. The wounds in both legs had not healed, and walking was difficult and painful. The shrapnel was still in my legs, in my buttock, and in my right elbow. It would take an operation to remove all the shrapnel, and the doctors at the camp infirmary did not have the necessary facilities and medicine to perform such surgery. The doctors did not even have any painkiller to ease my pain. They were only able to clean my wounds, add sulfur, and rebandage the wounds.

I saw the doctor every other day until, finally, the treatments cured the infection. It had taken a long month before the infection was healed, but there was nothing available for my pain. When I walked or moved my legs, the pain was sometimes almost unbearable, and I still limped badly. I was afraid that even when my wounds finally healed, I would still have a bad limp for the rest of my life. I was trying to work out a plan to help myself heal and to walk without a limp. Unfortunately, the Germans did not provide physical therapy for POWs. That's not at all surprising for people who cared so little for us that they still gave us soup laced with maggots. Even without physical therapy, and in spite of the pain, I kept forcing my right leg to straighten out in hopes of eventually being able to

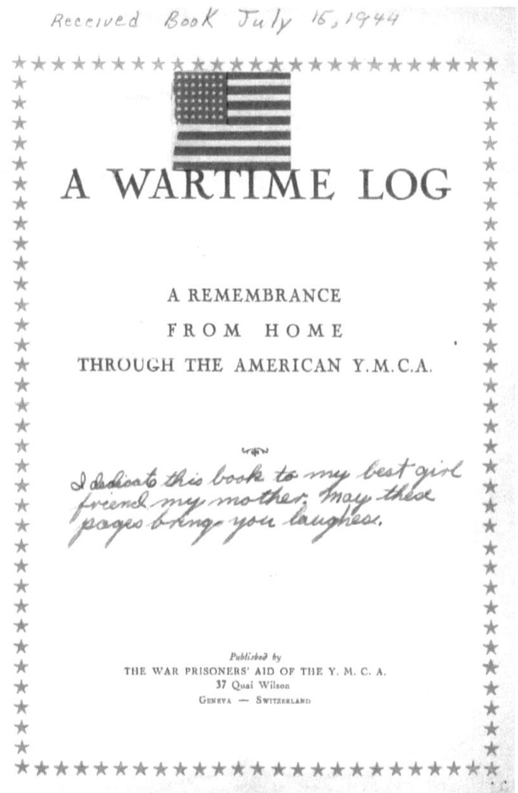

Front page of the log book provided by the War Prisoners' Aid of the Y.M.C.A. and distributed by the International Red Cross.

walk without the limp. It was very painful, but I persisted.

We did have some recreational time at Stalag Luft I, but not courtesy of the Germans. The International Red Cross sent volleyballs, soccer balls, and softballs and bats to the camp. Later we received books and playing cards. One time we received wartime logs, which were like diaries. I decided to use one to keep a log of my time in the camp. I drew some pictures and wrote in it from time to time, but I was careful not to write about the bad treatment, the lack of food, and the lack of medical treatment, or about anything of a military nature. During inspections the German guards went through our personal effects and sometimes even read our wartime logs. They wanted to see if they could get information about us or get any military information.

One day the International Red Cross shipments included some decks of playing cards. We were given one deck of cards for use in our room. That one deck of playing cards got used over and over again. We played whist, poker, hearts, solitaire, and all the different card games we could think of. It was another way for us to pass the time. We tried to be careful with the cards because we knew we might never get any more. But no matter how careful we were, the cards were used so much that the color, the spots, and the numbers were worn off.

As the days passed, we seemed to fall into a certain routine. We were sometimes able to supplement our meager food supply with fresh vegetable and eggs. Some of the German guards who lived near the camp with their families had small gardens. They grew vegetables and had access to fresh eggs. Some of the prisoners were able to barter with the Germans to get the fresh vegetables and eggs in exchange for cigarettes. The vegetables and eggs were a special treat for us when we could get them.

We began to understand what the Germans expected of us, and the men tried to comply with their rules to avoid any punishment. We even got used to the roll call when the Germans counted us every morning and night, and we got adjusted to being locked in every night. This is not to say that we felt defeated and without hope for the future. As American airmen, we were still proud men, and tried to maintain our dignity and pride at all times. We had faith in our country, and believed that America and the Allies would eventually win the war.

Every time I thought things were beginning to calm down and settle into a regular routine, something would happen to get the Germans angry. Whenever the Germans got angry with us, it always resulted in some kind of punishment. In our room, for example, we had the episode of the crawl space. The barracks floor was made of wood, and there was a small crawl space between the wooden floor and the ground underneath the floor. Even though the crawl space was small, it was just large enough for a person to crawl through it. The Germans, who we had nicknamed the goons, took turns crawling under the floor of the rooms in our barracks. Obviously, only Germans who understood English were chosen for this task because they hoped that by this method of spying they could listen to our conversations and get information about military operations.

Sometimes we heard them crawling under the floor, and sometimes we could see the light of their flashlight when the goons accidentally let it shine up through the cracks in the floor. We never said anything that would be of use to the goon under the floor, and ordinarily we did not pay any attention to them when they started crawling around. But one night, when we heard one of the goons crawling under the floor of our room, we just got fed up with their constant spying on us.

The goon stopped moving, and we knew he had positioned himself directly under the center of our floor. We were motioning to each other, silently pointing to the floor. Everyone now knew that the goon was under us. He had stopped moving and was completely silent, listening to our conversation. We continued talking to each other, but only small talk, like about girls, home, baseball, and about how we knew that we were going to win the war.

Sometimes when we had coffee left from a Red Cross parcel we kept a large metal pitcher of hot water on top of the heated stove in case someone wanted a cup of coffee. This particular night was one of the times we had a full pitcher of hot water on top of the stove. None of us liked to have the goons underneath the room listening to our conversations, but usually we ignored them. This night was different. One of the men stood up, quietly moved to the stove, and picked up the pitcher. He carried the pitcher of hot water over to a crack in the floor in the center of the room where we knew the goon was hiding. Slowly and quietly he held the pitcher over the crack and then quickly poured the hot water down through the crack into the crawl space.

We knew he had hit his target when the German started screaming. We thought it was pretty funny until the goon retaliated by firing his gun up through the floor. He wanted to kill us. Everyone jumped up on the bunks against the wall, hoping the bullets wouldn't hit us. The goon's shots came up through the floor in the middle of the room, and the bullets went into the ceiling. Thankfully none of us got shot. We hadn't expected the shooting. It was a close call, and we learned another lesson. We would have to be more careful in the future when we planned something against the rules. We expected the goons to invade our room to punish us in some manner, but nothing else happened that night.

The next day, during the regular morning roll call, the commandant of the camp came out to address us. He was very upset about a prisoner throwing hot water and injuring a German soldier. "If such an episode ever occurs again," the commandant warned us, "there will be extremely harsh punishment for all the men in the room. Your punishment for today will be to remain standing out here for the entire day."

While we were kept outside, we were allowed to walk around and talk to each other, but we were forbidden to enter the barracks all day. The guards in the towers watched us carefully while German soldiers were sent into our barracks to search for contraband. The search also served as just another form of punishment. They went through our belongings and stole our candy bars, cigarettes, and anything else they wanted. That was one of the reasons we always tried to carry our candy, cigarettes and whatever other small items we wanted to keep, with us at all times. The Germans also seemed to take great pleasure in overturning our mattresses, throwing the blankets on the floor and making a mess of the room. We, of course, had to clean up the mess when we were allowed back in the barracks.

I knew that some of the POWs talked about escaping, but so far, I had not heard about any escape plans. I knew that somewhere in the camp we had an escape committee, but I had never discussed it with anyone until one night the topic of escape was discussed in our room. Dwayne Gillette, one of the fourteen men in my room, had an idea about how he could escape. Thirteen of us gathered around Dwayne to hear about his plan. We were all excited and listened quietly to his escape plan.

Gillette's escape was timed to coincide with the British bombing raids. On the nights when the British bombed Hamburg, Rostock, or Berlin, their planes flew over Stalag Luft I to reach their targets. The camp's air-raid sirens sounded as the British planes passed overhead. All the lights in the camp were shut off, including the searchlights, and the camp was temporarily in complete darkness. Gillette had checked how long the lights stayed off. The time varied, depending upon which target the Brits were going to bomb. The British did not bomb in close formation like we did. Their lead plane would take off, and in one- or two-minute intervals the other aircraft would form a string of planes following the leader. Gillette was sure that he had the timing figured out, and he felt he could escape during the time all the lights in the camp were out.

The CO and the escape committee approved Gillette's plan. Within one week, he was ready to make his escape try. None of us in the room were ready to go with him, but we all volunteered to help him in any way we could. I wished I could go with him, but I was in no shape to attempt an escape. My legs would not hold up.

Gillette began timing the allied air raids. Three days later, Gillette announced that he had the timing all worked out, and he set the escape for that night. A few days earlier, after the escape plan had been first approved by the escape committee, we had begun loosening the floorboards. After the Germans locked us in our room each night, we worked on taking the nails out of the floorboards so that the boards could be removed in order to create a space large enough for Gillette to crawl through to the outside of the barracks. When Gillette said this was the night he was going, we were already finished and able to raise the floorboards so he could fit into the crawl space. As soon as the sirens sounded, all the lights in the camp went out. Gillette lowered himself into the crawl space under the floor and made his way through to the outside of the barracks.

We all raced to the shuttered window, but only a few of us were able to jump up onto the small table. There was a small six-inch-wide slot over the window. We tried to watch for Gillette, but it was too dark to see much of anything. But because it was pitch black outside, Gillette was able to crawl across the open ground to the barbed-wire fence without being seen by the Germans. The escape committee had given Gillette a wire cutter to cut a hole in the fence large enough for him to get through. He also had some chocolate D bars, and we gave him some more so he would have food to sustain him for a while.

There was a single strand of barbed wire about two feet high stretched on posts around the camp. This was the warning wire. Any POW who went beyond this wire would be shot. The warning wire was about twenty feet from the first barbed wire fence. There was another five feet between the first barbed-wire fence and the second, or outer, barbed-wire fence. In this five-foot space, the Germans had spread tangled, snarled barbed wire on the ground to about four feet high. Unfortunately, just as Gillette reached the first barbed-wire fence, the all clear sounded. Gillette had hoped to cut his way through both the barbed-wire fences and the tangled barbed wire between the fences.

Suddenly, the searchlights came back on again. We could see clearly now as one of the searchlights shined right on Gillette. The guard in the tower saw him at the fence. He could have shot Gillette right then and there, but instead the guard yelled something. Even though he yelled in German, Gillette knew that the guard meant, "Halt!" Gillette began to slowly crawl back away from the fence to the warning wire, praying that the guard would not shoot. The German guards with their dogs surrounded him. Gillette quickly raised his hands to surrender. As the guards grabbed him and marched him away, Gillette dropped his D bars on the ground, and yelled for us to pick up the chocolate bars and save them until he came back. We couldn't do that. If we went outside we would be shot. It didn't matter anyway, because the goons picked up the D bars and kept them.

The Hitler Youth soldiers were in the camp as guards when I first arrived at the camp, and there were many of them still there. They ranged in age from fourteen or fifteen to eighteen. At the age of eighteen, Hitler Youth members were usually transferred to the regular German army. It was the Hitler Youth soldiers who caught Dwayne in his escape attempt. The Hitler Youth members guarding us were very cruel and harassed us every chance they got. They did not need much of an excuse to shoot any of us. Dwayne was really fortunate that he made it back to the warning wire and was not caught between the two rows of barbed wire. We felt sure that the Hitler Youth guard would have shot him.

Dwayne had tried to guess which British bombing raid would force the Germans to keep the searchlights off in the camp long enough for him to escape. He timed the raids pretty accurately, but this night he guessed wrong. As punishment, Gillette spent seven days in solitary confinement in a separate building that contained all the solitary cells. When his time was up, the Germans returned him to our room. We were very happy to have him back.

Things began to quiet down after Gillette's attempted escape. We slipped back into our normal routine until one night we got the news that an airman in the room next to us had somehow caught and killed a cat. The men in our room were invited to the room next door to share in what they called a Pomeranian rabbit dinner. Obviously one cat wouldn't go too far for 28 men, but it was very unselfish of them to invite us to share. I missed out on this luxurious meal because I was late getting back. By the time I arrived, the food was all gone. Believe it or not, I was sorry I was too late to share in the meal. Once again things had begun to quiet down in the camp, but I knew that the peace and quiet would not last. The Germans never allowed it to stay peaceful.

CHAPTER EIGHT

Stalag Luft I: Things Get Worse

There were some good times in the camp, like when we were able to take our turn with the phonograph record player that we borrowed from our makeshift library in another barracks. The International Red Cross had given some record players and records to the American officers to be shared with the men. The library also contained books donated by the Red Cross. When it was our turn, we took the phonograph and records back to our barracks. Listening to music was a special treat for us. We heard Tommy Dorsey, Glenn Miller, Artie Shaw, Les Brown, Jimmy Dorsey, and many others. It was as if a little piece of home had come into our life. The record player had to be wound up to play, and when it stopped, someone got up and wound it again. We did not mind. We had no electrical outlets in the room, just that one small light in the ceiling, so an electric phonograph would not have been any use to us.

If it was a good day outside, we would put the phonograph outside the window, between the barracks, and play the records. The men from the other barracks would gather around. We usually had a big crowd. You could tell that most of the men listening were reminiscing about home and wishing they were back there. The music made us happy and sad at the same time.

These happy times never lasted long. We were always aware that somewhere in the camp the escape committee was diligently working on ways of escape. Gillette's attempt to escape had failed, but that would not stop other POWs from wanting to try. Tunnels were always being built somewhere in the camp. If successful, they would be the best way to get outside the camp without being shot. Digging tunnels was not easy to do. It took secrecy and dedication to the hard work needed for the hours, days, and months necessary to complete a tunnel. Many of the POWs were too weak to help. We lacked equipment and had to use whatever we could find or make. The diggers would use cans, makeshift shovels or anything else they could find. The men had to use some of the wooden slats from the beds in the room where the tunnel was located. The slats were necessary to shore up the tunnel and prevent it from collapsing.

Besides lacking equipment, there were two other major problems. One was trying to keep the Germans from finding out about the tunnel. The tunnel was usually built under the barracks in an area separated from the crawl space so that the goons who spied on us in the crawl space would not see the tunnel. The other problem was what to do with the dirt taken out of the tunnel.

One means of hiding the dirt was to put it in to small bags that were given to the men. The dirt-filled bags were hidden in the men's pant legs, and as the POWs walked around the outside field and between the barracks, the dirt was slowly released down their leg to the ground. The problem with this was that the dirt taken from the tunnel was much darker than the dirt on the outside ground. The men had to slowly grind the darker dirt and spread it with their shoes to blend in with the lighter dirt. This was a very long and slow process. It was also dangerous, if a German guard happened to see what they were doing.

A second means of disposing of the dirt was to hide it over the ceiling of the room. The barracks had slanted roofs, and when the ceilings had been built into the rooms, there was a good-sized space between the ceiling and the roof, much like a small attic in our houses at home. The tunnel diggers were able to hide dirt in that space. They had to be careful because if they put too much dirt in that hidden space, the ceiling might collapse.

The men in charge of tunnel digging were very inventive when it came to hiding dirt. They devised a third way of hiding the dirt, by using the outside latrine. The waste from the outside latrine only went down below the building into the cement vault, where it stayed until the Russians came to clean it out. When the dirt was thrown down into the vault, it seemed to just disappear in with the urine and other waste. By the time the Russians came to clean out the vault, the dirt would be mixed with the waste material, and blended in so well that it couldn't be distinguished as dirt from a tunnel.

Once the Germans pulled one of their terrorizing raids at about 2 o'clock in the morning. I don't think they had any real reason for the raid. It was just to keep us on edge, never knowing when they would come. The unannounced raids also gave the guards an opportunity to steal our cigarettes, chocolate bars, or whatever they could find. Everyone in the barracks was ordered outside while the Germans checked through the barracks. We were still half asleep as we went wearily outside. It was always a frightening experience when we were ordered out of the barracks in the middle of the night or early morning. The Germans hollered at us and threatened us. They used their rifles to push us out the door. Some of the guards had huge dogs with them. I was thankful that these big attack dogs were on a leash. Luckily for us, the guards kept them on their leashes, but we never knew if they would release the dogs to attack us. It was very unsettling.

On this raid the Germans found a tunnel in a room at the end of our barracks. They were furious as they destroyed the tunnel by caving it in and searched the entire room more carefully. They found the dirt hidden over the ceiling. There was nothing they could do about the dirt hidden in the ceiling because it was too early in the morning. They needed a larger crew, so the goons kept us outside our barracks all night and left two guards on duty. More Germans arrived around seven o'clock in the morning and entered the barracks. They went to the room that had the tunnel and began to drill holes in the ceiling. The hidden dirt came pouring down out of the holes and covered the floor, the beds, and the table. The goons had made sure that no more dirt would ever be hidden there. Even after they left and let us back into the barracks, small amounts of dirt that were still in the ceiling continued to seep down into that room for days.

Now that things had quieted down again, I had more time to think about different things. I remembered that when I first came into the camp I had trouble sleeping. Later on I could fall asleep, but would sometimes wake up in the middle of the night, wondering if my mother and father knew that I was still alive. Maybe they thought I was dead, and that upset me terribly. When we were in England, we were told that it was the duty of the commanding officer of the bomb group to notify families that their son, brother, or husband was killed, missing in action, or a prisoner of war. I did not know if my parents had been notified that I was alive and was a POW. My mother was a very religious person, and her faith would sustain her though this ordeal. But it still troubled me because I knew she would be very worried, especially if she had not yet been notified where I was. I kept praying that she would find out where I was and write to me. So far, noone else in my room had received letters or packages from home. We all hoped that news from our families would come soon.

One of the most important activities that occupied our time was keeping our bodies, our clothes, and our room clean. When I first arrived at the camp in April 1944, we had been deloused and given clean clothes, and so we were free from bedbugs, lice, and crabs. I had had enough of those insects in the Dulag Luft Interrogation Center to last me for a lifetime. It was easier for us to stay clean in the warmer weather of summer, but I should have known that freedom from the bugs wouldn't last for long.

As the war continued, many more allied planes were being shot down and the airmen captured. Some of these prisoners were being sent to Stalag Luft I. The camp was getting more crowded with these new prisoners coming in all the time. The new POWs were jammed into the already overcrowded rooms. The Germans did not bother to take the time to make sure that the new prisoners were deloused thoroughly. Soon the bedbugs and lice were once again spreading throughout the camp.

The warmer weather of May and June cheered us up a little bit. We naturally preferred the summer weather rather than the cold weather of April, when morale was not always at the highest level. The Red Cross had supplied us with sporting equipment like bats, baseballs, baseball gloves, basketballs, and soccer balls, but some of us were unable to participate. Quite a few of the men were in such bad condition from hunger, injuries, and sickness that they lacked the energy needed to participate in sports or any other kind of physical activity. Just walking around the compound was enough exercise, and even that began to drop off. Both the health and the morale of many of the men were at a low point, and they would skip any kind of physical activity and just sit down and wait — wait for the food rations, wait until it was time to go back to the barracks, wait until we heard from our families, wait for the war to end. We were always waiting for something.

One activity that we could still enjoy was reading, and we were very thankful for our makeshift library, a small room with the books, the phonograph, and the musical records. Any POW could go to the library, get the book or books he wanted and return to his barracks to read. Reading was the easiest activity. Reading did not require the use of any strength or energy, and it helped us to take our minds off our imprisonment for a brief time. We were all tired and hungry, and some of the men were so weak that reading was their only escape from the reality surrounding us.

One thing that could always make us temporarily more active was the occurrence of a special event. The event could be something good, like receiving our Red Cross parcels or getting a letter from home. Or it could be something bad, like being rousted out of our barracks by the goons or having the men in the barracks punished for some infraction of the German rules. One day during this hot summer of 1944, we had a really unusual special event. We were outside the barracks when suddenly the air-raid sirens went off. We were not ordered to return to the barracks, so we stayed outside to see the allied planes that would be flying overhead on their way to a bombing raid. It would be a great morale booster to cheer as we watched our planes flying overhead.

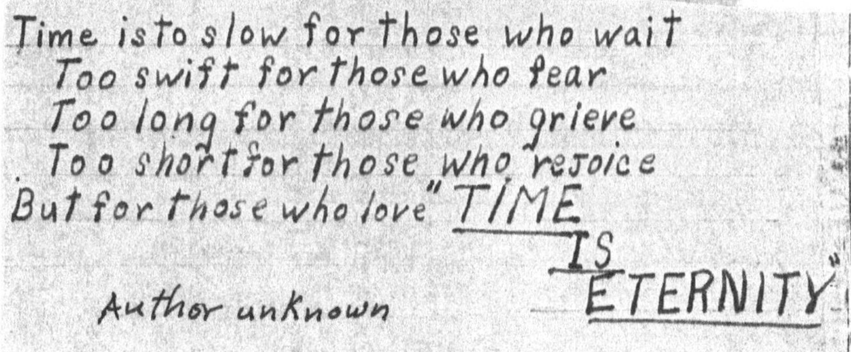

"Time," from my log book. Lonely POW staring out through the barbed wire.

The yards were filled with American and British airmen watching the sky, but we did not hear the loud noises usually made by squadrons of bombers. Instead, we heard the sounds of a single plane. It was a P-51 fighter. As the plane got closer, the pilot flew over the camp at about two thousand or three thousand feet. The whole camp went crazy at seeing an

American fighter. The prisoners began shouting and waving. The P-51 turned and came back at a lower altitude to take a closer look.

A German gunnery school was in a field next to the camp. When the pilot came flying over the camp at about 1,000 feet, the Germans at the gunnery school began shooting their artillery guns at the P-51. The flak from their guns hit the engine. The plane was badly damaged. The pilot managed to maneuver the plane higher so he could bail out. We could see the parachute open and the pilot drifting safely down. As soon as he landed, the Germans had him surrounded. They brought the flier to our camp.

We did not get a chance to speak to the pilot. The Germans led him right past us and straight to the solitary confinement cells. He spent ten days in solitary, and when the Germans were through interrogating him, he was assigned to a barracks. When he finally was allowed into the camp, everyone cheered and surrounded him. I wanted to know who he was, and where he was from, and what news he had for us. He was already answering questions from the men when I arrived. I could hear some of his replies about the progress of the war. He told us that the invasion had started, but we knew that already. But when he said that we were definitely winning the war and that the Germans were retreating, the men went wild, jumping up and down, waving their arms and cheering as loudly as they could. That was the most encouraging news we had heard for months. I wasn't able to get close enough to ask him any questions. There were too many POWs surrounding him and firing questions at him. After ten days in solitary he was exhausted, and said he needed to go back to his barracks. The excitement of meeting him and the good news about the war kept our morale up for many days.

I remember July 4, 1944, well for two reasons. Number one, it was our Fourth of July holiday, and number two, the Germans decided to make a search for a tunnel that same day. We never knew why these abrupt searches were made or why certain compounds were chosen for the search and others were not. The timing of the summer searches wasn't too bad because the weather was warm outside, but the searches were still disruptive. This Fourth of July, instead of being at home preparing for the big celebration, I was standing outside the barracks for the Germans' morning roll call.

Suddenly we saw German guards running toward the North 1 Compound. They stormed into that North 1 barracks to begin their search while all of us from the North 1 Compound were standing out in the field for roll call. After roll call we were ordered to stay outside in the sports field. There was nothing we could do except stand and watch as they entered the barracks searching for tunnels, radios and anything else they considered contraband. Unfortunately for us, the guards did not stop at contraband. They also used the searches to steal any chocolates, cigarettes and other personal items belonging to the prisoners. Sometimes I wondered whether the German commandant ordered these searches to punish us or to keep the guards on their toes, or maybe both.

We had radios hidden somewhere in the camp. The searches always made us afraid that the Germans might find them. The POWs built the radios out of parts bought from the guards and paid for with cigarettes and other available items. Our only connection with the outside world was from the men operating the radios. They listened to the war news. The latest news was quickly spread around the camp from prisoner to prisoner.

The Allied invasion at Normandy, France, had begun a few weeks ago, on June 6, 1944, and the Germans were slowly being forced back. The German guards continued to tell us that Germany was winning every battle. But thanks to our radio reports from the BBC (British Broadcasting Corporation), we knew that the Germans were not winning the war. I felt sure that some of the guards were aware of the radios in the camp because they would ask us how the war was really going.

We were not afraid that the guards' questions about the war were to trick us into revealing the location of a radio. We never mentioned where we got the news. The Germans made periodic searches for radios, but they never found the ones we had hidden. The radios were hidden very carefully inside the walls. The Germans searched thoroughly, but they never thought to break down the walls. Now that the war was going so badly for Germany, the guards no longer trusted the German broadcasts. They asked us what was happening so they could learn the truth.

Anyway, this Fourth of July was a nice, warm day, and at first we did not mind being locked out while the Germans searched the North 1 Barracks. Rather than feeling like a punishment to us, we felt good lying out on the sports field, looking up at the sky. The day dragged on past lunchtime. I was getting hungry. We began to get restless and looked around at each other, but it appeared that there would not be any food for us. Withholding food was another typical form of German punishment. Not only did the Germans not feed us, they ordered us not to use the outside latrine. Our compound leader, who was in charge of all 14 barracks in the North 1 compound, chose a small corner of the field and indicated that that part of the field would be the open-air latrine.

Instead of letting us back into the barracks at night, the Germans made us stay out in the field. As we lay down on the field looking up at the sky, we had a beautiful view of the stars such as the North Star and the Big Dipper. Now that it was nighttime, we had been without food for the whole day, and considering that we only received food once a day, we were getting very hungry. Usually we liked to carry our food and valuable belongings, like cigarettes and chocolate D Bars, with us at all times. I had my chocolate D Bars and cigarettes with me. We never knew when the Germans would schedule a search and steal these items. But some of the men were either caught by surprise or had no food to carry with them. All of us who had chocolate D bars or other food with us shared with those who had nothing to eat.

Some of the Germans made fun of us as we were lying down in the field. One of the goons reminded us that today was the Fourth of July.

"Did you forget that today was your Independence Day?" he asked as he laughed at us.

We certainly did not have our independence in this camp. We knew that the Kraut was just busting ass and everybody laughed. We believed that even though the Germans controlled our lives while we were prisoners of war, they could never really take away our independence. They would never change our thoughts and our love for our country.

Later in July 1944, we heard that some injured Americans and other allied POWs were being repatriated in exchange for German POWs who were wounded. This exchange of wounded prisoners was in accord with the Geneva Convention. I knew that I would not be one of the chosen ones, because there were other POWs more severely wounded and sicker than I was. The ones who needed severe medical attention were chosen first. There were a few POWs from Stalag Luft I who were chosen to be repatriated. One of those men was from a barracks near me. He was Lieutenant Don E. Folks from Spokane, Washington. When I heard that he was to be sent home, I gave him my home address and asked him to write and tell my mother and father that he saw me. Don was deluged with the same requests from the airmen to notify their families. He accepted all the requests.

During the summer months, we taunted the Germans when the daily bombing raids of the Mighty Eighth Air Force came close enough for us to see the contrails off in the distance as they were dropping their bombs in northern Germany. We would look up at the guards in the towers and yell at them, "Berlin kaput. Germans kaput." The guards became very angry. The German commandant posted orders on all the bulletin boards telling us that from now on when the air-raid siren sounded we were to go to the nearest barracks until the all clear sounded. Any prisoner not following these orders would be shot. The commanding officer of the North 1 Compound, Colonel Jean R. Byerly, told us to obey this order. The next time the air-raid sirens sounded, everyone obeyed Byerly's order, and headed for the barracks.

At the other end of our compound, one of the men began to run from the barracks he was in to the barracks next door. The goons were waiting for something like this to happen. They were still angry at the way we yelled at them when the air raids were happening farther away. One of the guards in the tower took careful aim, and without a warning, he shot the American in the head, killing him instantly. Colonel Byerly raised hell with the German commandant over the killing of one of our men. He also reported it to the Geneva Red Cross when they came to inspect the camp. I never heard

"Letter Home," from my log book, signed with my nickname, "Mousie."

if the inspectors did anything about it or not.

By October 1944 I had been in Stalag Luft I for six months, and I still had not received any mail from my family. The Germans gave us special forms to write letters to our families. We could not seal the forms. The Germans sealed the letters after they censored them. I had sent out my first letter to my mother on April 9, 1944, and it was now October. Six and one half months had passed since I was shot down, and all this time I was worried that my family thought I was dead. I had no way to know if they received my letter or not. I was really worried.

I will never forget the date. October 11, 1944. The first letter from my family arrived. "At last," was all I could think to myself as I opened the letter. It was a wonderful feeling to finally find out that my family knew I was alive. The letter was dated July 12, 1944, but it took three months for me to get it. In the letter my mother wrote, "Just received your card of April 9th, and also received a letter from the government giving us your address at the prisoner of war camp. The Red Cross told us the prisoners were being treated well."

I had to laugh at the sentence that said, "The Red Cross told us the prisoners were being treated well." My mother had no idea of how badly we were being treated. I would never be able to tell her the truth in my letters. There was no need to worry her any more than she was already worried about my being a prisoner of war. Even if I wrote anything about the bad treatment we were getting here, it would never get past the German censors, and I would probably get punished for writing bad things about the camp. I told my mother that I was well, and that we had sports, a phonograph and records to listen to, and plenty of food. I did not tell her that, even if we had regular sports, which we did not, I would not be able to play because of the wounds in my legs.

On October 20, 1944, I received my first package from my mother and father. It contained cartons of cigarettes. She had ordered them from a cigarette company, and the company shipped them directly to me at Stalag Luft I. The letters from home had improved my morale a great deal. I knew my family was well, and they knew I was alive. But receiving these cartons of cigarettes was as good as getting money to spend for items I might need. Everyone wanted cigarettes. I smoked before going

DEC. 9 - 1944

DEAR SON RALPH
WE ARE WELL HOPE YOU CAN SAY
the SAME. I RECIEVED MY ORDER
FROM WASHINGTON TO DAY. too
SEND YOU A BUNDLE AND CIGARETTS
I AM SENDING the CIGARETT TODAY.
AND getting the BUNDLE READY
FOR WEDNESDAY. to MAIL it toYou
thERE iS ONLY 2 DAYS A WEEK.
WE can go to the RED CROSS to
SEND you the BUNDLE thatis
WED. AND FRI, so I WILL HAVE MIND
READY. FOR WED. will SAY that
WE HAVE good NEWS. FROM
BUSTER. HE is ALL throught
NOW. HE WILL BE HOME FOR.
JAN. HE is OK. thANK GOD.
SONNY. EVERY BODY IS PRAYING
FOR YOUR SAFE RETURN. DID Not
get ANY. MAIL FROM you For
5 WEEKS NOW. the LAST, LETTER
I got WAS YOURS oF JULY 26. 1944
it took. 3 MONTHs to get HERE
HOPE that YOU ARE getting MY
MAIL oK. MIKE is still HOME
toMORROW i WILL RECIEVED FoR
you HOLY. COMUNION. WE ALL HOPE
AND PRAY that you WILL BE
HOME Soon NO SNOW yet

Copy of mail label to me from my family, concludes on facing page.

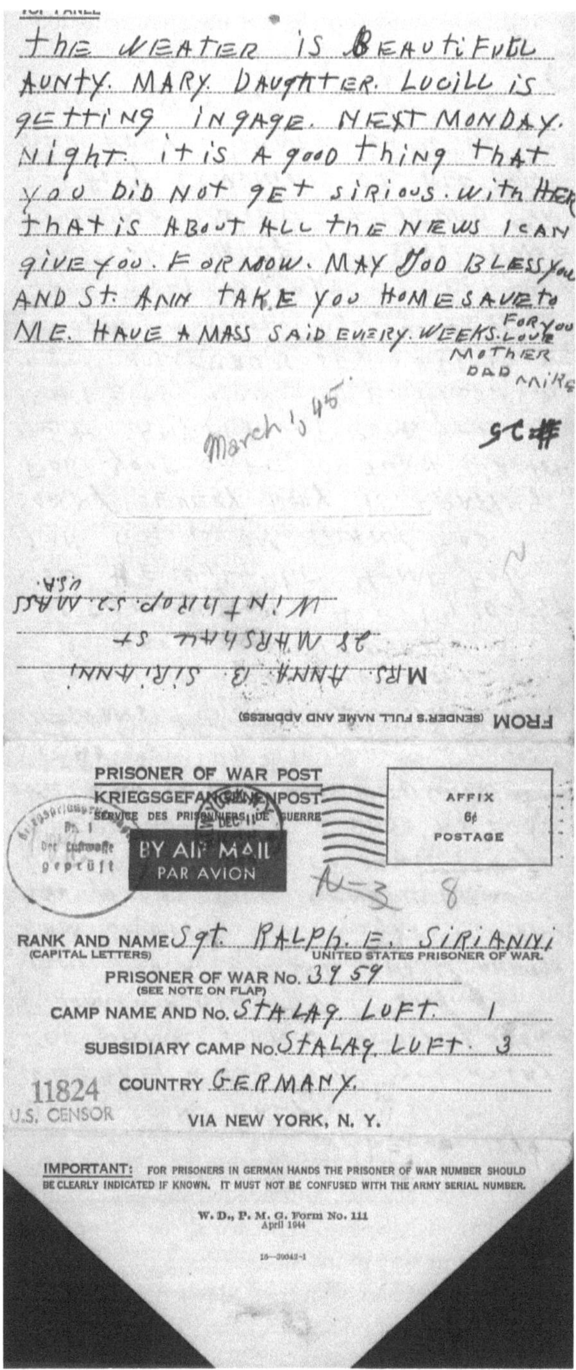

into the service and, like everyone else, I needed a smoke once in a while. We all saved some of our cigarettes to use in our bartering system.

On October 25, 1944, I received another letter from home that was dated August 28, 1944. My mother wrote, "It sure made me happy to hear that you play all kinds of sports." She added greetings from the family and said she looked forward to my getting home. Then she asked, "Do you get to go to church and confession?"

I answered her with another falsehood to ease her worries. I told her that we had a priest and that I went to Mass every Sunday. It was true that we had a priest and Mass, but I did not go to Mass every Sunday. By adding these falsehoods, I was not trying to please the Germans. I just wanted to make my parents feel better. Our mail was coming a little faster now, and I knew my mother got my answering letter, because on November 3 I received her September 18 letter. She wrote, "We are thankful that you go to church every Sunday, and that you have a good priest at the camp."

Even though it took a long time for the mail to arrive at the camp, my mother faithfully mailed her letters once a week, as she was allowed to do. I received a letter from my mother on Christmas Day, December 25, one day after my birthday. Her letter was dated October 11, 1944. She wrote that she had sent me a box filled with a jacket, sweater, shirt, shoes, and a couple of pairs of socks as presents for my birthday and for Christmas. The package was sent in October, but here it was December, and I still had not received any of the clothing my family sent. Now I was sure that the Germans had taken the package with the clothing. I guess some German soldier benefited at my expense.

I was very grateful that the letters were coming more regularly now, even though they pretty much said the same thing. I am sure it was difficult for my mother to know what to write, and I really appreciated her faithfulness in writing and keeping me informed about the family. When I got home I would give my mother an extra hug and thank her for the packages and letters she sent me for Christmas. But when I did get home, I would never tell her the details of my suffering in the camp, and I would never tell her about the falsehoods in my letters. They were only used to keep her spirits up, and once I got home, I would have no desire to upset her with the truth. I was satisfied that the misrepresentations about being treated well, engaging in sports, and going to Mass were justified to help ease her worries about me.

By the beginning of November the weather was getting colder and colder. The Germans were not overly generous with our supply of coal, and we could not keep a fire going in the stove all night. It was very cold at night, and we slept fully dressed with whatever clothes we could find. I even wore two pairs of stockings. I needed the extra clothing to stay warm enough to sleep.

With the cold weather and the lack of heat in our barracks, it did not take long for me to develop a bad cold. By Thanksgiving, my cold had developed into pneumonia. I could not get out of bed for roll call. One of the airmen told the guard that I was very sick and needed medical attention. The guard asked his superior if it was all right for three airmen to take me to the infirmary. Permission was granted, and three of my buddies carried me to the infirmary where I had been treated when I first came into the camp. The same two British doctors, and Jock and Taffy, the male nurses, were still there.

Thanksgiving was over and it was now into December and I was still sick in the infirmary. During the first two weeks, I was laid up in bed and couldn't move. The doctor gave me sulfur pills and made sure I drank plenty of water. The treatment did not help. My pneumonia was getting worse. I had terrible pains in my chest and could hardly breathe. Some of my buddies took turns coming to the main gate and waiting by the barbed wire for Jock or Taffy to come out of the infirmary and tell them how I was doing. They told my friends that I was doing as well as could be expected.

But I was not getting any better, and the next time the doctor came in to check my condition, I told him about the pain and the difficulty breathing. After checking me carefully, the doctor told me that my chest cavity had filled with fluid. The doctor said he would have to remove the fluid because it was preventing my lungs from expanding.

The doctor left the room and returned with a male nurse, who was carrying a basin and a very large syringe. After examining my chest, the doctor marked the left side with a pen. The infirmary did not have any Novocain or any other kind of painkiller to give me. Instead, the doctor sprayed something on my chest that made it very cold. The doctor said this spray would help dull the pain. I certainly hoped so.

I noticed that many of the patients from the other rooms came to watch what the doctor was going to do. There were so many people watching that I felt like someone must have sold tickets to a Broadway show, and I was the star. But I knew that they were really just concerned for me, and it was this type of care and concern that kept us going.

The doctor held up a large needle and pushed it in between my ribs. The insertion of the needle hurt like hell. I watched as he attached a large syringe to the needle, and began drawing out the fluid. As he emptied the syringe into the basin, I could see a thick yellow substance with traces of blood in it falling into the basin. The doctor repeated this procedure three times. The basin was filled with a lot of this awful looking stuff. A little later that night, I felt somewhat better, but the doctor told me there was still fluid in my chest. He said it would be necessary to repeat this procedure three days in a row, dropping the needle down a rib at a time. It was a terribly painful procedure. Finally, by the end of the third day, I began to breathe easier, but I was in pain and not fully recovered.

On December 23, 1944, I was still in the infirmary. The next day, the 24th, was my 21st birthday, but celebrating my birthday was the furthest thing from my mind. The day after that was Christmas, but even for Christmas, what was there to celebrate in this dismal prison camp? I really felt lonely and miserable here in the infirmary. Maybe I was feeling a little sorry for myself, but I was still sick and not in the mood for any celebration.

Just then, Jock and Taffy came into the room and stopped by my bed. I wondered what they wanted. Maybe I was being sent back to my barracks even though I still did not feel well. Much to my surprise, Taffy held out a small cake with one lighted candle on it. Both Taffy and Jock began singing happy birthday to me, and everyone else in the room joined in the singing, as I blew out the candle. I was very surprised and pleased that someone had remembered my birthday. Jock told me that my buddies from my barracks had told him that my birthday was today.

It was late in the afternoon, and my buddies could not come inside the infirmary to wish me a happy birthday because the infirmary was outside the gate, and prisoners were not allowed to go outside. Later that night, Jock and Taffy surprised me again. A Red Cross parcel had been delivered to the infirmary, and they used some of the parcel's contents to fix a birthday celebration for me. These Red Cross parcels were special Christmas packages with such things as a canned turkey, a can of cherries, some nuts, mixed candy, and jam. They also included pudding and fruit bars.

Even though I had started out the morning rather downhearted and not feeling well, I was considerably cheered up by the thoughtfulness of everyone for helping to celebrate my birthday. My 21st birthday was one day I would never forget. We continued our celebration the next day, Christmas Day. We used the remainder of the food that was in the Red Cross parcels to celebrate Christmas. It was a small, limited celebration there in the infirmary, but sharing Christmas with my fellow airmen was a good feeling.

I would have given almost anything to have been home for Christmas, but this birthday and Christmas sharing with the other prisoners had really cheered me up, at least for now. We were unable to have a New Year's celebration, but the enjoyment of our earlier celebrations stayed with me for a long time. For our New Year's time, we all hoped and prayed that the new year of 1945 would bring us our freedom.

On January 11, 1945, I was still in the infirmary recuperating from pneumonia. My right elbow had swelled up, and I was very uncomfortable. That day when the doctor examined me he noticed my swollen elbow. He asked me why my elbow was swollen. I told him that I still had shrapnel in my elbow but it had never bothered me until now. The doctor said he could take care of it by removing the shrapnel. With Jock's help, the doctor began to arrange the medical equipment necessary to operate on my elbow. He sprayed all around the swollen area on my elbow, using the same cold stuff he had sprayed on my chest. Soon my elbow felt cold, almost like it was frozen. The doctor tested to make sure that there was no feeling in my elbow. Then he began to cut around my elbow until he was able to reach the fatty tissue where the shrapnel was embedded. He removed the fatty tissue which contained the shrapnel and placed the fatty tissue aside on a piece of gauze. The doctor put six stitches in my elbow, bandaged me up, and my operation was over.

With the surgery over, I watched as the doctor dissected the fatty tissue and pulled the shrapnel out of it. The doctor held up three small pieces of shrapnel. He told me that the body's natural function is to form a protection against foreign objects. With the shrapnel in my elbow, my body had begun to amass fatty tissue around the pieces of metal as a form of protection. I asked the doctor for the pieces of shrapnel, and he gave them to me. I managed to save them all through my time in the prisoner of war camp, and to this day I still have them. The other pieces of shrapnel were still embedded in my body, and they have never been removed.

On January 16, 1945, five days later, Taffy came in to remove the stitches. After he cut the stitches, I asked him if I could pull them out. I don't know why I wanted to pull them out, I just did. Taffy said it would be all right since he had already cut them. I pulled out the stitches with the tweezers he gave me.

Another week went by. It was nearing the end of January 1945, and I was feeling better. The doctor notified the Germans that I was ready to be sent back to the barracks. I had come into the infirmary in November, the day before Thanksgiving, and had been kept there for nearly two months. In those two months that I had been sick, a lot of our airmen were shot down. The captured airmen were sent to Stalag Luft I. Our camp became so overcrowded that the airmen had to be crammed into the rooms. Where we originally had 14 men to a room, the Germans now jammed 24 men into a room. My room in the North Compound was filled to capacity, and the Germans sent me to a different barracks in the South Compound. It was typical January weather, very, very, cold. I was still in a weakened condition when I left the infirmary and the doctor gave me a blanket to take with me.

A German guard escorted me over to the South Compound. I did not have any time to stop and talk to my friends in my old North Compound barracks. The German took me directly to my new barracks. Things were a lot different in the barracks now, with twenty-four men in the room instead of fourteen. The sleeping accommodations in this barracks consisted of three large shelves built from the floor up on two sides of the room. The shelves were arranged three tiers high. Four men had to jam into the lowest level shelf, four more on the second level and four more on the third level, for a total of 12 men sleeping on one side of the room. The shelves on the other side of the room were built the same way with twelve more men crowded into them. Each tier was about the size of a king-sized bed, but definitely not as comfortable, especially with four men crammed in side by side. There were no separate bunks.

Each tier had four separate mattresses filled with wood excelsior and four blankets, one on top of each mattress. There was only one empty place on the second level, and I put my gear on it along with the blanket the doctor had given me.

In the South Compound I met Jerry Pucillo, who was from East Boston, Massachusetts. East Boston was about a mile from Winthrop, where I lived. Even though we had lived that close to each other, we had to go thousands of miles away before we met for the first time. Because we came from the same area, we had a lot in common when talking about our lives back home.

February, March, and April 1945 were terrible times in the camp. The allied bombing of Germany and the ground fighting in France and Italy began to take its toll on the Germans. We were excited at the news that the Germans might be losing the war, but they took it out on us, and we suffered even more. We used to get seven Red Cross parcels to feed 14 men. Now we had to feed 24 men on seven Red Cross parcels, and the packages did not always arrive when scheduled. And then, to make matters worse, after a few weeks we no longer received any Red Cross parcels. The rations the Germans gave us were cut in half, and the food was often rotten. While the German rations were never really appetizing, now they were so bad that we could honestly call the food downright garbage.

Rumors spread throughout the camp that the Russians were getting closer to Stalag Luft I. The Germans began to get frightened as things

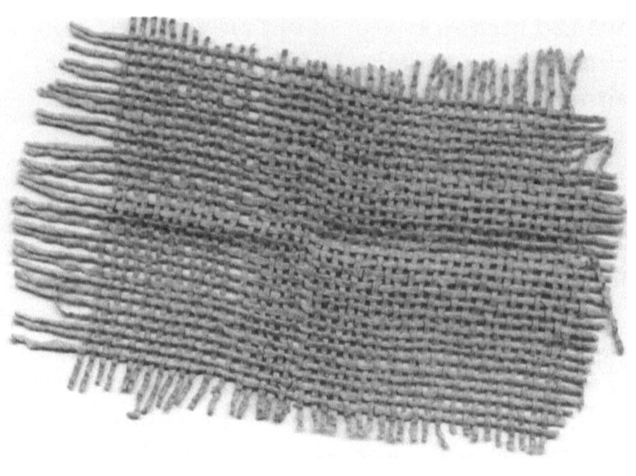

Before I left the camp, I cut off a piece of the straw sack to take home as a souvenir. The whole sack was filled with wood excelsior and used for a mattress.

got worse for them. All the regular guards and the Hitler Youth were transferred out of the camp to fight the Allies. Now we had mostly older men
guarding us. Some of them were even World War I veterans. Our new
guards were in their seventies and maybe even their eighties. With things
going so badly for the Germans, we began to get a bit apprehensive about
what they might do to us. It was obvious that these older guards were very
jittery. Regardless of their age, they had the guns and seemed nervous
enough to use them at the slightest provocation. We had no choice but to
wait it out and hope that rescue would come soon.

CHAPTER NINE

Stalag Luft I: The Last Days

By the end of January 1945, the war had progressed so fast in Europe that the Germans were forced to fight on three fronts, France, Italy, and Russia. The American and British air forces were bombing these countries day and night. The constant bombardments had a serious effect on German supplies and food. Camp water and electricity were only intermittently available to us. Unfortunately, this affected our health and safety. Because of the shortage of food, we had less to eat, and because of the shortage of water, it was difficult to keep clean. Under such adverse conditions, it did not take long for lice, bedbugs and vermin to return.

These were very cold months. We did not have enough coal to cook with or to keep a fire going to stay warm. We began burning the slats from our bunks and the wood from the ceiling of the barracks to keep the stove going so we could at least get some heat. The food the Germans gave us was worse than ever. It was often sour and rancid. Occasionally we got frozen potatoes, which were terrible. Many of the prisoners got the "GIs," our name for severe diarrhea.

As much as we bitched and complained during our early basic training back in the States, the rigorous training and discipline learned there helped us survive the mistreatment in the camp. The men who were well enough would help the men who were too sick to help themselves. We really tried to stay as upbeat and as healthy as possible to survive, and in many ways we succeeded. But now, after many months of imprisonment, the terribly cold weather, and the lack of food and water, the increasing infections and illnesses were wearing us down. My wounds had never been treated properly, and walking was very painful. The two months I spent in the infirmary with pneumonia only made me weaker. I believed that if the war did not end soon, many of us would not survive much longer.

On February 7, 1945, a large group of POWs came in from Stalag Luft

4. We watched them straggling in. They all looked to be in pretty bad shape. I saw Pop Grimshaw, who I hadn't seen since I left the Luftwaffe hospital over ten months ago. I yelled his name. He turned at the sound of my voice, and was surprised to see me. I yelled to him again, "How are you doing?" He answered back, "I'm doing OK, under the circumstances." I never got another chance to speak to him, as the prisoners were all kept on the move toward another compound. I never saw him again during our captivity.

When I first arrived at Stalag Luft I in April 1944, there were close to 4,000 prisoners. Now, in February 1945, some 11 months later, there were over 8,000 prisoners in our camp. In addition to the newly captured airmen being sent to Stalag Luft I, there were many POWs being transferred from Stalag Luft 4 to our camp. The Germans had to build new compounds to accommodate the increased population of American and British airmen. From three compounds that were in the camp in 1944, the South Compound (built in 1942), the West Compound (built in 1942) and the North 1 Compound (built in 1944), the Germans had added two more compounds, the North 2 Compound, in September 1944, and the North 3 Compound, in December 1944. The camp was extremely overcrowded, and there was a drastic shortage of food, heat, and water.

During February 1945, we often lost our electricity and water for a while. The lights were always turned off at around nine o'clock at night. The problems the Germans were having with the electricity often made the single light in our room go out much earlier than nine o'clock, and with the small window shuttered tight, our room was in complete darkness. We could not read or play cards. All we could do was lie on our bunks and wait for the daylight.

Before the war started going so badly for the Germans, we always had electricity and water all day, and the barracks lights were only turned off at night. I don't know why the electric lights in the barracks were turned off so much now. I didn't know if the Germans shut the lights off for some reason or if electrical problems kept causing power failures. Even when the lights in our barracks went off, the searchlights were not affected by any power failures, and they remained on all night throughout the camp. I was not sure, but I thought maybe the searchlights were on a separate generator system. The goons never bothered to explain anything to us. No matter what the reason for these problems, they existed, and we suffered all the more.

The German guards now realized that their army was in retreat and that they were losing the war. The supply of food was considerably decreased. They could not get the supplies and necessary equipment that they needed. Sometimes the water in the washhouse suddenly went off, and we could not wash ourselves or our clothes. We couldn't even shave.

We were very unhappy about the lack of electricity because it left us in the dark day and night in the barracks. Quite often when any kind of a bad situation arose in the camp, one of the prisoners would come up with an excellent idea to compensate for the latest problem inflicted upon us by the Germans. In this situation we desperately needed some light in our room, and the men were plotting and planning for some way to get light in the room. One of the men found a temporary solution by using a product from the Red Cross parcel.

The parcels often included a can of oleomargarine in its package. Oleo was a substitute for butter, which was scarce during the war. One of the men said he thought he could get us some light by using the oleomargarine. We had our doubts, but we patiently watched as he punched a hole in the top of the oleomargarine can and stuffed a piece of cloth into the hole. The piece of cloth served as a wick. He dipped the wick in and out of the hole to make sure he got some of the lard on it. Then he put the wick back in the hole with the lard part sticking out. A lighted match was put to the wick, and much to our surprise, we had light. It was a very crude lamp, and it did not light up the whole room, but it was a warm feeling to have some light. When we had two cans of oleomargarine available, we could put a "lamp" on each end of the table. These "lamps" were very smelly and gave off a lot of soot, but it was worth suffering the smell and the soot to get the light.

I was getting weaker every day and became so miserably ill with dysentery that I thought I was going to die. The Germans would not allow me to go to the infirmary because it was already too overcrowded. Things were so bad on the war front for the Germans that the goons no longer paid any attention to us or to our needs. They didn't even bother to delouse us anymore. The bedbugs and the lice were still there in full force. Food was scarce. I was sick, weak, and very depressed. Everything in the camp was getting worse, and I felt as if there was no hope for me to survive. Then, for some unexplainable reason, I slowly started to recover from my dysentery even though I had not had any medical treatment. I began to feel a little more optimistic about the future. Maybe, just maybe, we might make it through this terrible time of captivity.

As bad as our situation was, the Jewish airmen, both British and American, were in even greater danger. The Germans were getting worried, and they were beginning to take desperate measures. The guards pulled all the Jewish American and British POWs out of the camp's main population and isolated them in a section of the South Compound. The newly arrived prisoners of war told us how badly the Germans treated Jews. We were extremely angry that the Jewish airmen in our camp were being isolated.

The Germans were able to tell which men were Jewish by their dog tags. When we first entered the camp the Germans checked our dog tags, and the information on them was written into our camp records. In addition to our name, rank, and serial number on the dog tags, our religion was marked by a letter. J was for Jewish. C was for Catholic, and P was for Protestant. So it was easy for the Germans to pick out the British and American airmen who were Jewish. We were worried about what would happen to them. We realized that the Germans might be planning to punish them further or kill them. It was a very unsettling time, and even with our officers protesting such treatment, the Germans did not pay any attention to our protests.

By March and April 1945, we were happy to feel the warmer weather of spring. We were still hungry, sick, and worn out, but at least we were no longer freezing from lack of heat. Just about this time, word that the Russians were getting closer to our camp was spreading rapidly throughout the camp. We were excited. The Russians were our allies, and if they chased the Germans out, it meant freedom and home for us. We also heard that the British and Americans were advancing like hell on the Eastern Front. We were glad to hear that the Allies were forcing the Germans to retreat. We knew now that we were winning the war, and that information certainly boosted our morale, but our main concern was for the Russians to arrive at Stalag Luft I before the Germans decided to shoot us. The Russians were the closest, and we were relying on them to free us.

The tension we felt became almost unbearable. We faced fierce mental and physical suffering every day. We faced the threat of dying from sickness or starvation. We suffered from the increased punishment inflicted upon us as the Germans became more and more upset by the progress of the war and the closeness of the Russians. We still feared being shot by the goons. The Germans were obviously afraid of the Russians, who were rapidly approaching Stalag Luft I. We were afraid that the Germans would just shoot us and evacuate the camp. Our future looked grim. Sometimes I felt like I could not stand the suffering and the stress any more, and I just wanted to lie down and give up. But I could not give up. I did not want to die just as freedom was at hand. Nevertheless, I was constantly on edge, not knowing how the Germans were going to react as the Russians moved closer.

Even though I did not openly express my fear of dying with the possibility of rescue so close, I am sure that many of the other men had the same fear. The one thing that helped us stay alive and keep our sanity was the care and concern we had for each other. It was important for each of us to keep our minds clear, to share our food, to look out for each other, and to help each other survive.

On April 13, 1945, President Franklin D. Roosevelt died. The news came over one of our hidden radios, and runners were sent throughout the camp to notify all of us that Roosevelt had died. We were saddened at this news. Most of the prisoners gathered in their rooms, sharing their grief for the loss of our commander in chief, and praying for the war to end.

As a show of respect for President Roosevelt, we scrounged up all the black pieces of cloth that we could find. We tied the longer pieces around our left arm. The shorter pieces of black cloth were attached to our clothing over the left breast. We did this out of respect and mourning, and we defied the Germans by wearing our black mourning symbols out in the open. We did not care whether the Germans liked it or not. Roosevelt had been our president, our leader, and we owed him our respect. I was saddened to hear that President Roosevelt had died, but I was more determined than ever to try to keep my spirits up so as not to lose hope for our rescue.

By April 24 we could hear the sound of the Russian guns in the distance. The Russians were getting closer, but the Germans so far did not seem to be making any effort to evacuate the camp. We were nervous and apprehensive. The next few days dragged by as all kinds of rumors circulated throughout the camp. Word had even spread around the camp that Hitler had ordered the commandant to kill all the POWs before the guards left. From then on we were very careful whenever the German guards came near us. We also watched the guard towers, fearful that the guards might start machine-gunning us.

By now we had used up our oleomargarine lamps, and we were in almost total darkness in the barracks. The only light we had in our room came from the moon. The sliding shutter over the window was opened so we could get some air. In that little open space, we could catch a glimpse of the moon as a little moonlight shined in the room. At night, through that little space above the window, we could also see the bright flashes from the explosions of the Russian artillery barrage as the shells hit their target. The Russians were getting so close that sometimes we could hear the sounds of small arms being fired. Suddenly, a call from a POW echoed throughout the camp, and we could hear it through the open shutter. "Come on Joe," was the cry. And then, one by one, POWs from every barracks began to yell out through the little opening over their window, "Come

BARTH

HARD TIMES

Vol 1   No. 1   LAST 1   SATURDAY MAY 5th 1945   PRICE 1 D· BAR.

Editor F L E R INKPEN   Assoc 1st Lt N. GIDDINGS   Publisher 1st Lt D MacDONALD   Printing F LT J D WHITE

RUSSKY COME!

As seen by LOWELL BENNET. I. N. S. War Correspondent

RELIEVED!

Colonel Zemke intended to write this appreciation of the relief of Stalag Luft I, but unfortunately necessary duties have made this impossible. He has, in his own words, "taken a powder" to make final arrangements with the relieving Soviet forces.

It is therefore my privilege to introduce this Memorial Edition of the BARTH HARD TIMES.

During the successes, reverses and stagnant periods encountered during this struggle, our newspaper has faithfully recorded the German war communiques and expanded upon them in capable editorials.

With the redemption of a continent, our exile is ended. Our barbbound community will soon be a memory. So, on behalf of Colonel Hubert Zemke and myself, to all our fellow-kriegies: GOOD LUCK!

G. C. C. T. Weir.

WHAT D'YE KNOW- JOE!!

BRAITHWAITE FINDS UNCLE JOE

Contacts Russian Infantryman at Crossroads
Five miles South of Stalag One.

Major Braithwaite and Sgt Korson, our Stalag scouts, raced out to a cross-roads 5 miles south of Barth with the order, "find Uncle Joe". This was 8 p. m., May 1.

They searched southward, defying a rumored Russian curfew which was about as brief and emphatic as their own order: "EVERYONE stay put; anyone seen moving will be shot on sight."

Meanwhile, Wing Commander Blackburn's telephone crew were ringing numbers in Stralsund, hoping a Russian would answer the phone and we could break the big news of our presence. "Try the mayor," they asked the girl (who was still working Barth's phone exchange). "Not a chance," said she. "Barth's mayor poisoned himself and Stralsund's mayor has sprouted wings."

Scouts Braithwaite and Korson pushed on 3 miles. The scenery: thousands of people everywhere, sitting down, waiting.

POW newsletter cheering for the Russians. The newsletter was put out May 5, 1945, four days after the POWs' liberation by the Russians. The paper also indicates that it is Vol. 1 No. 1, and the Last 1. Price 1 D. Bar.

on Joe." The "Joe" they were calling for was, of course, Joseph Stalin, the Russian leader, because the Russians were the closest to us. The yelling grew and grew, getting louder and louder, coming from every barracks. Every once in a while the loud message was changed to "Come on Ike." This was for General Eisenhower and his troops to get here.

We knew that the Germans were getting more and more panicky as the Russians got closer. Then one day the SS suddenly appeared at the camp. The SS were the most feared men in the German army. They killed without mercy, and sometimes, it seemed, without reason. In the many months that I had been at Stalag Luft I, I had never seen any SS troopers in the camp. But they were there now, and that certainly was cause for us to worry. We felt sure that they must have come with orders from higher up in the German command. Our guess was right, and we did have cause to worry.

The SS did come with orders for the German camp commandant. They ordered the German camp commandant to force-march us out in front of the oncoming Russians. When the German commandant gave the order, Colonel Zemke, the American senior officer, defied him and refused to give the order to us. Even though Colonel Zemke knew that he might be shot for disobeying the commandant's order, he still refused to order us to march out of the camp. Instead, he ordered us to stay in the camp. We obeyed the colonel's order and stayed in the camp even though we might get shot for disobeying the commandant. Fortunately, the commandant decided not to punish anyone. The tension was mounting rapidly. We were all on edge, and most of us could only sleep for an hour or so at a time. We were constantly on the alert, and trying to be prepared for whatever might happen.

The next day Colonel Zemke ordered us to dig slit trenches next to our barracks. His hope was that if the German guards did get the order to kill us before evacuating the camp, some of us might survive in the protection of the trenches. Even if the Germans had already left the camp by the time the Russians arrived, the Russians might not know that. They could come in shooting and throwing hand grenades, thinking the Germans were still here. Of course, we did not know if the trenches would be enough protection or not. But we hoped so. At least digging the trenches gave us some hope of survival if the shooting was started by anyone. And just having a job to do in an effort to save lives helped to control some of the tension and anguish we felt. Some of the men used tin cans to dig the trenches, but most of us used our bare hands. No matter how scratched and sore our hands became, we tried to keep digging. We worked with all the energy we had left, and it still amazes me that as weak as most of the men were, we were able to finish digging the trenches.

Zemke knew that the Germans might evacuate the camp suddenly, and he organized a patrol to be ready to go outside the camp as soon as the Germans left. The patrol had some Russian-speaking men who would try to reach the Russians before they entered the camp. Their mission was to contact the Russian forces and tell them that the Germans were gone and that only allied prisoners were left in the camp. Zemke wanted to make sure that the Russians did not come in shooting, thinking the Germans were still there. Many innocent American and British airmen would get killed if that happened.

By now the Germans were really panicking. They were running throughout the camp, packing things, and getting ready to evacuate. They locked all of us in our barracks and left us inside with the doors and windows bolted. The Russians were so close now that the Germans fled in a panic without shooting us as they had been ordered to do. They just wanted to get out of the camp alive, and they hurried to their trucks and took off.

We couldn't see much of their evacuation procedures, as no one wanted to get near the small opening above the window. We had no way of knowing if shooting would start, either from the Germans retreating or the Russians advancing. It was a horrible experience, being locked inside in the dark and not knowing what was going on. It was a relief to know that the Germans were leaving, but we did not feel safe yet. We still didn't know what the Russians would do. When we felt sure the Germans had gone, we broke open the doors and got out of the barracks. The next day, Zemke sent the patrol out to meet the oncoming Russians. The men from the patrol reported back to Zemke that they were successful in their mission to tell the Russians that the Germans were gone.

After the Germans left, the searchlights were all turned off at night. We were exhausted, and lay down on our bunks to get some rest. The doors and windows were no longer locked, but sleep did not come easy. We knew from Zemke's report that the Russians had been notified that the Germans were gone from the camp, but we still did not know how the Russians would act when they got into the camp. We were keeping careful track of the dates. It was now April 30, 1945.

The next day, May 1, the Russians entered the camp. We were outside our barracks watching their arrival. If they aimed any guns our way, we were ready to dive into our trenches. The Russians, who rode their horses into the camp, looked like the Russian frontiersmen known as Cossacks. The Cossacks were wild and kind of scary, almost like shock troops. Wherever they went, they caused fear and hysteria as they killed, pillaged and plundered their way through Germany. The men and women riding their horses through the camp were shooting their guns into the air. These Russian soldiers were a frightening sight as they rode rapidly around the camp, with their horses rearing up on hind legs from time to time. We had to scurry out of their way or get knocked down by their horses. The Russian Cossacks wore fur hats, and had bandoleers of ammunition slung over their shoulders. Some of the riders had swords hanging from their belts as well as daggers sticking out from their belts. Some were shooting their pistols and rifles into the air. They seemed to be a very threatening group as they galloped around the compound.

Being liberated by these Russian Cossacks was a terrifying experience because many of them were drunk and out of control. It was their way of celebrating, and we didn't know what they were capable of doing. The camp was in total chaos. We were uncertain how far they would go with their shooting. Our emotions were at fever pitch for the few days that the Cossacks rode horseback through the camp. They pulled down the guard towers and the barbed wire fencing. They set fire to some of the German barracks and buildings. Colonel Zemke sent our interpreters to ask the Russian leaders to wait until we were evacuated before burning down our barracks. They agreed to wait, and they left our barracks alone.

In the middle of this mass confusion, I tried to find Pop Grimshaw, who had arrived at the camp in February. But because of all the confusion and chaos in the camp, I could not find him. I had heard that Bill Kemp, our first engineer, was in the camp, but I could not find him either. We were no longer under the control of the Germans, but neither were we completely free. The Cossacks and their guns ruled the camp.

For two days the Russians rode around the camp shooting their guns into the air. After the two days had passed, they finally stopped shooting and rode out to nearby farms where they slaughtered cows, pigs, and sheep for food to bring back to the camp. I was grateful for the peace and quiet and did not feel quite as threatened by the Russians as I had been at first. When the Russians returned with the food, they delivered some meat to each compound for the prisoners to share. When we got the meat, we lit bonfires to cook it. We cut the meat into smaller chunks and cooked them over the open fires. We used long pieces of stick cut from wood off our barracks to hold the meat over the open fires. Moving the meat-laden sticks in and out of the fire to get the meat cooked reminded me of roasting marshmallows over an open fire.

After being deprived of food for so long, many of the men were gorging themselves. Word was passed on from the American and British commanding officers for the men to stop gorging themselves. They had gone so long without proper food that they might get sick if they ate too much now. Notices were posted on the bulletin board in each barracks and on

Personalkarte I: Personelle Angaben

Kriegsgefangenen-Stammlager: ....

Beschriftung der Erkennungsmarke
Nr. 3959
Lager: St. L. I

Name: Sirianni

Vorname: Ralph Edward

Geburtstag und -ort: 24.12.23 – Boston

Religion: r/k.

Vorname des Vaters: Ralph

Familienname der Mutter: Anna

Staatsangehörigkeit: U.S.A.

Dienstgrad: Sgt. — Berufszehiger

Truppenteil: U.S.A.A.F. Komp. usw.:

Zivilberuf: Schüler — Berufs-Gr.:

Matrikel Nr. (Stammrolle des Heimatstaates): 31271422

Gefangennahme (Ort und Datum): 23.3.44 —

Ob gesund, krank, verwundet eingeliefert:

Lichtbild

Des Kriegsgefangenen

Nähere Personalbeschreibung

Haarfarbe

Fingerabbruck des rechten! Zeigefingers

Besondere Kennzeichen:

Name und Anschrift der zu benachrichtigenden Person in der Heimat des Kriegsgefangenen

Mutter: Mrs. A. Sirianni

28 Marslee St.

Winthrop/Mass.

Wenden!

Abschuß am 23.3.44 del. F.N. 190

Ital. + franz. Abstammung

Bemerkungen:

My German POW file.

the main bulletin board at the front of each compound. We were warned that some men might die from eating too much food at once. Within an hour or so, many of the men became very sick, and later some of the men did die of acute indigestion. The Russians also ate the food, but they did not become sick because they had not been starved as we had been. I was careful how much food I ate. I only ate small portions and did not get sick.

After we finished eating, someone said why don't we see what's in the German commandant's office. The Russians had stopped burning the buildings, and the main building where all the records of the camp were kept was still in one piece. Five of us agreed that that was a good idea, and we went to the main building. We looked through the closets, the file cabinets and the desks, searching for mementos to take home. The real score for us was finding the files that contained the pictures and personal records of each POW in the camp. I located my own file and those of several of my buddies. They were thrilled to have their picture and records as a souvenir of Stalag Luft I. Granted, it was not like a happy souvenir you take home from a vacation, but it was something we wanted to take and keep. Actually, it seemed kind of funny to think of ourselves ransacking the offices, after so many months of being locked up. Some of the men took boots, German uniforms, hats, and swastika emblems symbolic of the Nazi regime. I took a few small mementos also. In addition to taking my own POW file, I took a nice pair of German boots, a leather gun belt, and some other smaller items.

Later, I went to visit the infirmary. I wanted to see if anyone was still there. The British doctors were still there taking care of the injured and sick airmen who were unable to leave. Jock and Taffy and the other orderlies were still at the infirmary to help the doctors. I said my hellos all around. Just as I was about to leave, I spotted a scale in the corner. I remembered that when the doctor weighed me in September 1944, I weighed 140 pounds. From my original 160 pounds, I had lost 20 pounds from April to September 1944. When I had to go back to the dispensary with pneumonia in November 1944, the doctor weighed me again. I was down to 131 pounds. I really had not noticed the drop in weight too much at the time. I was still too sick. Now I stepped on the scale and, much to my surprise, I was down to 118 pounds. By now, I must have looked sickly and weak. No wonder I felt so weak all the time.

When I got back to the barracks, I heard that Colonel Zemke had left the camp in an attempt to reach the American and British forces. He wanted to make arrangements for the prisoners to be evacuated safely. Zemke accepted his responsibility to keep all of the former prisoners safe from harm, and to arrange an orderly evacuation. He put together a group of officers and noncoms to act as guards so that the men wouldn't leave the area. Not all the men were happy with the orders not to leave. Dwayne Gillette wouldn't obey the orders. He convinced the young Cossack leader to give him a horse so that he could join them and ride out with them to fight the Germans. When the regular Russian army arrived, the Cossacks immediately left the camp. Gillette rode off with the Cossacks. I never heard from him again. I was sorry that Gillette decided to leave and join the Cossacks, but I was not sorry to see the Cossacks leave the camp.

The regular Russian army was totally different from the Cossacks. They were more disciplined and followed military procedure. Unfortunately, they were not able to bring clothes, food, or anything to help us, but they did not mistreat us. The Russian army had a group of entertainers with them. We enjoyed watching them perform; it helped to occupy our time while we were waiting to be evacuated. The Russian entertainment group was similar to our USO that went around entertaining our troops. This was our only connection with the Russians while they were in the camp. There was no interaction or fraternizing between the Russians and us, but at least we were no longer afraid of being shot. We now felt safer and accepted the Russians as our allies.

It took Zemke a few days to make the arrangements for our evacuation, and then he announced that the B-17s would soon be here to get us out of Germany. Everyone was smiling now. We were very anxious to leave and yet, at the same time, some of us were a little apprehensive about going home. That may seem strange to some people, but the opportunity for freedom made some of us fear that freedom a little bit. Others were so excited about going home that that was all they thought about. This was especially true for the men who had only been in the camp for a short time. Fifteen months in Stalag Luft I had taken its toll on me, and I was apprehensive about going back into society as a free man. Would I be able to put my military training and my bombing missions behind me, especially the last mission when I was wounded and my plane was shot down? Would I be able to erase the cruel prisoner of war experience from my mind, and learn to adjust to civilian life again? There was no sense in worrying about civilian life for now. We knew that the planes were coming for us, so there was nothing to do but wait to be evacuated.

CHAPTER TEN

Going Home at Last

Within a couple of days after Zemke's announcement that the planes would be coming, we saw the first group of B-17s fly overhead on their way to land at the nearby German airfield. The sight of the planes energized the POWs, and we stood outside on the fields laughing and cheering. Bulletins were posted around the camp telling us to prepare for evacuation. The POWs were being evacuated according to the length of time they had been in Stalag Luft I. The British airmen, who had been in the camp the longest, were flown out first. A week later, the evacuation of our American airmen began. We were allowed to take only what we could carry. I remembered all the souvenirs we had gathered up from the German buildings to take home. We were limited as to how much we could carry and it was impossible for most of us to fit souvenirs together with our necessary gear. None of us was in very good shape, and it was a three-mile walk to the planes. We had to leave most of the souvenirs behind.

As I stared at all the liberated German items left behind, I thought to myself, "So what if we can't carry them on the plane. The hell with souvenirs. All I want to

German souvenirs I brought home.

132

do is go home." However, I did manage to pack a few small souvenirs to carry home with me. I kept my POW records and small things like a swastika, some military emblems from German hats, and other small items.

Finally it was my turn to go to the planes. I picked up my gear and, after fifteen long, horrible, frightening months, I walked out of the camp without looking back. We were led through the town of Barth, but there were no longer German guards to watch us, and no German civilians to attack us. We passed by the same railroad station where we had entered Barth. There were boxcars on the rails just like when we had arrived so long ago. As we walked toward the church, I looked up at the steeple that we had seen every day from the camp. While in the camp, that church steeple outside the camp seemed to be a symbol of freedom, and it felt good to finally be passing the steeple on our way home. We continued down the narrow street toward the arch under the church. The German people stayed off the streets, but we could see them staring out of their windows. They no longer dared to throw things at us or attack us. Instead, they remained in their homes and stared at us with frightened faces. They had lost the war and did not know what the future held for them.

Now that we were actually on our way home, we began to openly talk about how it would feel to be back with our family and friends. In the camp we had to struggle to survive. We came face to face with punishment and death every day, and we saw men die from starvation and illness. It was a rough life, and because of our feelings of anger and hatred at being locked up, vulgar language became a strong part of our daily life. This was something we did not wish to continue in our civilian life. I had been away from normal society for so long, I had a fear of not being able to readjust to civilian life. Too much had happened to me, and I was afraid it would be quite some time before I could adjust to being free. The horrors of Stalag Luft I would always be with me, and resuming a normal life again would be a challenge, not only for me, but also for the rest of the former POWs. When we finally arrived at the airfield, the B-17s were lined up and ready to take us out of Germany. Each plane could carry thirty-two former POWs. It seemed like the planes were taking off every two minutes, but it really may have been five- or ten-minute intervals between the takeoffs.

I was very emotional and excited as I waited to board the plane. It had been over fifteen months since I had been in a plane. I was looking forward to this particular flight because I was heading home, and no one would be shooting at me. After a few minutes there were thirty-two of us on the B-17, and we were ready for takeoff. This takeoff was, without a doubt, the most thrilling one of all. I had been in over a hundred flights, but they were involved with training exercises first and then the takeoffs for my missions. But this time the flight was very special. It meant going home after many months of captivity. On our way home we flew over some of the major German cities. We could see how badly destroyed these German cities were from our bombings. In a way, it was sad to see such once-fine cities devastated, but it was necessary to win the war.

I saw the Eiffel Tower as we flew over Paris, and I knew that we were close to our destination of Orly Field on the outskirts of Paris. When I looked out the window again, we were flying over Camp Lucky Strike. The camp was about two square miles filled with tents that were surrounded by roads running north and south, east and west. From the air it looked like a giant crossword puzzle. We landed at Orly and were transported by trucks to Camp Lucky Strike. Now that France had been liberated, there were other camps in the area near the city of Le Havre, all named after cigarettes. In addition to Camp Lucky Strike, there was Camp Old Gold, Camp Philip Morris, Camp Chesterfield, and others. These camps were originally set up as staging areas for men being sent to the front lines, but in 1945 many of the camps were temporary facilities for the men being sent home.

We were greeted much more pleasantly at Camp Lucky Strike than when we had been greeted on our first entrance into the German prisoner of war camp. Here everyone was smiling and laughing and helping us. We were deloused, and had wonderful showers where the water was plentiful and hot, and the soap was white and perfumed, a true luxury for us. We received new uniforms, socks, underwear, and brand-new GI shoes. It was like Christmas to us as we got all the things that we hadn't seen in a long time. After we finished our showers and got our new clothing, we were sent to the medical tent, where the doctors gave us a cursory physical. They said we would get complete physicals when we reached the States. I told the doctors that I still had shrapnel in my legs and buttocks, and the pain in my legs forced me to limp as I walked. They said that when we reached the States, the doctors would take care of my wounds. We were all in bad shape, but some of the former POWs were in such bad shape that they needed medical attention immediately. They were sent to the camp hospital. The rest of us were assigned to our quarters, which were tents rather than barracks. Four to six men lived in each tent.

I put my gear away in my tent and went out to find the mess hall. Camp Lucky Strike was a huge camp. Thousands of tents were divided into sections laid out alphabetically and numerically. It was very easy to find the most important tents because they were clearly marked. The first large tent that I was looking for was one that was marked "mess hall." Then I saw the one with a "latrine" sign on it. There were other mess halls and latrines around the camp, but these two were the nearest to my tent. Many of us made frequent trips to the mess hall to get something to eat, and later to the latrine for the diarrhea that sometimes affected us after the meal. After our starvation diets at Stalag Luft I, the sudden abundance of food at Camp Lucky Strike was overwhelming, so extra trips to the latrines were common.

The mess halls were open from early in the morning to 9 at night. Most of the food was prepared especially for us, and was intended to be a bland diet so that we would gradually get adjusted to eating normal food again. Also, the bland diet was planned so that we would not get sick, which might happen if we suddenly began a rich-food diet. When the Russians freed us from the Germans, we had that problem as some men ate too much food too fast after being on a near-starvation diet. Some got sick and some died. Most of the men here, like myself, were still in bad condition from nearly being starved to death, and if they overindulged at Camp Lucky Strike, sickness and death could happen. We were warned to eat light meals five or six times a day rather than eating huge meals all at once. After fifteen months of near starvation, the open mess halls were a luxury that I thoroughly enjoyed.

When I first entered the mess hall, I was amazed by the huge amount of food available. We had been deprived for so long that it was difficult to know where to start. Suddenly, all this wonderful food was placed in front of us. There was chicken, chicken soup, oatmeal, boiled eggs, and freshly baked bread. There was coffee, tea, milk, and eggnog to drink. The cooks even had prepared the old reliable, creamed chipped beef on toast, more popularly known to us as "shit on a shingle." The men who could not control themselves ate too much all at once in spite of the warning to eat lightly until they adjusted to the food. Some of these men got sick and vomited, while others got the GIs and had to keep running to the latrine.

One day in the chow line, I met one of the POWs from Stalag Luft I. We greeted each other and talked for a while as the chow line moved forward. During the conversation he said, "Ralph, if I remember correctly you're from Winthrop, Massachusetts. Right?

"Yes I am, and I can't wait to get back home," I replied. And then he told me that there was a guy from Winthrop in his tent, and he gave me his section and tent number.

We finally got our food and sat down to eat and chat for a while. I finished lunch before he did, and I left to search for the man from Winthrop. Camp Lucky Strike was huge, but I finally located the tent. I slowly opened the flap and looked inside. There was only one man inside the tent, and he was sitting on his bunk eating his chow. It was Dick Brown.

I recognized him right away. Dick had been a year ahead of me in school and Dick's younger brother, Bob, was also in school with us.

I yelled out, "Hey, is that Dick Brown?"

Dick looked up at me with a smile and replied, "It ought to be. I have been out in the sun all day."

I burst out laughing, and Dick joined in laughing. It was a corny joke, but I loved it. It was the most enjoyable laugh I had had in months. After Dick finished eating, we had a great time reminiscing about our town, our school and the good times we had back then. It seemed like a hundred years since I had been in Winthrop. Dick told me how he had been captured. He was a foot soldier, and he had been captured during a battle with the Germans. The Germans did not send him to a prisoner of war camp. They were retreating rapidly, and they moved him and some other allied prisoners along with them on their retreat. When the Germans holding him were captured, Dick was released and eventually sent to Camp Lucky Strike in preparation for his return home. We talked for a couple of hours in Dick's tent and thoroughly enjoyed sharing our hometown memories. I was very cheerful as I left the tent and headed back to my own quarters.

After eight or nine days in Camp Lucky Strike, trucks were provided to take us to a Liberty ship that would be our transportation home. The Liberty ship had been converted and equipped for troop transportation. Each deck had hundreds of two-tier bunks, and as a result, the ship was very crowded. They wanted to get as many men on the ship as they could safely without endangering the men or the ship. I, for one, did not care how crowded it was. I just wanted to get home. So far, I had traveled by trains, trucks, planes, and even a streetcar, but this was my first experience traveling by boat, and I was looking forward to it. This Liberty ship would bring me closer and closer to my home. Reportedly, the voyage would take about five and a half days to get to New York. I looked forward to getting started. I planned on catching up on my sleep. There would be enough to eat, and maybe I could gain some weight back.

While on board the ship, I met Charlie "Buddy" Bachini from Winthrop. Buddy and I had been in school together, and had not seen each other for years. Just like when I met with Dick Brown in Camp Lucky Strike, Buddy and I had a grand time talking about our hometown. After the ship left port and was just out of sight of land, Buddy became seasick. He was so sick he couldn't get out of his bunk. He had a pail by his side every day. To give him a helping hand during his illness, I emptied the pail every day and washed it out before bringing it back to Buddy. After my meal was over, I brought something back for Buddy to eat, hoping that he would eat a little and feel better. But the sight and smell of any food only irritated his seasickness and made him sick all over again. I stopped bringing anything but water.

The second day out to sea, all kinds of horns and sirens started blasting throughout the ship. The engines were stopped, and we were ordered to turn out on the main deck. We were still at war with Japan and we thought maybe some Japanese ships had made it to the Atlantic and were going to attack us. A message over the loudspeaker calmed our fears a little by informing us that several German floating mines had been spotted. The navy gun crews had already manned their 20mm and 40mm cannons, and were firing at the mines, blowing them up with great accuracy. The last thing anyone aboard the ship wanted was for the ship to be damaged or sunk by German mines. It only took the navy gun crews about twenty minutes to blow up the five or six floating mines. I breathed a huge sigh of relief. That was enough excitement for me. I hoped the rest of the trip would be more peaceful. I did have to have a bad tooth pulled while on the boat. Having the tooth pulled wasn't too bad because they used Novocain to kill the pain. But I had no other medical treatment while on the boat. Fortunately, the rest of the trip was fairly peaceful, and it was not until we reached New York Harbor that all of us became excited again. Now I really believed that I was going to get home safely.

It was late afternoon when we arrived in the outer harbor, and the tugboats came out to bring our ship into the harbor. The men in the tugboats were blowing the ships' horns. Streams of water were shooting up into the air from the fireboats. The police boats joined in our homecoming celebration by sounding their sirens. There were giant "WELCOME HOME" signs on the end of the piers jutting into the harbor. There were thousands of people all along the shoreline holding more welcome-home signs. It was quite an amazing welcome-home scene.

It was just turning dark when we dropped anchor a few hundred yards in front of the Statue of Liberty. They were not ready for us to disembark yet, and we were called down to dinner in the mess hall. After dinner I went back on deck and found a nice spot to sit and admire the view. The Statue of Liberty was all lit up, and what a beautiful sight that lady was to us. It was almost as if she was personally welcoming us home. During the war, the Statue of Library remained in the dark because of the blackouts. But the lights had been turned on a few days before we landed.

It was a beautiful May evening, and we were prepared to stay on deck all night, even if we dozed off once in a while. This was one of the moments we dreamed about during our captivity. I know how I felt, so without even exchanging a word, I knew how the other fellows felt. We all had the same emotions as we looked at the Statue of Liberty. We had sacrificed a lot and suffered tremendously, but seeing our own country safe and sound made it worth all our efforts and sacrifices. We fought the enemy the best way we knew how. Yes, we suffered, but it was worth it to help keep our country free. Patriotism was at a very high level with the returning veterans, and we could see that same patriotic feeling from the civilians and military personnel who welcomed us home.

The next day I was still just as emotionally choked up as I had been the night before. A band was playing, and thousands of people were still lining the docks and the streets. Many of the people were waving signs with messages like "WELCOME HOME" and "GOOD JOB." We waved back at them as we boarded the buses that were waiting to take us to Fort Dix, New Jersey.

We each had a physical and a debriefing at Fort Dix, and then were issued light summer uniforms. The physical was a complete one from top to bottom: eyes, ears, throat, and everywhere else. My legs were still bent, and I could not straighten them out. I still had some pain and the scars were very bad. The doctor looked at my legs and asked me if the shrapnel had been removed. I told him no. The doctor's response was, "Later on, before you are released, the doctors will check your legs to see what they can do." There wasn't much I could say to that, except to hope that sooner or later the shrapnel would be removed, and I would be able to walk without limping in pain.

The debriefing was not very enlightening. As former POWs, we were gathered together in groups and given advice. For example, we were told what we could and could not talk about with the press or our families and friends. We were not to discuss our treatment by the Germans as POWs. We were still at war with Japan, and I guess they felt that if our experiences were widely known that the Japanese treatment of POWs under their control might get worse. I'm not exactly sure why we were told to keep quiet, but I had no desire to relive the past 15 months, so keeping quiet did not bother me at all. Then, at the end of the debriefing, they notified us that we would be getting a six- to eight-week leave. That was good news. Nobody mentioned to me about further treatment of my wounds or about going to a VA hospital.

As soon as I was finished with the debriefing, I headed for the phones. The army had arranged for the installation of banks of phones so that we could call our families. There were long lines of men waiting at the phones, but I eventually got my turn. My mother answered the phone, and I said, "Hi, Mom. It's me." When my mother heard my voice she cried, "Ralph, Ralph," and became so emotional that she couldn't talk anymore. My father came on the phone. I told him I was fine and in good health.

"It's really great to be back in the U.S. and talking to you," I said. "I should be home in about a week. I love you all."

We said goodbye, and I hung up the phone. We really could not say much over the phone, but just being able to hear my father's voice boosted my morale. I would soon be back in Winthrop. After months of war and months in a prisoner of war camp, I guess a person should be happy to be free. And I was glad to be free, but I was also depressed and worried about the future.

A week later I was on my way to Fort Devens, in Massachusetts, along with some other Massachusetts servicemen. My stay at Fort Devens was only one night. No other doctors examined my wounds. I hoped the doctors would check my wounds after I returned from furlough. I still had the shrapnel in my legs, and sometimes it was very painful to walk. When I was issued a six-week furlough, from the first week in June 1945 to the middle of July, I just wanted to get out of there and go home. I called my father, and he drove to Devens to pick me up.

My father was never much of a talker, but on the ride back to Winthrop, I could sense that he was anxious to talk. I was sure he had a lot of questions he wanted to ask me. When he noticed my limp as I walked to the car, he asked me what had happened to my legs. My brief reply was, "I got injured when I was shot down, but I'm fine now."

"Are you sure you're all right?" he asked.

"Yeah, I'm feeling fine," I replied.

I wasn't really feeling fine, but it was difficult to answer a lot of questions. I did not want to discuss my injuries, and I definitely did not want to talk about the camp. I was not ready yet.

My parents had never been informed about my injuries. They had not even known that I had been very ill with pneumonia from December 1944 to January 1945. They did not receive the notice about my pneumonia until May 1, 1945, which was only three weeks ago, and I was still in Stalag Luft I. May 1 was the day I would never forget. It was the day the Russians took over the camp and liberated us.

My father's question about my injured legs disturbed me and I began to feel some of my despair and worry returning. My legs were bothering me, and I was very conscious of my limp. I had tried so hard in the prisoner of war camp to exercise and force myself not to limp. Nothing worked. I still limped, but I did not want people to keep asking me about my injuries. When I got home, I hoped to strengthen my legs and be able to walk normally. To prevent my father from asking any more questions on the ride home, I kept him busy answering my questions about my mother and my brother, about family and friends, and about what was going on in Winthrop.

When we arrived home that afternoon, my mother was waiting at the door. She began to cry when I came to the door. She hugged and kissed me, and then cried some more. I reassured her that everything was OK now, and she didn't need to cry. She stopped crying and wiped her tears away. Actually, neither of us knew what to say to the other. Then she asked me if I was hungry. I think this was her way of trying to get things back to normal. I really did not feel like eating at that moment. For a few minutes I almost felt like I didn't belong there. Everything seemed different now. I felt somewhat uncomfortable being home after my long ordeal at the camp. But it seemed to me that my mother needed time to adjust to my being home, and I said, "Yes, I am hungry." She began to busy herself by fixing me a nice, home-cooked meal.

When lunch was ready, I sat down at the table with my mother and father and pretended to be delighted with the lunch. I knew in my mind that I was glad to be home, but at the same time, I was happy that there were only the three of us there. My brother had not returned from his summer job in a resort in upstate New York. I did not realize until then how challenging being home would be for me. For fifteen months I dreamed of nothing except being back home, and now that I was there, I was unsure of myself. After all those months of living under the most horrible conditions, it was difficult for me to suddenly readjust to a normal family life. I would have to try to spend more time with my mom and dad so that I could get reacquainted with my family and feel more comfortable at home.

The next morning my parents came into my bedroom with breakfast on a tray. They thought that I would enjoy breakfast in bed. I was overwhelmed by their thoughtfulness in trying to welcome me home, but breakfast in bed was not for me. I told them I would be more comfortable sitting at the kitchen table having breakfast with them. They said that was fine and went downstairs with my breakfast tray. I got dressed and joined them for breakfast in the kitchen.

The next few days were a little unsettling as I tried to adjust to being home while at the same time my parents were trying to adjust to the changes in me. One of my most difficult adjustments was carrying on a conversation with my family. I know that sometimes my family felt like I did not want to talk to them, but I was not ready to talk about the war or my prisoner of war experiences. Even harmless conversation around the table unnerved me. It wasn't that I did not want to talk about everyday things with them, but rather that I was scared. On more than one occasion I had used the rough language we used in the camp. One time I was sitting at the table with my parents and wanted the salt shaker. The words came out of my mouth automatically. Without thinking, I said, "Pass me the f...... salt shaker."

The use of the swear word, the gruffness of my voice, and forgetting to say please, startled my mother. She was embarrassed, and so was my father. When I saw the looks on their faces, I was so ashamed that I wanted to get up and run from the table. Instead, I apologized to my parents and told them that the use of swear words was common in the camp. Swearing was a way to express our feelings about being held captive in the camp, and for a person like me who never used such language before, it became an outlet for my tension. Soon, swearing became a habit at the camp. Now that I was back home, I was trying hard not use those words anymore, but sometimes, especially when I was frustrated or remembering the camp, they just popped out. Gradually I learned to be very careful when I spoke, for fear that the swear words would come out at the wrong time. It would have been nice if I could have just said to myself, "You are home now. Stop using those words and that gruff tone." But it doesn't work that easily. Stalag Luft I stayed with me for a long time.

Later, when I did talk a little bit about my wartime experiences to my family and friends, I still had to be very careful of my language and not use the swear words commonly used by us in the German prisoner of war camp. I had already made mistakes, like startling my family when I swore while making a simple request for that salt shaker. I continued to be extra careful about my language. I wasn't always successful. One day I was explaining to my parents how excited I had been to receive their package with the cigarettes in it. Instead of just telling them how happy I was to receive the package, I said, " I was so glad to get your package that I held it up for my buddies in the barracks to see, and yelled 'Hey, guys, look what I got! Six f...... cartons of cigarettes.' My buddies were really excited for me."

I was greeted by dead silence as my mother and father stared at me. Suddenly I realized what I had just done. Again I had startled them with my rough language and gruff voice. They never criticized me, but the expression on their faces said it all. Once again I apologized to them. It was a totally new situation to them. I had never heard my mother or father be impolite or use such words. Courtesy and politeness were expected in my house. I had been brought up to be polite and I never used swear words. I asked my mother and father to please be patient with me, and they said that they understood. They seemed to know that these problems were the result of my experiences in the war and my imprisonment by the Germans. They knew I was trying hard to readjust to freedom and civilian life.

Everything I did in these first weeks home reminded me of the prison camp in some way. One day I went into the supermarket to get a couple of items. It was my first time in a food store since I had been home. As I walked up and down the aisles, I marveled at all the food that was available. It brought back memories of the camp, with its starvation diet. We certainly wished we had such food back then. Even though I was out of the camp and safe at home, somehow I kept relating everything I did and saw to the camp. Even the sight of the pet food set me off. I couldn't help thinking that in the camp we ate food that people would never think to give to their pets. But here, in America, even the dog and cat food had to pass inspection before it can be sold as pet food. I couldn't help but wonder if all these people moving up and down the aisles realized how lucky they were to be in America.

A few days later, when my mother was busy, my father said he wanted to talk to me alone. He said that he had a very strange story to tell me, and he was hesitant about telling it. I urged him to tell me. My father told me that one night around 2 o'clock he was awakened by my mother's crying and thrashing around in the bed. He was afraid she was having a bad dream, so he woke her up. But even when awakened, she continued crying as she told my father that she saw me standing at the foot of her bed. Of course that was impossible because I was still overseas. Eventually, both my mother and father were able to get back to sleep.

But the story was not over. My father said that when they went downstairs for breakfast the next morning, they discovered that the kitchen clock had stopped at 5 A.M. that morning of March 23, 1944. And they were startled because that clock had never stopped before. My parents had had it for years, since they were married, and they only had to set it once a year. My father said that after a few days, they both recovered from what he believed was my mother's bad dream, even though my mother insisted that it was not a dream and that she did see me. They got the clock fixed and tried to put that night behind them. I remembered the clock well, having practically grown up with it, seeing it every day in our kitchen. It never had stopped, and now, after being repaired, it was still in the kitchen working fine.

My father was finding it very difficult to finish the story, but I convinced him to continue. He told me that on April 10, 1944, they got a telegram from the War Department that said I was missing in action. It was quite a blow to them, for fear that I was dead.

The memories of that night of March 23 came back to them again when on May 5, 1944, they received a second telegram from the War Department notifying them that I had been shot down on March 23, 1944, and was in a prisoner of war camp. March 23, 1944, was the night that my mother told my father she saw me standing at the foot of her bed, and it was the day the clock stopped. My father told me he could not explain why my mother had her vision of seeing me that night or why the clock stopped on that particular date. He said he just wanted to tell me what had happened to them. I did not know why or how things like this happen to people, but I was glad my father told me the story.

The next day I talked to my mother about seeing me in her vision and about the clock stopping on the exact day I was shot down. She didn't say too much about it, but she vowed that she saw me that morning standing at the foot of her bed. Her dream or her vision, call it what you will, kept my mother's faith strong in the belief that I was alive. She was so sure about the vision being real. She was mystified about the stopping of the clock at the exact time I was shot down, but she said it just gave her more assurance that I was still alive. I was glad that she was able to talk to me about the incident, and whether it was a dream or not, I believed that she did see what she said.

As the days passed, I gradually began to feel a little more comfortable at home. My parents were planning a welcome-home party for me. They only invited relatives because they thought it would be easier for me to see family at my first welcome-home party. They were right. It was too soon for me to be surrounded by too many people at once. I did enjoy seeing my relatives again, and the party was fairly quiet. No one asked me what it was like in the prisoner of war camp, and I was grateful for that. Mostly they just welcomed me home and told me how happy they were to see me.

My Uncle Dom told me that when my parents notified him that I had been liberated from the German camp in May 1945, he went right out and bought a half-gallon of Black Gold rye whiskey. He knew I would soon be

The Black Gold Rye bottle that my uncle gave me at the welcome-home party. We labeled it with the date of my liberation from the camp and with the date of my welcome-home party for me to keep as a souvenir.

home and that my parents would have a welcome-home party. Uncle Dom saved that half-gallon bottle of whiskey until the night of my party. At the party he presented the bottle of Black Gold rye, and said, "Welcome home, Ralph." Uncle Dom and my father put labels on the bottle, one label had the date of my liberation from the camp, and the second label had the date of this welcome-home party, July 8,1945. Of course, during the party the contents of the bottle were enjoyed by some. When the party was over and the bottle was empty, I put it aside to save as a memento of the evening.

A couple of days after the party with my relatives, I decided it was time to try to contact my friends and do some visiting. Most of my friends had been in the armed forces also, so I would have to call around to see who was home. The first person I called was my best friend, John Moriarty. John and I played football in high school and he was home on leave from the Navy. We talked on the phone and arranged to get together that evening. We had a great time talking about the "good old days" in school, about our friends and relatives, and about how everyone was. But neither of us talked much about our experiences during the war. John was a chief petty officer in the navy and served on an LST. He saw action in the invasion of the Japanese-held islands, such as the Marshalls and the Marianas. I talked a little about my service in the Army Air Corps. I never mentioned my POW experience, and I had no desire to talk about the camp at all. John and I just wanted to have a nice night out.

Two days later, John had arranged for us to go out on a double date with two girls that we had known in school. I borrowed my father's car and picked up John, and then drove to pick up the two girls. The girls said that they were happy that we had come home from the war safely, but after that the war was not mentioned again. We had a terrific night out for dinner and dancing. I had a little trouble dancing because of my injured legs. I did all right for a few dances, until my legs began to hurt. Then I quit dancing, but we still stayed there and enjoyed our time together. By midnight I was pretty tired and was glad that we all decided it was time to go home. I drove the two girls home, and then drove John home.

As we sat in the car outside his house, John said, "Come on in for a cup of coffee." I knew how he felt. We were both trying to adjust to our family and friends again, and we were not ready for this night to end.

It was close to 2:30 in the morning. We were still sitting at the kitchen table talking and drinking our coffee when John's sister, Mary, came downstairs and sat with us. I apologized if we woke her up. She said it was no problem. She just heard the voices and wanted to join us. I hadn't seen Mary since we were in school, and it was nice to meet her again. Then John's mother appeared in the doorway. She also sat down and joined us.

About a minute later, Jean, another one of John's sisters, came into the kitchen and sat down with us. We had awakened most of the family. But they didn't seem to mind. We stayed there talking until the wee hours of the morning. This was the first time since I had been home that I felt completely relaxed about talking with people. I didn't talk about Stalag Luft I, but I was able to talk about how much I liked being in the Army Air Corps and how much I loved flying. Besides having a great night, the next best thing for me was that I never slipped up and said a swear word. I just enjoyed myself talking with the people around me that night. The next day I received a telegram from Fort Dix saying that my furlough had been extended until the first week in September. That was good news. I was beginning to enjoy my time at home.

A couple of days later, I called John to see if he wanted to go out on a double date that night and maybe go to dinner and a show. He said OK, and before he could suggest a date for me, I asked him if he minded if I asked his sister Mary to be my date for the evening. He said it was all right with him if it was all right with her. I had really enjoyed meeting Mary again and talking with her. John couldn't make it that night, and said the next night would be great. I told John to let me talk to Mary. When she came on the phone, I asked her if she would like to go out with me on a double date with her brother, John, and his date. She quickly replied with a yes.

We decided to go to Frankie Mac's Nightclub in Revere. They had an excellent floorshow. I enjoyed everything: the floorshow, being with friends, and especially being with Mary. She was a good listener, and a very understanding person. Mary seemed to sense my reluctance to talk about the war, and she didn't ask me any questions about my prisoner of war experiences. I still wasn't ready to talk about the horror of the camp. John's leave was over and he had to report for duty with the Navy. Mary and I still continued to go out together. In fact, the more we went out together, the more we began to enjoy each other's company.

I will never forget the double date we had with Mary's married sister, Elaine, and Elaine's husband, George. It was August 14, 1945. We went to a late-afternoon movie in Boston. In the middle of the movie, the picture abruptly stopped and the lights came on. A voice came over the loudspeaker announcing that the war with Japan was over. The Japanese had surrendered. Everyone jumped up and yelled enthusiastically, shaking hands and hugging. The movie did not start again. The theater lights stayed on. The movie no longer mattered, anyhow. Everyone was too excited to sit and watch it. We wanted to go outside and celebrate.

The streets were packed with people yelling and cheering. Horns were blaring, church bells were ringing, and sirens were sounding everywhere. People were kissing, and crying, and hugging each other. The streets of Boston were rapidly filling with more cheering people. The Boston Common was so crowded that you could hardly move around. We got caught up in the crowd and stayed outside celebrating for a couple of hours. We finally got tired, and worked our way to a nearby restaurant where we could sit down and order some food. Everyone in the restaurant was buzzing with excitement also. I was extremely elated about the ending of the war with Japan, as I am sure all these people were. It meant we won. There would be no more fighting and no more killing. The servicemen would soon be home, and for me, it especially meant that I would be getting a discharge fairly soon. Mary, Elaine, George and I continued our celebration by having dinner in the restaurant.

The next few days went by fast, and I received another telegram from Fort Dix telling me to report to Mitchel Field in Long Island, New York, when my furlough was over on September 5, 1945. Mary and I were seeing each other on a steady basis, and I was going to miss her when I had to leave.

Finally the day came when I had to pack up and leave my family and Mary, and report to Mitchel Field. I did not know what my assignment would be, nor did I know when my discharge would be forthcoming. The accommodations at Mitchel Field weren't too bad. We had twenty-four men in the barracks, but we were still not overcrowded. We had single beds complete with blankets, a pillow, and a comfortable mattress. Even if we had been a bit crowded, which we were not, I would not have complained. This was a lot different from our rooms at the POW camp where we first had 14 men in one small, cold room, sleeping on wooden bunk beds with poorly made mattresses infested with lice. Later, when the Germans squeezed 24 men into each room by adding wooden shelves, one on top of the other with four men sleeping on each shelf, the crowded rooms became almost unbearable. Sometimes it amazed me that I could take such pleasure in the small things now allowed us, like a comfortable bed, a blanket, and the availability of food whenever I wanted it. I used to take all these things for granted, but not anymore. My months in the German prisoner of war camp taught me what it meant to lose my freedom of choice, and I would always fight for the right to be free.

Mitchel Field had a dayroom where we could play cards, ping-pong or pool. There was an excellent library in another room. We were not required to prepare for inspections, and we didn't even have to make our own beds or clean up the room. There were German POWs at Mitchel Field, and they were assigned the task of making the beds and cleaning the barracks. Along with not having to make beds or clean up, I really enjoyed not having to get up early in the morning and turn out for reveille. We were still recovering from our ordeal as former prisoners of war. Many of us were not in good shape physically and, in some cases, mentally. The pain of our injuries, the suffering from the bad treatment given us by the Germans, and the memories of the camp were not easy to erase from our minds.

I had only been at Mitchel Field for a few days, waiting for an assignment, when I began to realize that there were not going to be any future assignments. I was not given any duties to perform. I felt more like a visitor than an airmen waiting for orders. In fact, Mitchel Field seemed to be a temporary location for some of us as we waited to be discharged. I was given a class A pass that entitled me to leave the base whenever I wanted to. All I had to do was show the pass at the gate and I could leave. There was one restriction, however. I could not go any further than New York City. This meant that I could not use the pass to go home to Winthrop.

It was only a one-hour train ride from Long Island to New York City. Sometimes a group of us would go into New York City to see a movie or a stage show. I remember the time I saw the Andrews Sisters in a stage show. Most of the men in the service admired the Andrews Sisters because they were always entertaining the troops. I thought they were great. Sometimes my buddies and I would walk around Times Square after the show, and then go get something to eat before we headed back to Mitchel Field.

Since we had nothing to do back at the base, we went to New York City as often as we could. A USO was located in Times Square, and we stopped in occasionally. We always had a good time visiting the USO. We did not have much money, and the food, coffee, and entertainment were free for servicemen. The USO was well known for the excellent shows they often put on for the servicemen. It was at this USO that I saw a television for the first time. The television screen was very small, but we didn't care how small it was. I was fascinated sitting there watching a football game on the TV. I really didn't care who won or lost. I just enjoyed watching television for the first time. We had never had one at home.

One day when I was in New York, I decided to test the rules of the class A pass. I was curious to find out what would happen if I tried to get on a train leaving New York for Boston. There was a train at the station just getting ready to pull out for Boston. I walked right up to the MP who was checking the passes of military people, and showed him my pass in preparation for entering the train. But the MP was not fooled at all, and he knew the rules of the class A pass. He would not allow me to get on the train leaving New York. I had hoped to pass inspection, but I was prepared for rejection, even though I was a little disappointed. At least the MP did not make any plans to report me. He just refused to let me get on the train.

My family wrote and kept asking when I was coming home. I told them I did not know when, and I would call them as soon as I found out. It was difficult just hanging around. My buddies and I didn't make as many trips into New York City as we had when it was all new to us. There was a building on the base where movies were shown, and we went just to kill the time. I received letters from Mary, and wrote back to her as often as I could.

Then one day I got a letter from Mary saying that she and her parents were coming to New York in a few days to visit Mary's Aunt Alice. Aunt Alice lived near Times Square, and Mary's letter said they would be staying with her for ten days. She added her aunt's address and telephone number for me to call them. I had been a little bored and depressed because I couldn't get home, and there was nothing to do at the base to keep me busy. I had not been using my pass very much the past few days, but now, with Mary coming to New York, my class A pass was really going to be worth having.

I talked to her on the phone when she arrived in New York, and from then on we spent almost every day together. We went everywhere together, to the movies, out to lunch, out to dinner, and sometimes just for long walks. I wanted to spend every minute with her that I could, and I hoped she felt the same way. I was very happy when I was with her. Even thoughts of my hardships in the Stalag Luft I camp began to fade away. Or at least I thought those bad memories were fading.

One night Mary and I got back to her aunt's house late in the evening after returning from dinner and a show. It was rather late for me to get back to Mitchel Field. I could catch the late train, but I would not get back to the barracks until around 2 A.M. Mary's aunt had a three-bedroom apartment. The aunt had her room, Mary had the second bedroom, and Mary's parents had the third bedroom. But they all agreed that I should stay over and go back to Mitchel Field the next day. My class A pass allowed for staying overnight in New York if I wanted to. Aunt Alice said that if I did not mind sleeping on the living room floor, she could give me a pillow and a blanket. I thought sleeping in the living room was a better idea then spending another hour or two traveling and not getting back to Mitchel Field until two in the morning.

Everyone went to bed, and I tried to get comfortable on the floor. It wasn't too bad. But with the lights turned out and the room now in total darkness, thoughts of the POW camp suddenly came back to me. I remembered the lice-infested beds we had to sleep on. I remembered trying to sleep in the freezing-cold rooms without heat and without enough blankets to keep warm. I remembered trying to sleep when I was so hungry that my stomach was hurting. I tried to get these thoughts out of my head. Did I mind sleeping on the floor with a soft pillow for my head and a nice blanket wrapped around me in a house with friends? No, I did not mind. As far as I was concerned, sleeping here was like being at the Ritz. These sleeping accommodations were still a thousand times better than the horrible sleeping accommodations I had suffered with for fifteen months as a prisoner of war of the Germans. Enough, I told myself. I could not keep dwelling on the camp. Soon after that, I fell asleep.

Mary's ten-day vacation was over. She and her father were going back to Winthrop. They both had to get back to their jobs. Mary's mother was staying in New York a little longer to visit with Aunt Alice. I hated to see Mary leave, but I understood that she had to get back to work. I went to the railroad station with Mary and her father to see them off. I tried to ease my sadness by reminding myself that I would be discharged soon and could go home.

When Mary left, I did not go into New York as much as before. I went more often to the movies on the base. Mary continued to write, and I wrote back, and sometimes called her. I preferred to talk to her personally on the phone rather than just send letters. I stayed in close contact with my family by phone and by mail. There wasn't much for me to do at Mitchel Field. I was still just killing time waiting for my discharge.

On November 1, 1945, one of the lieutenants told me to get ready to go home because my discharge would be processed on November 4, 1945. I was delighted. I couldn't believe that my time to go home had finally come. I couldn't sleep that night. The next day I packed and unpacked and packed again. I practically wore out the floor in the barracks pacing up and down. By November 3, I had my gear packed for the final time and was ready to go. The next day, November 4, I received my official discharge papers and my back pay for all the time spent in the POW camp. I was sent to Fort Devens, in Massachusetts, along with some other Massachusetts servicemen who were also being discharged. I was thrilled knowing that I would be home for both Thanksgiving and Christmas for the first time in two years.

We had to show our discharge papers at Fort Devens, and they put us up for the night. I called my father to come and get me, and the next day he arrived. I did not hesitate at all. I just got in his car, and we drove out through the gate. There was no turning back now. I had mixed emotions, both good and bad, about leaving the Army Air Corps and reentering civilian life. It wasn't just a furlough anymore. I had to readjust to home, family, friends, getting a job, and making my own decisions again. I did not know what to expect, and I was not sure how I would handle the future. But I was eager to get home and try.

There were thousands of servicemen being discharged at this time, and one of the top priorities for most of us was to find a job. The U.S. Government had a program for discharged veterans who were unable to find jobs. Under this program, an unemployed veteran could get twenty dollars a week for nine weeks to help out until he could find work. Quite a few veterans, including many men I knew, signed up right away. We called this program the Nine-Twenty Club. Any veteran with an honorable discharge who was unable to get a job was eligible to receive this money. I did not have a job yet, but I did not want to sign up for the Nine-Twenty Club. I wanted to get to work as soon as possible.

Mary and I were going steady, and preparing for marriage.

I had been a welder before going into the Army Air Corps, but jobs in that field were scarce. I did not have a high school diploma because I had left high school to work in the war effort before joining the Army Air Corps. Mary and I were now going steady, and I was determined to find a job as fast as I could. Mary was a telephone operator for the telephone company, and I thought it might be good for me to try to get some kind of a job with that company. I knew it would not be as a telephone operator because those positions were mostly for women. But maybe there was something available that I could apply for.

I decided to give it a try, and went to the telephone company in Boston to apply for a job. The girl at the front desk gave me an application form to fill out. Just as she was about to hand me an application on a white sheet of paper, she asked if I had a high school diploma. I said no because I left school and went into the Army Air Corps. She quickly withdrew the application and handed me one on an orange sheet of paper. I asked her what was the difference between the while application she first had and the orange one she was now handing to me.

She replied that the orange application was for a janitor's or an elevator man's job, and she gave me that one because I did not have a high school diploma. I immediately turned and walked out of the office without saying a word. I was furious and remained angry all the way back to my home. I was insulted, and thought that with everything I had been through during the war, this was the way returning veterans were treated. I knew I could do better than that. But now I knew for sure that the first thing I had to do was get my high school diploma at night school. Unfortunately, I was not able to go back to school right away. I still needed a job.

The next day I was talking with Nick Crosby, a friend of mine, and I told him what had happened to me at the telephone company. Nick asked what kind of a job I was looking for. "Welding, if I can get it," I replied. Before I enlisted in the Army Air Corps, I had learned welding in a shipyard where I worked to help in the war effort.

"My father is a foreman at the Bethlehem Steel Shipyard," Nick said. "I could talk to him to see if anything is available, if you want me to."

"Definitely." I said. "I would really appreciate it."

True to his word, Nick called me the next morning to tell me I had an appointment with his father at the shipyard that afternoon. I kept my appointment with Mr. Crosby, Nick's father. I couldn't believe my good fortune when he hired me then and there as a welder. I was grateful for the opportunity Mr. Crosby was giving me. It was a good feeling to have a job. It was not an easy time for some of the discharged veterans to take up where they left off in civilian life. Many of my friends who had been in the service were still not working.

In May 1946, after I had been working steadily for six months, I gave Mary an engagement ring and asked her to marry me. She said yes, and on September 15, 1946, we were married and went to Canada on our honeymoon. I was happier than I had been in a long time. I had a job, a wonderful wife, and thoughts of the prisoner of war camp were fading from my mind. Adjustment to civilian life was beginning to work very well for me, even though I was not yet completely sure of myself. I could not explain the feeling I had that maybe things could still change for the worse. This sense of foreboding seemed to be embedded in my mind, and sometimes it was difficult to ignore it. I did not have my high school diploma yet, and I still hoped to go to night school. But my wife and my job came first, and by the time Mary and I returned from our honeymoon, I had put aside all doubtful thoughts and prepared to report back to my job at Bethlehem Steel.

Mary and I had rented a small apartment in my parents' house. When we arrived back home from our honeymoon, my mother greeted us, and at the same time handed me a telegram that had come a couple of days earlier. I thought it was a message from some friend congratulating Mary and me on our marriage. I opened the telegram. It was from the Bethlehem Steel Company. The message was short and not so sweet.

"Mr. Ralph Sirianni. Due to the fact that we have to lay off some workers, this telegram is to notify you that your services are no longer required at Bethlehem Steel."

I was devastated. Just when I thought I was getting my life back in order, this message shook me up. What would I do now? Where would I find work? Jobs were scarce, with hundreds of veterans in the area unable to find work. In those times, when there were layoffs, the pattern usually was last hired, first fired. With only a few months on the job, I fit that pattern. Mary was still working as a telephone operator, and we had some money saved, so we would be all right for a while. I had been planning to start night school to get my high school diploma, but that was impossible now. It was time to start job-hunting all over again.

Two days later John Tacelli, my godfather, called me. He heard I was looking for a job and said he had something I might be interested in. John was opening a gas station and auto repair shop in Winthrop. He asked if I would like to come to work with him. I didn't even ask him what the job was. I just said, "Yes."

I worked for John for two years doing all sorts of odd jobs. Whatever job I was asked to do, I did it. I greased cars, washed cars, replaced batteries, added new brake liners, pumped gas, and did any other job I was told to do. I certainly did learn a lot about cars, but I knew that this was not what I wanted for a future career. Nevertheless, I stuck with the job out of necessity to make a living.

One day when I arrived home from work, I found a package waiting for me. I was surprised because it was from the Army Air Corps. The package contained my medals. There were eight medals and one citation, listed as follows:

1. Two Purple Hearts, one for being wounded when my plane was shot down, and a second Purple Heart for my injuries in the prisoner of war camp.

My medals.

2. The Air Medal, which airmen received after five combat missions.

3. Prisoner of War Medal, which was engraved, "For honorable service while a prisoner of war."

4. Good Conduct Medal, engraved, "For Good Conduct."

5. The American Campaign Medal, engraved on the back, "United States of America, 1941–1945."

6. The European, African, Middle Eastern Campaign Medal, engraved on the back, "United States of America, 1941–1945." I received this for serving in the European area.

7. World War II Medal, engraved "World War II" on the front and "United States of America, 1941–1945. Freedom from fear and want. Freedom of speech and religion." This medal was granted to all veterans who served during World War II.

8. Presidential Citation — 388th Bomb Group. Individual citations were given to each member of the 388th Bomb Group.

As I looked at these medals and read the engraved words on them, I felt very proud for having served in the Army Air Corps. There was a certain amount of satisfaction for having done my duty for my country. But

As a police officer, I am guarding a damaged building in Winthrop after a vicious hurricane struck.

seeing these medals also brought back memories of my time served: good memories and bad memories. For the first time since I had been discharged from the service, memories of the bad times in Stalag Luft I came back to me. I had been too busy getting married, finding a job and supporting myself and my wife, to dwell on what happened in the war. But now, as I looked at the medals, I recalled the physical suffering, the hunger, and the death of some of the airmen. I was very sad as I put the medals back in the box, sad for all the pain and suffering inflicted upon us, sad for the death of many of my fellow airmen, and sad for all the veterans who had gone through these ordeals. This was the first time I had flashbacks about Stalag Luft I, and it was very unsettling. I had hoped I could put the past behind me and get on with my life.

While still working at the gas station, I joined the Winthrop Police Department as a special police officer, a position that would not interfere with my day job. Special police officers were on call for when needed in the evenings. We were paid for whatever hours we worked, and this helped supplement my income.

I really enjoyed my work as a special police officer, and decided to take the police exam to become a full-time officer with the Winthrop Police Department. The civil service exam courses were scheduled nights for six months. While still working at the gas station days, I attended the night classes and passed the civil service exam for policemen. From 1949 to 1954, I worked as a full-time police officer with the Winthrop Police Department. I liked my job because I was helping people and it certainly was not boring. Nevertheless, I had a feeling of wanting to move on. I still felt a deep commitment to be involved in public service, but police work was not the answer to my public service commitment. I was not sure yet what or where that new commitment to public service would be.

It was now 1955. Ten years had gone by since our liberation from Stalag Luft I. I no longer had doubts about adjusting to civilian life or the fear of being unable to take care of a family. The horrible atrocities and the brutal treatment we received in the German prisoner of war camp seemed to have almost disappeared from my thoughts. My mind was on the future now, not the past. I thought that the memories of my time in the camp would stay out of my life from now on, but I would eventually learn that these bad memories were deeply rooted inside me. And when I least expected it, Stalag Luft I would come back into my life.

In 1955, there was an opening for a health officer in Winthrop. I took the civil service exam for health officer and passed. The Board of Selectman appointed me to serve as the Winthrop health officer. I left the police department and served as Winthrop's health officer from 1955 to 1964.

Even though I was more deeply committed to public service, I did not forget my goal to finish school. While working days as the health officer, I went to Winthrop High School nights for two years and finally received my high school diploma. This was an especially proud and satisfying time for me.

In 1963, while still serving as the Winthrop health officer, I decided to run for an elected public office as a representative in the Massachusetts House of Representatives. The opening was to begin in 1964, and I believed that, if elected, I would be better able to serve both the people of Winthrop and the people of the commonwealth of Massachusetts. I was now as determined to stay in public service as I had once been determined to become a gunnery airman in the U.S. Army Air Corps. I had a love for flying then, and a love for public service now.

I defeated three opponents in the Democratic primary election, and went on to win the election against my Republican opponent. I resigned my position as the health officer and became a member of the Massachusetts House of Representatives, serving from 1964 to 1974. Because of my background in public health and as a former police officer, the speaker of the House appointed me chairman of the Public Safety Committee. In 1964 Governor Endicott "Chub" Peabody appointed me to the Massachusetts Public Health Council. The Public Health Council dealt with the public health concerns of the commonwealth of Massachusetts. This was a special appointment made by the governor as representative of the executive branch. In 1971 Governor Frank Sargent reappointed me to the Public Health Council. I served voluntarily on this council for two six-year terms, from 1964 to 1978.

My main ambition from the time I was discharged from the Air Corps was to serve the public, and I was fortunate to be able to fulfill this ambition. By 1974, nearly thirty years had gone by since my experiences in the camp. The horrible memories seemed to have gone further and further back in my thoughts. I had missed a lot of things in my early life because of the war. I didn't finish high school until years later. I never got the chance to go to college or play football again. My teen-age years were spent at war and then, later, in a prisoner of war camp. It took me years to recover from my wounds and the suffering in the POW camp, but I never regretted joining the Air Corps and serving my country. And now I had fulfilled my ambition to serve the people of my town and my state. In 1974 I retired from the Massachusetts Legislature, but I stayed on the Massachusetts Public Health Council until 1978. Mary had left her job at the telephone company, and we were raising a family. My daughter, Kristine, had already given birth to our first grandchild, Krisy, and a couple of years later

As a representative of the Massachusetts Legislature, I met with President Lyndon B. Johnson in Washington, D.C.

our second granddaughter, Jamie, was born. Mary and I wanted to spend more time with our family and to do a little traveling.

Even though the bad memories of the camp were not bothering me anymore on a day-to-day basis, I could never forget the ordeal that we went through as prisoners of war. I kept in touch with some of my *Heaven Can Wait* crewmembers. We talked about ourselves, and what we were doing in civilian life. We also talked to each other about our experiences as prisoners of war. I subscribed to a magazine entitled *The EX-POW Bulletin*, published by the American Ex-Prisoners of War Organization. *The EX-POW Bulletin* kept us up-to-date about all the news, events, and information pertaining to former prisoners of war. In fact, it was an article in this bulletin that led me back to Stalag Luft I.

CHAPTER ELEVEN

Revisiting Stalag Luft I
Years Later

One day when I was reading *The EX-POW Bulletin*, I saw a story about a tour being planned for former POWs and their wives to visit Germany. The tour was from April 24to May 7, 1985. The itinerary of the tour would take the travelers to England, Holland, Germany, and Poland. The members of the tour would visit the former sites of two German prisoner of war camps, Stalag Luft I in Germany and Stalag Luft III in Poland. May 1985 was the fortieth anniversary of the POWs' liberation from Stalag Luft I and III. The main purpose of the tour was to celebrate the liberation of the POWs from these two camps. On May 1, 1945, the Russians had entered Stalag Luft I, and we were freed from the Germans at last.

Mary and I decided to take the tour to visit the Stalag Luft I Memorial site and the other sites. On April 25, 1985, Mary and I met with the tour group in England at Heathrow Airport. The tour guides were waiting for us at the airport, and we were bused to the Tower Thistle Hotel in London. One of the guides waited at the airport for the remaining members of the tour group, who were arriving a little later. They would also be escorted to our hotel.

Mary and I checked into our room and began unpacking. I took a look out the window and saw the famous Tower of London. It was very impressive looking, and it was within walking distance of the hotel. I told Mary to come and look out the window. She did, and as we both stared at the landmark. I said to Mary, "Let's go visit the Tower of London as soon as we finish unpacking." She agreed.

It only took us a few minutes to get to the Tower of London, and we began our walking tour. We were pleasantly surprised to be greeted by a guide known as a Beefeater. He was dressed in a special red uniform and a red and black hat. Beefeaters were the men who took people on tours of the Tower of London, explaining its history and upcoming events to the tourists. One of the requirements for becoming a Beefeater was that he had to have served with special distinction in the British military. Once a former military man was accepted as a Beefeater, he and his family lived in an apartment in a special section inside the Tower of London.

We said hello to the Beefeater. He smiled and said, "Welcome to the Tower of London." Then he asked us where we were from and what brought us to England. I told him I was an ex–POW on the way to Germany with other former POWs and their wives. We were going to visit Barth, in East Germany, to see the memorial placed at the site where Stalag Luft I had been situated, and then on to Poland to see the memorial at the site where the Stalag Luft III POW camp had been.

The Beefeater held out his hand and showed us a large ring on his finger. I looked at it closely and could see that the figure of a man crawling under a piece of barbed wire was carved on the ring. This Beefeater had also been a prisoner of war. He told us that he

POW tour brochure.

That's Mary talking to the Beefeater who sang with me.

had been a prisoner of war in Germany, but he had been one of the fortunate ones who escaped and made his way back to England. The ring was an honor in remembrance of his successful escape from a prisoner of war camp.

I asked him if he knew the words to the song "Anne Boleyn," about the queen who had been beheaded in the Tower of London. He chuckled and said, "Oh, yes indeed. I know all the words by heart." Suddenly he began to sing the song, and without even thinking what I was doing, I joined in with him. We continued singing the song together.

Mary was standing in front of us smiling. When we finished the song, I heard applause behind me. I turned around and was surprised to see people standing behind me, smiling and applauding our performance. I had no idea that the people were even there. For a short time, while singing that song, the years were erased. It was not 1985. It was 1944, and I saw myself in my prison cell listening to the British prisoner in the next cell singing the song of Anne Boleyn over and over again. I quickly brought myself back to the present. I shook hands with the Beefeater as Mary and I said goodbye. After a little more sightseeing, we returned to the hotel. I never did remember to ask the guide why they were called Beefeaters.

That evening our tour group was treated to a dinner in our honor at the Tower Thistle Hotel. The tour guides had arranged for the dinner in advance. The town crier, dressed in his medieval uniform, was standing by the dining room door. As each of us entered the dining room, the town crier asked our name, and then read our name aloud from a list he held in his hand, thus announcing our arrival.

Before dinner, the Reverend Gerald Wilbur, from Franklin, Maine, gave the invocation. Reverend Wilbur was a member of our tour group. He had been a former POW imprisoned in Stalag Luft I. After the invocation, we enjoyed an excellent dinner. When the dinner was over, the first speaker was Lieutenant Colonel Richard Neal, the air attaché from the U. S. Embassy. He welcomed us to England and then read a telegram from President Ronald Reagan and his wife, Nancy, recognizing the fortieth anniversary of our liberation.

The telegram was addressed to Mr. Phil Gibbons, c/o The Tower Hotel, St. Katherine's Way, London E1 9LD, England. Gibbons was the leader of our tour group. The telegram read as follows:

> Nancy joins me in wishing you and your colleagues every blessing as you mark the anniversary of your experiences as prisoners of war and of the end of World War II. It is especially fitting that you should come together to commemorate your sacrifices on behalf of freedom and to honor the memory of fallen comrades.
>
> This is also an opportunity to celebrate the spirit of reconciliation we in the West have achieved in these past four decades and to reaffirm our commitment to the ideals of peace and human dignity and the values we share in common as free people.
>
> We owe you a debt that can never be repaid, but I know that your heroism will be remembered always. On behalf of the American people, I say, well done and God bless you.
>
> Signed, Ronald Reagan

It was a wonderful feeling to be recognized by our president, and while there were other dignitaries who also spoke, the words from President Reagan made me feel proud.

Stefan Staniszaeski, Poland's ambassador to Great Britain, spoke in his own language. As soon as he finished, an interpreter stood and read the speech in English so we could understand what was said. When Alexry Nikiforou, the consular for the Soviet Embassy, gave his speech in Russian, an interpreter then translated his speech into English for us. Ron Nield, an RAF wing commander, also gave a short speech, in English, of course. After the dinner and the speeches were over, the Reverend Wilbur ended the ceremonies with a blessing. Then we were able to move around and get a chance to meet and talk to some of the dignitaries, especially the ones who spoke English.

We had a good time talking with each other at our tables. This was the first time I had been able to meet with other POWs in a group like this. It brought back memories of the camp. I felt at ease with these men who had suffered through the same ordeal that I had been through. I was very impressed by the whole event. I considered it an honor to be recognized by such distinguished men, and to be remembered by the president of the United States.

The next day the tour guides had three buses available to take us to the south English coast. From there we went by a hydroplane boat to Holland. There were three buses at the dock ready to take us to our hotel in Amsterdam. We had a wonderful two days in Amsterdam, and were able to do a lot of sightseeing. Just as we were preparing to leave, a Dutch tour guide was assigned to each bus. They were to continue the tour with us through Germany and Poland.

Our next destination was Rostock, East Germany. Rostock was very close to Barth, where Stalag Luft I had been located. After World War II ended, Germany had been separated into East Germany, under Russian control, and West Germany, under Allied control. Rostock and Barth were both located in East Germany. With the Berlin Wall sealing East Germany off from the rest of the world, it was not the most pleasant place to be visiting. But our goal was to visit the site in Barth where Stalag Luft I had been located, and then go on to Poland to see the Stalag Luft III memorial site. To fulfill this goal, we would have to eventually cross over from West Germany in to East Germany.

From Amsterdam we went to Hamburg, and spent the night in West Germany. The next day we traveled to Lubeck, where we had time to do a little sightseeing, and then went a short distance to Selmsdorf, where we stopped at the East German checkpoint. We did not have any problem at the checkpoint. The inspection was very quick. The East German guards entered each of our buses and looked at everyone's passport. They didn't ask any questions and they didn't check any luggage. It only took us an hour or so to go through the checkpoint. I was surprised because we had been told that it usually took three or four hours for a group our size to be checked by the guards before being allowed to enter East Germany. I should have known that there had to be a reason why we passed through the checkpoint so quickly, with very little checking done.

Three East German tour guides were waiting for us on the other side of the checkpoint. These three young ladies were assigned as our tour guides for the next six days in East Germany. The three Dutch guides stayed with us, but the East German guides would be showing us around and explaining things. As if assigning three guides to watch where we went and what we did was not enough, six East German motorcycle policemen were also assigned to go with us for the next six days.

Looking at these stern East German policemen made me feel as if we were under restraint and would have to be careful of what we did and said. I was not comfortable being escorted by these men. They reminded me of being guarded in the prison camp. The policemen were all about the same height and weight, and they looked so much alike that it was difficult to tell one from the other. They were dressed alike in brown leather jackets, brown pants, and black boots. They also wore the customary helmets required of motorcycle policemen. The East German guides had smiled and welcomed us to East Germany, but none of the East German motorcycle policemen were smiling.

One of the wives on our bus commented, "Isn't it nice of them to give us a motorcycle escort?"

A former POW near the back of the bus replied, "Sure, but don't forget they are also there to watch us."

That man had the same sense of foreboding as I had. These policemen

East German motorcycle police escorts.

were not really our friends, but rather our watchers. They were not here for our benefit, but for the benefit of the East German government.

We arrived at our destination at the Rostock hotel in time for dinner. Mary and I went to bed early so we would be rested for our visit to Barth. The next morning we had a quick breakfast and our tour group prepared to leave on the buses for the 45-mile drive to Barth. We reached our destination in less than an hour. As the buses approached Barth, the first thing I saw was the church steeple, the same church steeple that I had seen every day when I looked outside the camp. Because this church steeple was outside Stalag Luft I, it had become a symbol of freedom for me and the other airmen while we were prisoners in the camp. When I got off the bus in front of the town hall, I looked around at the other men, who were also staring at the steeple. Some of them were quietly explaining to their wives what the steeple had meant to us. It was easy to see that they were experiencing the same emotional turmoil that I was.

Everyone was off the bus now, and as I turned around I saw that the Barth train station was still operational. This was the train station that was near Stalag Luft I. A train had brought us from the Dulag Luft Interrogation Center to the Barth train station. I remembered the train pulling into the station and the German guards ordering us to get off. I couldn't see Stalag Luft I from the station, but I knew it was about one mile away. More memories were flooding through my mind as I recalled the long, painful walk to the camp. My legs were so sore and the wounds were so painful that walking was difficult. I had been very apprehensive about what awaited us in the Stalag Luft I prisoner of war camp. Seeing the station now held no fears for me, but the sight of it still brought back the bad memories, and I could feel the sting of small tears in my eyes. I remembered the two airmen who helped me walk from the Barth train station to the camp. They were weak, hungry, and exhausted. But they each took hold of one side of me and held me up on the mile walk to the camp. I never would have made it without their help. I often wished I had learned their names so that I could have found them later and thanked them.

The Lord Mayor Zeller was waiting at the town hall to greet us. He invited us to enter the town hall and enjoy a midmorning snack. After we finished, we went back outside to the public square. Already, over a thousand people were in the public square waiting to greet us. Some of these people were old enough to have been living in Barth during our captivity in 1944 and 1945. Maybe some of them were the ones who yelled at us or threw rocks at us when we first arrived at the camp. But that didn't matter now. It was May 1, 1985, the fortieth anniversary celebration of our liberation, and all the people here, young and old, were cheering for us.

The mayor and some Russian dignitaries were standing on a newly erected reviewing stand. A band was playing some lively music. Some children approached the reviewing stand and handed each of us a paper dove attached to a small stick. Mary asked the little girl who gave her a dove if the girl would sign her name and address. The girl understood because she had English in school. Mary told her that she had a granddaughter about the same age, and perhaps they could become pen pals. The girl wrote down the information.

The music finally stopped and the speeches began. When the

Round identification markers of the 40th anniversary of the POW liberation, 1945–1985, given to the tour members to put on their luggage.

ceremonies were over, hundreds of real white doves were released into the air as a tribute to our liberation and as a symbol of peace. We watched the doves fly off into the distance. It was an inspiring sight. By now it was lunchtime, and we were invited back to the town hall, where we were treated to lunch.

After lunch, people from the tour went in all different directions around the town. Mary and I headed straight for the church. I just stood there looking at it for a few minutes. People would not be able to imagine how important this church and its steeple had been to me for fourteen months of captivity. Further down from the church was a huge arch over the road. The columns were on each side of the road and joined together above the road. It was like an entrance to the town.

I wanted to walk through this arch again. When we were liberated, we walked through the arch to the airfield farther down the road, where we boarded the B-17s as free men. I can't even begin to explain how emotional it was for me to see this church close up and to be walking through the arch again.

As we continued our walk around the town, everyone greeted us very pleasantly. The children were our most enthusiastic greeters. All the members of our group had made special plans for the children. Before we began our tour, we asked Phil Gibbons, our tour organizer, what kind of gifts we could bring into East Germany for the children of Barth. We were allowed to bring in such things as souvenir pens, key rings, small American flags, gum, candy, Kennedy half dollars, and other small items. Everyone on the tour had purchased these gifts in the United States, and had stored them away in with their luggage. Once we began giving out the gifts to the nearby children, word must have spread through the town that the Americans were giving things away. More and more children began to surround us, looking for something to remember the Americans by. I hoped that we had accomplished two things by our visit and our offer of friendship and gifts. One, I believed that the children were now made more aware of the fact that World War II really took place, and two, I hoped that we had shown the children and the townspeople that we could forgive and become friends instead of enemies.

We finished giving out all our presents to the children and got on the buses to go to the site where Stalag Luft I used to be. As we got nearer to the site, which was just outside Barth, I could see that each of the former POWs on my bus was experiencing the same emotion that I was. Memories from the past were beginning to come back to me again. I could visualize the camp as if it was still there. Forty years had passed since I was a POW, but now it seemed like yesterday. For a moment it was rather unsettling.

Many of the Barth townspeople were already at the site, waiting to greet us as we got off the bus. The first thing I saw was a huge granite monument with a bronze plaque on it. The monument was located approximately where the entrance to the POW camp had been. I moved closer to it and read what was on the plaque. The words indicated that this was the site of the Stalag Luft I POW camp for American and British Airmen, and that the Russians had liberated the camp on May 1, 1945.

Four 30-foot-high flags were placed around the monument. One was a Russian flag, one was a British flag, the third was an American flag, and the fourth flag, honoring all servicemen, represented the German Democratic Republic, often known as the GDR. The monument and the flags were a memorial to the former POWs of Stalag Luft I and to the Russians who had liberated the POWs. Seeing this beautiful memorial honoring both the former prisoners of war from Stalag Luft I and the Russians who liberated us was a very emotional experience for all the former POWs and their wives.

Many of the men were crying because they were reliving their past experience as POWs. It was difficult for the women to visualize the POW camp being on this beautiful site. Nevertheless, tears came to their eyes because of the suffering of their husbands as they shared their remembrances of the camp. The men were talking to each other and pointing out where things had been located in Stalag Luft I. One man said, "Over there was where the North Compound was." "Yes," said another POW, "and right over there is where the parade field was." Others pointed to the spot where the latrines had been. They continued pointing to certain areas around the site until finally one man said in a solemn tone, "I can see the church steeple from here." Everyone was silent as they turned and looked off in the distance at the steeple that had been the symbol of freedom during their captivity.

Finally it was time to get on the buses and continue our tour. When we had first arrived at the Stalag Luft 1 memorial site, we were told to leave packages and other items on the bus. Mary left her paper dove behind. When we got back on the bus, Mary discovered that, not only was her paper dove gone, but also everyone's paper dove was missing. While they were at the memorial site, somebody entered the buses and took every paper dove. We never recovered them, and we never found out why they were taken.

We left the Stalag Luft I memorial site, and our next stop was the former site of the Ravensbruck Concentration Camp, which was also just

Mary looking at the sculptures at the Ravensbruck Memorial site.

outside Barth. The site was only about two kilometers from the Stalag Luft I site. Ravensbruck was gone, and our guides told us that the cement factory we were now looking at was located on the original site of the concentration camp. When I looked at the Ravensbruck Memorial, I saw that the bronze sculptures on it were very graphic, and the sight of them brought tears to my eyes. The sculptures showed the suffering of the men, women, and children who had been in Ravensbruck. These bronze sculptures brought back my time at Stalag Luft I. Just after our liberation, Ravensbruck was liberated. I saw the stacks of dead bodies. I saw the emancipated captives who were brought to our camp hospital. Many of them died within a few days. The sight of these bronze sculptures depicting the life of the inmates being tortured and dying brought back the memory of the horror and decay that we smelled after Ravensbruck was liberated. Of course, I did not really smell that fear and decay now while standing at the Ravensbruck Memorial, but I felt as if I did. No one could ever tell me the Holocaust never happened. I was a witness, and the memories are still with me.

The wreaths have been placed on the Ravensbruck Memorial site by these veterans. I am second from the left, in the white coat.

I was glad when it was time to put the wreaths at the bottom of the Ravensbruck monument. Two members of the Soviet delegation carried a wreath and carefully placed it down at the monument. We also had a wreath to place there. Phil Gibbon, our tour director, chose six former American POWS to place the wreath. He chose me, Calary Beltman, George Fernades, Neil Weiss, Max Castner, and James Gray. Neil Weiss carried the wreath, and the other five of us acted as escorts.

When the ceremonies were over, we went back to Barth. Lord Mayor Zeller and other local officials hosted a luncheon for the Soviet delegation and us. Each Russian man in attendance had a significant role in the liberation of the POWs in Stalag Luft I. General Juri Naumenko was the former battalion commander of the Russian soldiers who liberated us. Retired Colonel Jakow Swinfow was the leader of the Russian group of soldiers who entered our camp. Sergeant Nikolai Kiyowda was the first regular army Russian soldier to meet the POWs at the gate. There were others who also made speeches. We enjoyed the luncheon except for the speeches. The speeches took a long time because they were given in English, German, and Russian with follow-up translations. When the ceremony was over, we returned to our hotel in Rostock.

A special dinner was planned for us that night at the Rostock hotel. Members of the East German government and a Russian general hosted the dinner. This dinner and the concluding ceremonial speeches did not last as long as the previous ones. We even finished early enough to have time to sit in the hotel lobby and relax after dinner. One of the East German guides had announced at dinner that the ceremonies we attended earlier had been televised and taped. He wanted us to gather in the lobby because he was going to replay the tape for us. I thought that was a great idea and I looked forward to seeing it.

The guide unlocked the door of a small closet and rolled a TV set and VCR out into the lobby. He plugged the cord into an outlet and turned the equipment on. An East German television crew had done an excellent job of recording our activities at the Stalag Luft I Memorial. It was very interesting to see the ceremony and to see ourselves on the videotape. I wouldn't have minded having a copy of it to take home, but we were not offered that opportunity. When the program was over, the guide quickly disconnected the equipment, rolled it back into the closet and locked the closet door. It wasn't difficult to see that the East Germans were so strict that they even went so far as to control what their people could see on TV. In fact, they even controlled the TV itself. We fought a war so that people could live in freedom without fear. But, somehow, the East Germans never got that freedom. In 1985, when we were on our tour, Germany was still divided into East Germany and West Germany. The Berlin Wall separated the two Germanys. None of us ever thought that the Berlin Wall would eventually come tumbling down and East and West Germany would join together as one country, Germany.

After we saw the videotape, some of us stayed in the lobby to relax and talk. I went to the bar to get a round of drinks to carry back to the eight of us sitting together. As I left the bar, I noticed a man and woman who were sitting at the bar watching our group. On my way back to the group with the drinks, I said hello and smiled at the man and woman as I passed them. A few minutes later the man came over, pointed to me, and then in broken English, he said, "You prisoner of war. Me too, in United States." He introduced himself as Lother Petzole and pointed to his wife and said her name was Christine.

I said, "Why don't you and your wife join us?"

When Lother and his wife sat down with us, he told us he had been in the German army. When he was only18 years old, he was captured in North Africa and sent to America, where he remained a prisoner of war for five years. He told us he had been treated well in the American prisoner of war camp. I did not explain to him how badly I had been treated as a POW in Germany. We were on a friendly visit to Germany, and I did not want to bring up our terrible treatment at the hands of the Germans so long ago.

Lother and his wife were just visiting Rostock. Their vacation was over, and they were returning to Dresden the next morning. Mary and I were pleasantly surprised to learn that they lived in Dresden. Our tour group was going to stop in Dresden for four days. We enjoyed Lother and Christine's company and told them we would like to meet with them again when we get to Dresden. Lother said that we would have to get permission from our East German escorts first.

I asked one of our Dutch tour guides if she would ask permission from the East German guide for us to meet Lother and his wife in Dresden and take them out to dinner. The East German guide said that it would be all right. When we told Lother and his wife that the visit was approved, and that when we did get to Dresden they were to be our guests at dinner, Lother and Christine were delighted. We shook hands all around, said our farewells, and added, "Until we meet again." It was a shame that the lives of the East Germans were so closely regulated, but at least Mary and I did everything by the book and got permission in advance.

The next day we left Rostock and headed for East Berlin, where we stayed at the beautiful five-star Hotel Interpol. By now we had been ten days on the tour, and our group had done everything together: traveling in the buses, attending the ceremonies, eating our meals, and going sight-seeing. But that night in East Berlin, I thought, just for once I would like to go someplace special for dinner. While Mary and I were in our hotel room preparing to join the group for dinner in the hotel, I suggested to her that maybe we could go out to eat at a local restaurant. She agreed and we picked out a restaurant from a brochure. It was named The Ratskeller. It sounded intriguing to us.

We stopped at the desk in the lobby so I could exchange a hundred-dollar bill for East German marks. The desk clerk asked why I wanted to do that. Desk clerks don't usually ask that kind of a question, and I was a little bit perturbed. "Excuse me, miss," I replied, "but that is none of your business."

She immediately called the manager, who was not too thrilled either that I wanted East German marks. He reminded me that we were having dinner here in the hotel, and it was already paid for through the tour group. It was evident that they did not want to change my money, but I was persistent.

I could not figure out what was so wrong with wanting to go to a restaurant outside the hotel. As far as I knew there was no rule against it. I looked the manager straight in the eye and replied, "My wife and I are aware that the hotel dinner is already paid for, but we want to try someplace different." I showed him the brochure advertising the Ratskeller.

The manager looked around for a moment and, after a brief hesitation, he agreed to change my money, but not my hundred-dollar bill. He would only allow fifty dollars to be exchanged for marks. The way the manager was looking around at a man in a brown coat, I was beginning to feel a little uncomfortable. When the man nodded his head, I was sure that he was giving the manager a sign that it was all right to exchange the money and let us go out to the Ratskeller.

The doorman got us a cab and told the driver where we wanted to go. I watched the route the cabdriver took to be sure that we could find our way back again. As we drove by the Elbe River, I noticed that the streets were empty. We did not see any people walking on the sidewalks and there were only a few cars in the streets. When the driver stopped in front of a doorway, he said, "Downstairs," and pointed to the door.

As I followed Mary into the Ratskeller, I saw a car pull up to the curb and a man get out. He wore a felt hat, and had a long, dark-brown leather coat over his suit. He seemed to take an unusual interest in us, and I was convinced that he had followed us to the restaurant. The maitre d' hurriedly moved forward and showed us to a table. He did it so fast that it seemed almost as if he knew we were coming. Meanwhile, the man in the brown leather coat had entered the restaurant and went over to speak to the maitre d.' They were both looking in our direction. I was not sure if I was getting paranoid or not, but I sensed that the maitre d' had been told that we were coming, and now he and the man in the leather coat were talking about us and watching carefully. In spite of being watched, Mary and I were determined to enjoy our dinner.

As Mary was looking around the restaurant, she said it almost looked like a romantic movie setting. It looked like a really good restaurant, but we were surprised to see that there was only one couple seated over in the corner. Except for us and the couple, there were no other customers in the place.

We were ushered to our table and ordered drinks. A few minutes later the couple left, and we were alone except for the waiters and the maitre d.' It gave us a weird feeling to be the only ones in such a large restaurant. Our dinners came, and we enjoyed them. I was still a little nervous and tried not to let Mary know that I was. But she sensed my nervousness and asked, "Ralph, why do you keep looking behind me?"

"The man in the brown leather coat is here now, and he's watching us," I said.

Mary turned her head and saw the man talking to the maitre d' and staring at us. We had finished our dinner and it was time to leave. I paid the bill, tipped the waiter, and asked him to call us a cab. Quite some time passed and we were still waiting for the cab. Mary said, "It's taking a long time for the cab to come." Mary could see that I was getting nervous.

"Yes, too long," I replied. "Let's see what's holding up the cab."

We went up to the man at the desk to asked where our cab was. He replied very abruptly, "No cab. Take subway."

Then the maitre d' said he was unable to get a cab. He walked with us to the exit door at the top of the stairs and pointed to a subway, and went back into the restaurant. There was no way we wanted to go into the dark subway. As we went outside, I told Mary exactly how I felt about our situation. "Mary," I said, "we're in trouble. We were followed here by that man in the brown coat and he might still be watching us. Going into the subway is out. We don't know the language, and we might get lost. We will have to walk back to the hotel."

Mary was a little uncertain as she asked, "Do you know the way, Ralph?"

"I have a general idea, so let's go," I replied.

We were in the business district surrounded by high buildings, many of which were adorned with life-size statues. The streets were deserted. We were the only two outside on the sidewalk.

Mary and I started walking to the hotel. We followed the route back that the cab had used to take us to the Ratskeller. The streets were totally deserted. We walked toward the Elbe River. As we were getting nearer to the hotel, a car went by us. A few minutes later the same car drove by us again. It was going a little more slowly this time. The driver must have gone around the block and come back to check on us. We both were scared, and I said, "Don't stop. Keep walking." It was 11 P.M. and there was no one else on the streets. Mary asked me if I was sure we were going in the right direction. "Yes, I'm sure," I replied. "We came over the Elbe River to get to the Ratskeller, and there's the bridge over the Elbe straight ahead."

We crossed the bridge on the pedestrian walk, and when we reached the other side we still did not see the hotel. We began to walk faster. Soon we saw a glow in the sky quite a distance ahead of us. "Mary, look there," I pointed. "See that glow in the sky. It has to be the hotel. It's the only place that would cast that much light. Let's run as fast as we can before that car comes back."

Mary kicked off her high heels, picked them up quickly, and we began running toward the light as fast as we could.

As we got closer to the lights, we could see that it was indeed the Hotel Interpol, and we tried to run even faster than before. We burst through the doors all out of breath and surprised the man at the desk. Sweating, huffing and puffing, I looked at the man and managed to ask, "Where is the bar?"

Standing in the safety of the hotel lobby was a good feeling, but we were still shaken by the whole event. We needed to sit down and get a drink to calm down. Our Dutch bus drivers and tour guides were relaxing in the lounge. We were delighted to see people that we knew. As we stood before them, pale, sweaty, and out of breath, they were very concerned. They all jumped up at once and told us to sit down and tell them what had happened to us.

I told them about our harrowing experience, and how we had to make our own way back to the hotel on foot. Mary still had her shoes in her hands. She told the Dutch guides how she had to take off her high heels so she could run fast. They saw her feet covered by ripped, shredded nylons. And then she added, "Never in my wildest dreams did I ever expect to do long-distance running, especially without shoes."

I also told them about the car that we were sure was following us. They were shocked by our story and said we were lucky not to be picked up by the East German police. They were really relieved that we made it back safely, and so were we. The guides then impressed upon us to always stay with the group, and never wander off by ourselves.

Later, in our room, I lay in bed thinking about our adventure. What an absolutely stupid thing Mary and I had done. We hadn't told anyone in our group where we were going. We could have been arrested by the East German police and disappeared behind the Iron Curtain forever. For the rest of our time in East Germany, I would never again depart from the group. Just the thoughts of being arrested and put in an East German prison scared me. I had no desire to become a captive of the Germans again. Fortunately for Mary and me, we managed to get back to our tour group The next day, Mary said she had a hard time sleeping that night. She said her mind was whirling with the thoughts of what could have happened, since no one in the group knew that we had left the hotel. If the police had picked us up, we would have just disappeared. It was very frightening. No one would miss us because the people on the tour did not always eat at the same tables or ride in the same bus all the time. Also, there was no roll call. I told her I had the same thoughts, and we were very lucky to have gotten back to the hotel safely.

The next day we were allowed to go through Checkpoint Charlie into West Berlin for some shopping and sightseeing. Before leaving, we asked the three East German women who were our guides if there was anything

Checkpoint Charlie guard post where Mary and I crossed over into West Germany to do some shopping.

they would like for us to bring back from West Berlin. They told us to bring back magazines or newspapers so they could catch up on the news from West Germany. I was surprised that they did not ask for stockings or other things they could not get in East Germany.

Mary and I picked out some magazines, newspapers, lipstick, stockings, and candy for them. We put the items in our shopping bags with our purchases, so that it just appeared as if everything was our own shopping items. We could have been in trouble if they had checked our bags. The East Germans did not want outside newspapers and magazines in their country. If caught, people who broke this rule could be punished for bringing them in. Fortunately, we were not checked on the way back and got through the checkpoint safely. In the late afternoon we returned to the Hotel Interpol in East Berlin in time to prepare for our trip to Poland. We gave the gifts to the three East German women guides. They were very thrilled to get the items.

In East Berlin we had to get a separate visa to visit Poland. Once we received the visa, we were able to enter Poland and by 10 A.M. we crossed the border into Poland and were soon on the way to the Stalag Luft III memorial site. The German motorcycle policemen were left behind in East Germany. A different police escort welcomed us in Poland. They were there as an escort and as a gesture of welcome from the authorities as we proceeded to the memorial site. These policemen were not here to watch or control us like the East German police did.

The Stalag Luft III area had a memorial and a museum with artifacts from the Stalag Luft III POW camp and from the sites of former concentration camps in the area. After the speeches were over, some of the former POWs from Stalag Luft III placed wreaths at the foot of the memorial monument.

We also went to the gravesite and memorial for the British airmen who had escaped from Stalag Luft III in what has been called "The Great Escape." On March 24, 1944, 76 POWs escaped from Stalag Luft III, all at the same time. Only three of them made it back to England. The other 73 were recaptured over a short period of time. Some of the men were imprisoned again, but 50 of the recaptured POWs were murdered by the guards while supposedly being taken back to the camp. They were ordered off the trucks to stand in a field where, they were brutally shot down. These airmen had been executed by the Germans as an example of what would happen to all POWs who tried to escape. The order to kill prisoners who tried to escape came directly from Adolf Hitler, and some of the German officers, especially in the Gestapo, were quite willing to carry the orders out. After Hitler was dead and the war was over, those Germans who were responsible for carrying out this atrocity were tried and convicted as war criminals.

I had only been in Stalag Luft I a few days when I heard rumors about a large group of prisoners escaping from Stalag Luft III at the same time. We did not have all the details, but we were excited about their escape, and hoped that they all made it safely back to England. The Germans put new posters up all around our camp warning us that any prisoners trying to escape would be shot. I did not learn about the murder of some of the recaptured prisoners until much later. It was a sad day for me and for all the prisoners in our camp when we did hear the news of their deaths.

It was time to leave the Stalag Luft III memorial site, and by 3:30 P.M. we were on our way to Dresden. That evening Mary and I were expecting to meet Lother and Christine in the hotel lobby. While Mary was getting ready, I told her I would go downstairs and wait for our guests. Just as I entered the lobby, Lother and Christine came in. There was another person with them, a young man whom I did not know. I was surprised to see a third person because we did not expect anyone to be with them. I wondered if he was a person assigned by the East Germans to watch over our meeting. I must have had a bewildered look on my face because they were quick to introduce their son. Their son had driven them to the hotel and was going to come back to drive them home when we finished dinner. After a brief introduction and handshaking, Lother's son left to meet with friends. I had asked two of the Dutch guides to join us for dinner to help interpret for us. Lother's English was not yet the best it could be, and his wife did not speak English.

We had dinner in the hotel and stayed there until three in the morning enjoying each other's company. The two Dutch guides were enjoying

Mary and I have our special dinner in Dresden with Lother Petzole and his wife, Christine.

themselves and stayed, chatting with us the whole night. We had a fantastic evening. Lother's son had arrived earlier to drive his mother and father home. They were having such a good time that he went to the bar and patiently waited for them. We finally had to break it up because Mary and I, and the two guides, had to be up early the next morning for breakfast. We were going to visit the Meissen Porcelain Factory just outside Dresden. Mary and Christine exchanged addresses before Lother and his wife left. Then Mary and I went up to our hotel room.

The next morning our group left the hotel early to visit the porcelain factory. It was located just outside Dresden in a town named Meissen. The factory had a long history, dating back to the eighteenth century. Over the years it had grown to be one of the most famous ceramics makers in the world, and was still active in 1985 when we were there. The factory was also famous for making its Dresden china. It was quite an experience to watch the workers create and decorate the porcelain vases, plates, and other items. This trip to the porcelain factory was quite special for the wives. They enjoyed watching the beautiful things being created right before their eyes. I was more amazed to see that the factory had survived the Allied bombing raids. Dresden had been heavily bombed during World War II, and we could see many newer buildings that had been built after the war. But the Meissen Porcelain Factory was a much older building and it looked like the bombs had never touched it, even though it was only a few miles away. After the tour was over, we returned to Dresden for the night. The next morning we left for Frankfurt, our last stop in Germany before returning home.

In Frankfurt, we went on a sightseeing cruise on the Rhine River. After the emotional strain of visiting the POW sites and recalling the unpleasant time in the POW camp, it was great to just relax on this cruise. The next morning we were bused to the Frankfurt Airport, where Mary and I got our plane for Boston.

The trip through England, Holland, Germany, and Poland was very exciting. Mary and I had a wonderful time. But there were also times when the trip was very emotional for me. Most of the time I was happy and had fun, but there were other times when my wartime memories came back to haunt me, and I felt sorrow. Over the years I had tried to put my wounds and my prisoner of war experience behind me. This trip back to Germany made me realize that the memories of the suffering I had endured in the camp would never leave me. The memories had just been hidden for a while, but revisiting the past had begun to bring the pain and the horrors of the war years back to me.

I was very glad that my wife, Mary, had come with me to share my past, even though we did not discuss my wartime experiences in detail. Mary told me that it was good for her to meet some of the other POWs and their wives and to be able to talk to them about the war. The wives could learn how their husbands had been affected by being prisoners of war, and they could see how their own lives had been affected as the wives of former POWs. All in all, it was a worthwhile trip, but it was very good to be back home in Winthrop.

CHAPTER TWELVE

Searching for the Plane's Crash Site

In 1986 we received a letter from Lother, the German we had met in Barth while he and his wife, Christine, were on vacation. Lother wrote that because he was now sixty-five years old, he would be allowed to travel outside East Germany. His wife, who was not yet sixty-five, was not allowed to leave the country. Lother hoped that he could stay with us for two months. He was limited to only two months on his trip out of the country. With his wife and family still in East Germany, he had to return on time or they would suffer the consequences. Mary wrote back and said we would be delighted to have him as a guest for the two months he was allowed.

In April 1987, Lother took a plane from East Germany to New York. I was afraid he would have trouble getting from New York to Boston. I also knew he was not permitted to take much money out of the country, so I decided to meet him in New York. Then I would pay for his ticket to Boston and fly back to Boston with him.

We soon discovered that Lother had learned over the years to speak English a little better. He was very anxious to see everything he could in America. We took him all around Boston and the surrounding area for sightseeing. We also drove to Maine to get some of their famous lobster. Lother had promised his neighbor in Dresden that he would try to visit the neighbor's relatives in Rhode Island. We did that and had a nice afternoon visit with them.

Lother was amazed by many of the things we took for granted. Our freedom to travel wherever we wanted delighted him. At first he expected to be stopped by guards asking for identification, but as we crossed state lines from one state to another, he finally stopped watching for guards.

When he came food shopping with us, he could not believe his eyes at the amount of food that was available to us. On one shopping trip we were putting some oranges, apples, and bananas in the shopping cart. Mary and I had chosen all the fruit we wanted and were ready to move on. I was concerned when I noticed that Lother was standing very still and watching us intently.

"What's wrong, Lother?" I asked.

"In East Germany we cannot get such quantities of food," he replied. Then he told Mary and me how he had waited in line for a long time just to get three oranges to bring home to his family. Later he told us other stories of life in East Germany. For example, he had waited seven years before he was allowed to buy a used car. We already knew his wife was not allowed to leave the country, and he reminded us that he was only allowed to take a small amount of money out of East Germany. That's why he had very little money for use on this trip. For us, as Americans, it was difficult to picture living under such restrictions as Lother and his wife had to endure.

I had seen the strict rules and constant surveillance imposed upon the East Germans when I was there in 1985. I had also had fifteen months of being subjected to loss of freedom in Stalag Luft I in 1944–45, so I could truly sympathize with Lother and his family. Lother and I had many conversations about being prisoners of war. Sometimes it surprised us that, even though we were once enemies and had both spent time in prisoner of war camps, him in America and me in Germany, we held no animosity toward each other. We had both been extremely happy when World War II ended. At the end of the two months, Lother went back to Dresden. I could well imagine that when he returned home he would astonish his family with stories about America.

It was sad that Lother had to go back to such a restrictive life, but he had to protect his family. I remember telling him that it wouldn't be long before the Berlin Wall came down, and the Iron Curtain would no longer exist. He replied, quite sadly, that he did not believe that would happen. In 1988, Lother's wife notified us that he had passed away. Shortly thereafter, on November 9, 1989, the Berlin Wall was opened and thousands of East Germans crossed the border into the West. There were celebrations for days, and people began to break pieces off the Berlin Wall for souvenirs. I was very sorry that Lother had not lived to see the Berlin Wall come tumbling down.

Over the years I had kept in touch with some of my *Heaven Can Wait* crewmembers. I had been in close touch with George McFall and his wife Elaine, and with Walt Pawlesh and his wife Marg. We kept in touch by phone and by letters. George and Elaine came to visit with Mary and me in Winthrop and in our cottage in New Hampshire. Walt had visited us twice, once in New Hampshire and once in Winthrop. It was really great to be able to see them from time to time. Later, Mary and I visited George McFall and Elaine at their home in Arizona. They lived part of the year in their Wisconsin home and part of the year in their Arizona home.

In 1992 when Walt suggested to me that we have a crewmembers' reunion later in 1993, I thought it was a good idea. So far only the three of us, George McFall, Walt Pawlesh, and me, had been able to keep in touch. We hoped maybe some of the other crewmembers and their wives would be able to join us in a reunion. Walt said he would make all the arrangements, and he did. He notified the other crewmembers that the first reunion of the crew of *Heaven Can Wait* would take place in Myrtle Beach, South Carolina, in June 1993.

Out of ten crewmembers, five were able to come to the reunion. In attendance were: Ralph Sirianni and Mary, George McFall and Elaine, Frank Irizarry and Blanca, Bill Kemp and Alene, Walt Pawlesh and Marge. Roy Eggman had passed away, and his wife Judy represented him at the reunion. Alan "Pop" Grimshaw had passed away. Ed Brazies was too ill to travel, and we did not get any response from Willy Krupitsch or Ernie Alcorn.

Counting wives and crewmen, there were eleven of us at the reunion. We spent three great days talking over the good times during our training at Ardmore, Oklahoma. We especially remembered Frank Irizarry's chandelle episode that almost caused the plane to crash, and made Walt and me fly around inside and hit the ceiling of the plane. After we had managed to land safely, George McFall had taken Frank aside and chewed him out. We never did know what McFall said to Frank, so now Walt and I took Frank aside and asked him to tell us what McFall had said. Frank said, "McFall yelled at me, and said I endangered the whole crew. He told me that he never wanted to see anything like that happen again." Then Frank added, "George really gave me an ass-chewing, and you guys know that I never did anything like that again."

Then we talked about the ice storm that almost caused us to crash. I especially remembered this close call because it was on the day of my twentieth birthday, Dec. 24, 1943. I recalled going out with the whole crew to celebrate my birthday that night, and we all remembered being thankful to be alive after that close call.

Walt brought up the possibility of going back to Germany to find out where our plane had crashed, but no one seemed interested except for Walt and me, so we dropped the subject. We had three great days at Myrtle

Beach, and then the time was over. No one suggested setting another date for a reunion for the next year, so we said goodbye to each other and headed for our homes.

But a reunion did take place in 1994, in Tampa, Florida. Our plane had been shot down in 1944. We all knew that we had been lucky to survive our ordeal of being shot down and captured by the Germans. Since 1994 was the fiftieth anniversary of being shot down, we were ready for another reunion. Frank Irizarry lived in Tampa and he made the arrangements. For the first reunion we had five crewmembers and six wives. At the Tampa reunion we had six crewmembers and seven wives. In attendance were: George McFall and Elaine, Frank Irizarry and Blanca, Willy Kemp and Alene, Walt Pawlesh and Marg, Ralph Sirianni and Mary, Ernie Alcorn and Paula, and Judy Eggman, representing her husband, Roy Eggman. Ed Brazies was in a veterans' hospital and was too ill to come. Willie Krupitsch did not respond to our invitation, so we did not know what had happened to him.

We had a good time getting together again and talking over old times. We also talked about how much we all enjoyed the first reunion in 1993. The first reunion had helped to bring us closer together. At the 1994 reunion we were able to discuss our wartime experience in more depth. It was very emotional for us because we talked about being shot down and how we tried to take care of each other. I had warned Walt to bail out or else he might have gone down with the plane. Ernie Alcorn had bound my wounds and helped me get my parachute on and bail out. He parachuted out right behind me. As we talked about what we did, and how, even though wounded, we helped each other, we could not hold back the tears.

A reporter from the *St. Petersburg Times* wrote an article telling about our Tampa reunion. She began her article with the following statement: "Fifty years after they were shot down and taken prisoner by the Nazis, the surviving crew members of a B-17 meet again in Tampa for a tear-stained reunion." She was right. It was a very emotional, "tear-stained reunion" where we finally got a chance to open up our feelings to each other.

We remembered our deceased crewmembers, Pop Grimshaw and Roy Eggman. And then the six of us crewmembers voted unanimously to make Roy Eggman's wife, Judy, an honorary member of the *Heaven Can Wait* crew. Judy had been with her husband and with us during our training at Ardmore, Oklahoma. We often all went out together to dinner, to the movies, or to go bowling in the evening. She came to the reunions in place of Roy, and we felt she deserved to be recognized as an honorary crewmember.

Walt once again mentioned the possibility of going back to Germany to see where our plane crashed, but nobody else, except me, seemed interested, so we dropped the subject again. The reunion ended, and we all went back to our homes. No one made plans for the next reunion.

One day I heard from Walt that his wife, Marg, had passed away. The funeral and burial was going to be at Arlington National Cemetery in Washington, D.C., instead of in Pittsburgh, where Walt lived. I flew to Washington to be with Walt for his wife's interment in Arlington National Cemetery.

In 1996, George McFall called me from his home in Wisconsin. He and his wife, Elaine, were getting ready to celebrate their fiftieth wedding anniversary, and Mary and I were invited, as was Walt Pawlesh. Mary and I drove to Pittsburgh to get Walt, and then we went on to Wisconsin to share in the celebration of George and Elaine's anniversary.

We met in Tampa, Florida, again in 1997 for another reunion. Three years had passed since our last reunion. Frank Irizarry, who still lived in Tampa, and Walt Pawlesh got together to make the arrangements for our third reunion. We had five crewmembers and three wives attending this reunion: George McFall and Elaine, Frank Irizarry and Blanca, Ralph Sirianni and Mary, Bill Kemp, and Walt Pawlesh. Bill and Walt's wives had since died. Ed Brazies had been in a veterans' hospital and had died there. We learned that Willy Krupitsch and Ernie Alcorn had also passed away.

We were saddened to hear about the loss of more of our crewmembers, and we talked about them and remembered them at this reunion. This 1997 reunion gave us a chance to meet once again. The bond between us as crewmembers was never broken during the years, and we kept in touch. Walt and I talked again about going to Germany to find out where our plane crashed, but no one else was interested. For the third time, Walt and I dropped the subject. We had no way of knowing that this would be our last reunion.

In January 1998, Walt called me to talk about finding the plane.

"Ralph," he said, "why don't you and I just go ahead and do it? Let's go to Germany and find out where our plane crashed? We're not getting any younger and now is the time."

On May 11, 1998, we were on a plane heading for Frankfurt, Germany. Walt and I were the only ones who went. The other remaining crewmembers were not interested in making the trip. Walt's wife had died, and my wife, Mary, did not come with us.

We arrived in Frankfurt on May 12 and stayed at the Wings Hotel on the outskirts of Frankfurt. The next morning we drove to Hanover, stayed overnight, and left for Neinburg the next morning. We had read in the

Notice of *Heaven Can Wait* crew's reunion in Tampa, Florida, 1997.

official Army Air Corps records that our plane had crashed near the town of Neinburg. So I assumed that Neinburg was the town where I had been temporarily kept when I was captured.

When Walt and I arrived at Neinburg, we discovered that the town had both a new and an old town hall. The first thing I wanted to do was take a look at the old town hall. It did not seem familiar to me. Walt and I walked around the building, and I was puzzled. I told Walt that this was not the building as I remembered it. The more I looked around, the more certain I became that this was not where I had been temporarily held by the Germans. If I was right, then we were in the wrong town.

We went to the mayor's office in the new town hall to get some information. We introduced ourselves to the mayor's secretary, who spoke excellent English. We told her we were looking for the site where our B-17 crashed in 1944. She was just beginning to search her files when the phone rang. She picked it up and said hello in German. She was quite surprised, as she held the phone out to me and said, "Mr. Sirianni, this call is for you."

Walt and I were even more surprised than she was. Who could be calling me in Germany? As I reached for the phone, I was afraid that it might be someone from Winthrop and that something was wrong. "Hello," I said cautiously.

Walt Pawlesh (right) and I leave for Germany in search of our own B-17's crash site.

"Mr. Sirianni, my name is Enrico Schwartz." The voice on the phone continued, "I live in Cologne and am actively involved with a group that tries to locate the sites of aircrafts that had been shot down during World War II. Do you remember the number of your plane?" Enrico had a list of all the downed aircraft in the area and where they were shot down. He also knew the numbers of all the planes and whether they were B-17s or B-24s. He had obtained this list from the American government.

Walt remembered the number and repeated it to me. I told Enrico the number was 42–31745. I could hear the rattling of paper over the phone as Enrico looked through his lists. A few minutes later he said, "Your airplane went down 55 kilometers north of Neinburg near a town called Wildeshausen. If you wish to see the site, I'd like to suggest that you leave Neinburg and return to your hotel in Hanover. Tomorrow morning drive to Wildeshausen. I will make reservations for both of you to stay at the Quality Hotel Huntelal in Wildeshausen. After you check in, go to the town hall and ask for Alfred Panscher."

When Enrico and I finished the phone conversation, I looked at Walt and asked, "How did Enrico know my name? How in the hell did he even know we were here?" Walt shrugged his shoulders. He didn't know either. I should have asked Enrico, but I didn't think of it then. I was too excited about finding out where our plane went down.

The next morning we drove to Wildeshausen and went right to the hotel. Within a half an hour, Walt and I were out of the hotel to start our search. The first thing I wanted to do was find the town hall. Wildeshausen was a small town and it did not take us long to find the right building. I knew right away that this was the place where I had been taken by the German guards. As we approached the building, I said to Walt, "This is it. This is where I was first taken as a prisoner of war."

The building was no longer a town hall. It was now a tourist information center and restaurant, but I recognized it nevertheless. I could see that the original round watering trough for the donkeys and horses was still in the square next to the building. The scaffold where I thought the Germans were going to hang me was gone.

When Walt and I got closer to the watering trough, I felt disturbed and became emotional. I could feel the tears in my eyes. I had had a bad time there, and it began to come back to me. I was standing on the very spot where the cart I was riding in had stopped under the scaffold. I could picture the scaffold, and I remembered my fear that the Germans were going to hang me. I had to shake off those memories for now, and continue our search for the site where our plane crashed.

The cellar where I had been kept was now a restaurant and cocktail

I am standing in front of the building that was the old Town Hall, where I was temporarily imprisoned just after I was captured. The building now contains a restaurant and a tourist center.

lounge. Walt and I went downstairs to have some lunch there, but when I got into the restaurant, I changed my mind. I did not want to stay there, in the same room where the Germans had held us. I was not ready yet.

"Let's come back later," I said to Walt. "We can come back for a drink and to take some pictures." Walt agreed.

We went to the burgermeister's office in the new town hall. Enrico's friend, Alfred Panscher, was waiting for us. He was the town historian and spoke English. After we introduced ourselves, I asked him where our plane had crashed. Alfred said he would take us to the site of the crash. As the town historian, Alfred had become part of a network of people all over Germany who were dedicated to finding World War II downed airplanes and the bodies of MIAs. The members of this network were all volunteers.

We left the town hall and walked down the street until Alfred stopped at a house where we saw a man painting. The man was in his sixties. Alfred called to him in German and explained who we were and why we were there. "His name is Heinz Vanhorn," Alfred told us. "He saw your plane come down."

Heinz stopped painting and walked toward us. Alfred introduced us and we shook hands. Heinz was smiling and seemed to be eager to tell his story about our plane. Alfred translated for us. Heinz said he remembered the day of March 23, 1944, very clearly. It was a frightening day for all of the people in the neighborhood. Heinz was only a young boy, still in school, but he had a clear memory of the crash. He described seeing the plane come down. It hit the ground so hard that it bounced up and down three times, sliding along the ground until it finally came to a stop. On the way down the plane narrowly missed the Schutte family's house.

After Heinz finished telling us the story of the crash, we thanked him for taking the time to talk with us. Then Alfred said, "Now we can go see the Schutte house. Mr. Schutte is not at home now, but he will meet us later at his house."

Alfred wanted to show us how close the Schutte family home was to the crash site. Then we would be able to understand what a close call it was for their family as the plane came crashing down so close to their house. On the way to the Schutte house, Alfred described the area as it had looked during the war. The area was mostly farmland in 1944 with very few houses. But now, in 1998, there were many houses in the area, and most of the farms had disappeared and had been replaced by the beautiful homes.

Later that afternoon we returned to the Schutte house and met with Mr. Schutte. Alfred Schutte was a teacher who taught deaf children, and he also spoke excellent English. Schutte was only 14 years old when our plane crashed. We walked around to the back of his house, where Alfred pointed to the exact location of the crash. The plane crashed so close to the house that it was a miracle it had not hit the building.

Alfred and his brother were in school when the siren began to sound the air-raid warning. The teachers told everyone to get home as fast as they could. Alfred and his brother were halfway home when they heard the roar of a plane overhead. The plane seemed to be heading toward their house. The terrifying noise of the plane scared them because they were afraid the plane would hit their house, and their mother was there. As they got closer to their home, they saw the plane flying over their house, just barely missing it. Alfred heard the loud noises as the plane crashed in back of the house.

Alfred saw the fire trucks arriving, and then he saw his mother standing outside the front of the house waving to him and his brother. They ran to their mother and embraced her with hugs and kisses. She had been worried about them, and they had been worried about her. Now they were all smiles and very happy that they were still alive.

Then, Alfred told us that he ran around to the back of his house. What he saw there was very frightening. The plane was on the ground and flames were coming out of it. An American airman was trapped inside the plane. Another American, with the help of some of Alfred's neighbors, was trying to pull the wounded airman out of the plane. It was a difficult task because the plane had slid along the ground as it crashed and was dug deeply into the dirt. The American officer and the neighbors were frantically digging the dirt out from around the plane so they could reach the wounded man inside. The flames were spreading rapidly and the heat was almost unbearable. The men kept working, trying desperately to save the man caught inside the aircraft. Alfred was frightened, and he moved further away from the plane. He knew that it could explode at any minute

As Walt and I listened to Alfred's description of the attempted rescue, I knew from what he described that it was our captain, George McFall, working with the neighbors to save his crewman. I knew it was Pop Grimshaw who had been trapped in the burning plane. Finally, with the flames getting closer and closer, McFall and the neighbors had been able to pull Pop out of the plane. I didn't find out if the plane eventually exploded or if firemen got the flames out.

When Alfred finished telling his story, we followed him back to the front of his house. He wanted us to wait while he went into his house to

Alfred Schutte gave me pictures of the crashed plane that he had taken as a boy.

get something to show us. A few minutes later he came back out with a .50-caliber bullet in one hand and some pictures in the other hand.

"I found this bullet near the wrecked plane," Alfred said. " I also have a heavy flight jacket that I found near the plane. It was burned, but I saved it anyhow."

He had not brought it out with him, and we didn't ask him to go back in and get it. Then Alfred showed us pictures of the remains of our plane. One of the pictures was of the tail section. Walt and I were shocked when we saw how badly the tail section was broken apart. After we looked at the other pictures, we realized how miraculous it was that the crew remaining with the plane had survived the crash.

The news of our being in Wildeshausen had spread, and a reporter and a photographer had come to interview us. The reporter's story, along with a picture of Walt, Alfred, and me, appeared in the newspaper the next day. The article was, of course, in German, but I got a copy to bring home with me.

Alfred and his wife, Maria, invited us to stay for dinner. After dinner, the four of us went to the restaurant in the old town hall where I had been kept as a prisoner. We went just to have a beer and enjoy some more conversation. Because Walt, Alfred, and Maria were with me, I felt I was

Alfred and Maria Schutte and I stand in front of the old Town Hall, now a tourist center and restaurant.

Having dinner in the restaurant that was the cellar where I was first imprisoned. I am on the left; next from left to right are Walt, Alfred Schutte, and
Alfred's wife.

ready to face the memories that the room brought back to me. Everyone
was so cheerful. They saw this place as a nice restaurant, but I still saw it
as a place of captivity and suffering. Nevertheless, I managed to drink my
beer and enjoy the conversation with everyone.

Before we left the restaurant to return to our hotel, Alfred asked Walt
and me if he could drive us on a sightseeing tour around Wildeshausen
and the surrounding area the next day. We agreed, and at 9 A.M. Alfred
arrived in his car. As we traveled down the curving roads, I could see how
much the whole area had changed. Alfred said the population was around
1,500 people in 1944, and now the population of Wildeshausen had risen
to about 18,000. We could see for ourselves that most of the large farms
were gone, and private homes now dotted the landscape.

Sometimes the memories of the war came flooding back into my mind
and upset me. I had been hoping that the previous reunions and the finding
of the site where our plane had crashed would enable me to face the past
and move on to enjoy my retirement. The people in Germany were wonderful, not like the Germans I had known in 1944 and 1945. These people
had been friendly and eager to hear our story. But now it was time to leave
Wildeshausen. When we got back to our hotel, I told Alfred how much

we appreciated his kindness and his help. He smiled, shook our hands, and wished us well on our journey back home.

The phone rang that night just as we were packing. It was Enrico calling from Cologne. He wanted us to stop in Cologne so he could spend some time with us and show us around. Walt and I were delighted to extend our trip. Enrico arranged our reservations at the Hotel Mondia in Cologne. We drove there the next morning, checked into the hotel and met with Enrico.

Extending our trip was a very wise choice. We stayed four days in Cologne. Enrico drove Walt and me everywhere. We went sightseeing, and later visited with Enrico's mother and father and had lunch at their home. On our last night in Cologne, Enrico invited us to have dinner with him and his girlfriend, Swetlna. We enjoyed the dinner and the company, but both Walt and I were getting tired of traveling. It was time to get to Frankfurt and catch our plane back home. I told Enrico that we were leaving the next day.

The next morning we packed our luggage, brought it down to the lobby, and checked out. Enrico had said the night before that he wanted to meet us at the hotel before we left. We were putting our luggage in our rented car when Enrico drove up. He told us he was going to drive his car ahead of ours to lead us out of Cologne and onto the main highway leading to Frankfurt. When we reached the road leading to the main highway, we stopped our cars just off the road to meet and say goodbye. Enrico got out of his car

Enrico (in the middle) and Walt (right) join me in visiting Cologne. Enrico shows us a .50-caliber machine gun that he found after the war.

and walked to our vehicle to wish us a safe journey home. We shook hands and thanked Enrico for all he had done for us.

That night, Walt and I stayed at the Wings Hotel in Frankfurt, and the next morning we were on our plane heading home. I was thinking how lucky we were to have been able to make this trip. Ever since our reunions in 1993, 1994, and 1997, I have had a desire to talk more about my time in Stalag Luft I. Walt and I had both had a deep desire to find out where our plane had crashed. And now we had done that. Seeing the crash site and hearing the people's story about the crash, I felt like the final chapter of my World War II experience was closed. At least I thought it was closed now that the missing link, the site of the plane crash, had been found. But unfortunately, this feeling of euphoria was only temporary.

At the time of this trip, 1998, fifty-four years had gone by since I had been a prisoner of war. But I was soon to find out that the experience of being a POW never goes away. Sometimes it was shunted aside in my memory, but as the years went by, the horror of being a prisoner of war kept coming back in my dreams and in my mind. I understood now, after the trip to Germany, that you couldn't forget, no matter how hard you try. You could not blot out the horror from your life. Those memories will always be with me.

Many POWs must have had some of the same flashbacks and disturbing memories recurring in their lives just as I have. It surprised me to have everything come back to me so late in my life. I did not have these nightmares earlier in my life after my discharge from the Army Air Corps. Maybe the flashbacks did not occur earlier because I was so glad to be home and so busy finding a job, getting married, and raising children and grandchildren. Gradually I began to have occasional glimpses of the bad times at the German camp, but I was able to suppress them and continue on with my life.

But a few years ago the bad dreams and memories of the cruelty at the camp came back time and time again. Sometimes I woke up in fear after a bad dream about being back in the camp. It was almost as if I was really back in the prisoner of war camp. Night after night my dreams sent me back to the camp. I dreamed of the terror of being shot down and captured by the Germans. The brutal treatment of the airmen came back to me in my dreams, and I saw the men dying one by one. My wife said that while I was still asleep, I would thrash about in the bed. I knew I had to do something about these continuing nightmares because they were getting worse and more frequent. But I did not know what to do.

For the next few years I tried to fight off the memories of Stalag Luft I and to live a normal life. We did not have any more crewmember reunions. Many of our crewmen had died: Pop Grimshaw, Roy Eggman, Ed Brazies, Willie Krupitsch, and Ernie Alcorn. Bill Kemp's wife had died, and Walt Pawlish's wife had died. It was now 2002, and I was soon to hear from another voice out of the past.

One day in May 2002, Mary's niece, Judy Burditt, and her husband Bob came from New Hampshire to visit us. They seemed very excited and said that they had something to tell me, and they wanted to do it in person. One night when randomly searching the Internet, they found a web site about Stalag Luft I. They checked the listed names of the former POWs and found my name, but they also found Mickey McGuire's name and current e-mail address.

Judy and Bob knew that I had been looking for Mickey for a long time. He was in the same room as me in the North Compound. I had been searching for him for years, but he moved out of Gloucester and I had no idea where he went. I was surprised and pleased that Judy had found him.

Judy e-mailed Mickey, telling him they were relatives of Ralph Sirianni, and that Ralph had been searching for him a long time. Mickey answered her right away, saying that he had been looking for Ralph for a long time also. Mickey gave his telephone number and wrote, "I'm in California. Tell Ralph to call me."

Judy handed me a copy of Mickey's e-mail with the telephone number on it. I was too emotional to call Mickey right away, but it only took a few minutes for me to calm down and be ready to talk. I dialed his phone number and after two rings, I heard a deep voice say, "Hello."

"Mickey, this is Ralph Sirianni, I said." "I've been looking for you for a long time." Mickey replied that he had been looking for me also and was surprised and delighted to hear from me. He was living in California, was married, and had seven kids, all grown up. After chatting with Mickey for a while, I asked him if there was any way we could get together. He said that he and his wife would be in Gloucester in a couple of weeks to visit some relatives, and that maybe we could get together then.

Mary and I made arrangements with Mickey and his wife to meet us at the Hilltop Steak House in Saugus the next Tuesday. I told Mickey we were also inviting Judy and Bob, since they were the ones responsible for this reunion.

Four days went by. Time seemed to be dragging. Finally it was Tuesday evening, and Mary and I left our house and drove to the Hilltop Steakhouse. We checked in with the hostess, and were sitting on a bench waiting for Mickey and his wife. A man and a woman walked right by us, and I heard the man ask the hostess if Ralph Sirianni was here yet. I jumped up and yelled, "Mickey!" He turned quickly to look at me and, with a smile on his face, he yelled "Ralph!" We hugged each other, and the tears flowed. The people nearby probably thought we were crazy, but we didn't care. Of course, Mickey and I had changed a lot over the past 56 years, but when I saw him enter the restaurant, I knew it was Mickey right away.

I had booked a table for six people in the restaurant, but when we told the hostess that this was a World War II POW reunion, she arranged for us to have a small private room where we could have dinner and talk without being interrupted. Judy and Bob arrived just then, and we went into the private room.

It wasn't until after dinner that Mickey and I started talking about the camp. I talked about Dwayne Gillette's attempted escape, and then I mentioned the tunnels. Many of the airmen helped out with the tunnels, but I always wondered why no one ever asked the men in our room to help with the tunnels. I told Mickey that I always wondered if they didn't trust us. We were all willing and eager to help.

Mickey looked up at me in surprise. "That's not true," he said. "They trusted the men in our room. 'Bugs' Kappen and I had been helping with the tunnels by carrying Red Cross cardboard boxes out of the barracks. The boxes were filled with dirt from the tunnels. Laundry was placed on top to cover the dirt and fool the Germans. We carried the boxes to the outside latrine and dumped the dirt down the hole."

"I never knew you and Bugs did that, I said." "Why didn't you ever tell us?"

"We couldn't tell you, Ralph, or anyone else," Mickey explained. "Bugs and I were sworn to secrecy by the officers of the escape committee. We were ordered not to tell anyone what we were doing. The fewer people who knew, the better."

We had been at the restaurant about four hours when Mickey said he and his wife had to get back to Gloucester. We all enjoyed the opportunity to get together, and we made arrangements to keep in touch with each other. During that time together, I never mentioned the problems I was having with the flashback memories of the camp. It did not seem like the appropriate time. So I never asked Mickey or any other of our crewmembers if they had the same problems I was having.

But I knew one thing for sure now. I no longer wanted to suppress my wartime experiences. I wanted to end the horrible dreams. I had never talked about my time in the camp to my family or friends, but now I needed to get everything out in the open. Then maybe the bad dreams would stop. I made two major decisions. First I decided that I wanted to tell my story to my family so they could understand what I had been through. Then maybe they could understand what I was going through now. My second decision was to seek the help of a psychologist who would help me understand these flashbacks and memories.

One way to tell my story was to write a book about my wartime experiences, but I had never written a book before. I contacted a friend, Pat Brown, who had already published a book, as well as some articles. She agreed that I had a story that needed to be told. Together we wrote this book. Telling my story and getting it out in the open has been very beneficial to me. My family now knows the whole story that I had kept bottled up inside me for many years. The bad dreams have not completely stopped, but they do not occur as often. Hopefully, someday they will disappear altogether.

Appendix A:
Ralph's POW Log Book

The Red Cross had distributed logbooks to the POWs. The title on the front of the book's hard cover was *A Wartime Log.* Underneath the title was a picture of the Liberty Bell. Many of the POWs filled their logbook with their hopes and with stories of the camp and their fellow POWs as well as poems and drawings. They had to be careful what they wrote in the logs because the German guards had access to everything in the barracks, including the logs. Nevertheless, the kriegies (POWs) managed to show how they felt.

The first page of Ralph's log was clearly a warning to the Germans. He wrote:

DANGER

NOTICE

Warning to those who are about to look thru the pages of this book.
The contents of this book are mostly made up by some Kriegies who have
no scruples. Now that you have been warned, you may leave this book
alone, or venture forth and learn how the peasants live.

Signed, R. E. Sirianni

On the next page Ralph drew a map of Germany, France, and the surrounding area. He marked the area where he was held prisoner, and attached a small American flag over the area. The flag was given by the Swiss Red Cross. The title page was next, *A Wartime Log, A Remembrance from Home through the American Y.M.C.A.* On this page Ralph had placed another small American flag and wrote, "I dedicate this book to my best girl friend, my mother. May these pages bring you laughter."

But there was nothing in the log to bring laughter as we know it. It was a special kind of humor mixed with sadness, frustration, and a longing for

197

freedom. There were many poems, some original, some remembered from before the war.

Ralph wrote in his log:

> Our death they called our glory.
> They were lying.
> The glory was in living
> Not in dying.

Most of us remember the old story about the man who had no shoes. He was feeling sorry for himself until he saw a man with no feet. The POW version in the log was:

> I had no shoes and I murmured
> Until I saw a man with no feet.
> I had no shoes and I murmured
> Until I saw a Kriegie with two pairs
> And I screamed!

Poems and pictures were a favorite way for the POWs to express themselves. Bob Hope was noted for traveling to entertain the troops. He usually ended his entertainment with a song, "Thanks for the Memories." Here is the POW version as written in Ralph's log.

> Thanks for the Memories
>
> Thanks for the memories
>   Of flights to Germany
> Across the cold North Sea
>   With blazing guns we fought the Huns
> For air supremacy
>   How lucky we are!
>
> Thanks for the memories
>   Of ME 109s
> Of flak guns on the Rhine
>   They did their bit and we got hit
> And ended our good time.
>   We hate them so much!
>
> We drifted far out of formation
>   We ditched, and what a sensation.
> And now to sweat out the duration
>   Our job was done. We did have fun — so
>
> Thanks for the memories
>   Of days we had to stay
> In Stalag "Seven A"
>   The cabbage stew which had to do
> Till Red Cross Parcel Day.
>   How thankful we are.

When reading the log, one can sense the anger and the frustration of the POWs, and yet, they maintained their sense of humor and hope for the future. One page in Ralph's log had the name of things remembered and missed, and things wished for. In addition to home and family, such things as Dick Tracy, Bob Hope, Wonder bread and Maytag washers were remembered and missed. Wishes for the future were expressed in short terms like, "New drive in '45." "Home alive in '45." "Back to the sticks in '46." "Out the gate in '48." "Across the Rhine in '49." The hope of survival and the memories of home and freedom never left their thoughts.

From Ralph's Log: "Nov. 23, 1944. Thanksgiving day back in the States. Was thinking of the football game I played in two years ago. Also of the one going on today with Mike (Ralph's brother) as a cheer leader. Had to stay in sack all day — have a bad cold and it's raining out. At night we had the phonograph. Thinking of home."

Thoughts of home often saddened the POWs because they so desperately wanted to be home. Yet, at the same time, the thoughts of winning the war and getting home kept their hopes up, and helped them survive their terrible ordeal in the prisoner of war camp.

Time seemed to move very slowly for the POWs as they waited for freedom. Ralph drew a picture entitled *TIME*, and signed it "Mousie." All Ralph's drawings were signed with his nickname, "Mousie." The picture shows a very sad, lonely, cold POW looking out through the barbed wires that keep him a prisoner. He is leaning on a large hourglass in which the contents are dropping to the bottom very slowly. Below the picture is the following poem by Henry van Dyke:

> Time is too slow for those who wait
> Too swift for those who fear
> Too long for those who grieve
> Too short for those who rejoice
> But for those who love "Time is Eternity."

Most of the POWs followed their officers' rules and helped each other in times of need. But not all the airmen were able to suffer the starvation diet imposed upon them. A few broke down and disobeyed the rules. Obeying their officers' rules and sharing with each other was essential to survive in the camp. In his log Ralph told of an episode where the rules were broken.

"March 21, 1945. Last night an officer was caught in the ration room. When the guys caught him, they beat him up. I saw his accomplice, and am writing out a statement to give the Colonel."

Time passed slowly for the prisoners of war, and conditions in the camp were getting worse. So far, Ralph had been imprisoned in the "bag" (the camp) for a year. He wrote: "March 23, 1945. Well here it is, a year in the bag. It seems more like ten years. We haven't had R. C. parcels for over a month. My stomach thinks my throat is cut. All we been eating is Rutabaga, turnips, and very few potatoes."

Freedom comes at last. Ralph's log has a very brief description written on the dates the Russians entered the camp and freed the prisoners of war.

> April 30, '45. There has been a lot of activity around for the past couple of days. We have been hearing Russian artillery for the past week. Hope and pray that I get home O.K.
>
> May 1, '45. Did not go to bed at all last night. Plenty of action last night. Jerries still blowing up ammo and other stuff. The Jerries evacuated at 23.30 hours last night. Our boys took over the towers at 02:00 hours this morning. I am Cpl. of the Guard and have five men under me. We start on shifts today. Russians are 18 miles from us now. Should be home by June. Tonight the Russians got here and took over the place. The guys went mad and run all over the place.
>
> May 2nd. The tanks are all over the place now. Today they put American, English and Russian flags up on the poles. I can't name or write all the things that have happened today."

There was just too much happening at once to write it all down, but Ralph remembered everything that happened. Now that the Germans were gone, and the POWs knew they were free, thoughts of home became the most important concern. They wondered how long it would be before the planes came to take them out of the camp. The men talked about all the things they were going to do when they got home. The last page in Ralph's log gives us a glimpse of that feeling.

From Ralph's log:

When I Get Home

> First day I want to spend with my mom, dad, and kid brother. Second day I will look up all my buddies and relatives. I also will get a date to go out that night. We will go to some nice Nite Club, have supper, see a good floor show, then take in a movie. The third night I want all my relatives up the house for a big party. From then on I will do everything I want to, and try to make up for the good times I missed when in the bag.

As told earlier in the book, Ralph eventually did all the things he wanted to, just not as fast as he wanted. No matter how hard he tried to forget about his prisoner of war experiences, the past always came back to haunt him.

Appendix B: The Last Mission as Told by the Pilot, Lieutenant George McFall

Lieutenant George McFall was Ralph Sirianni's pilot on their last mission, when the plane crash-landed on March 23, 1944. Ralph and two other gunners in the back of the plane had already bailed out before the plane crashed. Here is George McFall's story about how he and the remaining crewmembers survived that crash:

The mission was officially designated as Mission #84 of the 388th Bomb Group. Our planes were taking off at thirty-second intervals. The procedure for takeoff and for getting into our formation was carefully planned. With nearly one thousand planes flying over the eastern part of England at the same time, it was important to follow the procedure. Our target was Brunswick. As we were just heading out over the English Channel, my navigator, Lieutenant Brazies, told me we were ahead of schedule. Our fighter protection was not at the

Lieutenant George McFall, skipper of the *Heaven Can Wait* B-17 crew.

appointed place. My crewmembers were asking where the fighters were. I told them over the intercom that the fighters were not due for another twenty minutes. We could not wait. We had to continue on with our mission without any fighter protection.

As we got nearer to our designated target, the German FW-190s attacked us. There were forty or fifty German FW-190s flying nearer and nearer to us. Our group was one of the first targets, and the FW-190s swarmed in on us. The German fighters seemed to be everywhere. Our bomber was being shot to pieces by the German 20mm cannon fire. Our gunners were shooting back as rapidly as they could.

I saw both American and German planes being shot down. One German fighter collided with a bomber and both the fighter and the bomber began to fall. Then they both exploded. A few minutes later I saw one of the bombers on my left get hit and both the pilot and copilot were killed. The bomber caught fire and went into a steep dive toward the ground. The remaining members of the crew were able to bail out. It was impossible to avoid the attacking German fighters.

Part of a propeller on one of our four engines had been shot off, and our plane began to vibrate. A second engine caught fire and lost power. By this time we were out of formation. This made us an even easier target for the Germans. I called to our bombardier, Lieutenant Eggman, "Salvo the bombs." I hoped that by dropping the bombs, I could get better control of the airplane. If we eventually needed to make a crash-landing it was better not to have a full rack of bombs that would most likely explode when we landed.

But releasing the bombs did not improve the performance of our damaged plane. The rudder had been hit and it swung to the left and jammed into the far left position. I had very little control of the plane. The German rockets were flying by very close to the fuselage. I had no choice but to run for home in the hopes of saving the plane and my crew.

Just then, one of the waist gunners began screaming into the intercom. He had been hit by an exploding 20mm shell. Also, our oxygen system was damaged and would soon be unable to function. I had to fly lower. When I began to dive toward the ground, I saw a German fighter approaching from the left. Then suddenly a row of bullet holes appeared in the wing of my plane. Sergeant Alcorn, my radio operator/gunner, fired at the fighter and successfully shot it down. But our plane was now very badly damaged.

As the speed of our bomber increased, I was not able to trim the plane. I had to brace myself between the back of the seat and the steering wheel to keep the plane in a dive. The intercom had been damaged and was now out of order, so I couldn't use it to tell my copilot Lieutenant Frank Irizarry to help me. Frank had assumed that we were going to crash, and he began to pull on his wheel instead of pushing. I yanked off my oxygen mask and yelled at him to push, not pull. He understood and began to push. Between the two of us, we were able to hold to a steep dive. My goal was to get into the layer of clouds at one thousand feet above the ground. The German fighters were still following us and my gunners were still firing at them.

We made it into the clouds and the Germans could not see us anymore. Unfortunately, I soon became aware that the plane was picking up ice from the clouds. Ice can change the shape of the wing, and it would affect the control of the plane. I had to go below the clouds, and soon we were flying a few hundred feet from the ground. I only had one aileron and the elevator for controls. The other aileron had been damaged. It was not easy trying to keep the plane under control. A few minutes later, I saw that our left wing was covered with a sheet of flame. Now I was sure that we could not stay airborne much longer. I pulled the throttles back and looked for a place to land.

There was a small, marshy stream just ahead, and I thought this might be a good place to land. But I could not control the plane. We were going too fast. Just ahead of us there was a bluff that was higher than our elevation. My copilot also saw the cliff and yelled, "Mac, we're going to crash!"

"No we're not, Frank," I replied. Those engines that were still functioning supplied just enough power to get us over the edge of the bluff. It was such a close call that the ball turret beneath the plane hit the crest of the bluff. A few seconds later we came crashing down into the middle of a German farmer's cabbage patch. The plane skidded along the ground, pushing a pile of dirt ahead of it. Eventually we stopped, but it was a close call. We were within fifty feet of hitting a farmer's house.

My crewmen were getting out of the plane as fast as they could to run away from the burning plane. I was still in the plane but since I did not have my safety belt on, it was easy for me to get up and out of the plane. It was customary for us to unfasten our safety belts during long flights, as the belts were too confining to leave on for hours at a time. I saw that Frank still had his belt fastened and was having difficulty getting it unfastened. I stayed in the plane and reached over to unfasten Frank's safety belt, and we both made a very rapid exit.

Once outside the plane, I became more aware of the extent of the damage to the plane. Frank and I had exited through a hole in the side of the plane where there wasn't supposed to be one. The other members of the crew were already quite a distance away from the plane. I stopped a short distance from the plane to take off some of my equipment like my "Mae West" life preserver and my flak suit. Just as I began to move farther away, I heard a voice coming from the plane. "Mac, you aren't going to leave me, are you?"

I was shocked. Someone was still on the plane. I think this upset me worse than all that had gone before. To think we almost left a crewmember in a burning plane was a horrible feeling I would never forgot. I went back to the plane and discovered that Sergeant Pop Grimshaw, our left waist gunner, was still in the plane.

During the crash he had slid partly out of the plane. He had one leg in the plane and one leg buried in the dirt. He was partly trapped under the plane. I think this was the only time during our ordeal that I actually lost control, even though it was for a short time. The proof of my lack of control was the fact that in my hurry to save Pop, I grabbed a quart fire extinguisher from the plane and tried to use it to put out a thousand gallons of burning gasoline. I soon realized that this was ridiculous. The fire was too strong to be affected by a quart fire extinguisher. By now the other members of the crew had run quite a distance from the plane, as they properly should have. I yelled, and caught the attention of two of them, and called them back. They immediately began to run back toward me.

In the meantime a farmer came out of his house and ran toward us waving his arms and shouting in a questioning manner, "Boom? Boom?" I assured him that there were no bombs in the plane. Then, by making the motion of a man shoveling, I showed him that we needed some shovels. The farmer understood and ran to his barn. In a few minutes he returned with two shovels and another man to help. Finally we managed to dig the dirt out from under Pop Grimshaw's leg and pull him out of the wreckage. His leg was broken, but otherwise he was all right. Frank, my copilot, and Roy Eggman, my bombardier, were now standing beside me, and we carried Pop away from the plane. When we got farther away, we all watched the plane burn. It was not a pleasant sight, but we were lucky to be alive. I turned to Frank and said, "Well, that's all she wrote." Forty years later, at one of our crew reunions, Frank reminded me of that statement.

Our plane had crashed near a small farming village about forty-two kilometers west of Breman. There was no place for us to run to, and as we stood there watching the plane burn, it wasn't too long before the German home guards and the local police took us into custody. The Germans knew that B-17s carried a ten-man crew. When they could only find seven of us, they began searching the area.

We assumed then that three of our gunners, Ralph Sirianni, Walt Pawlesh and Ernie Alcorn, who were in the rear of the plane, had bailed out. They must have sensed that the plane was going to either blow up or crash. Because the intercom was damaged, they had no way to contact Frank or me, so they bailed out.

Under German guard and with the villagers following us, we were escorted to the basement of a building where other allied airmen were being held. The local German guards were armed with machine guns, and they carefully guarded us. Within an hour or so, regular German army personnel arrived and took control.

Later that same day four of us, myself, Frank Irizarry, Roy Eggman,

German guards captured the rest of the crew, and stand by McFall's plane until it can be removed. Picture taken by Alfred Schutte as a young boy.

and Ed Brazies were taken outside. We had no idea why we were being taken out or where we were going. Once outside, I saw Ralph Sirianni, my right waist gunner, lying on some straw in a cart pulled by a pair of oxen. Ralph had been wounded. He was so pale that I felt sure he was dead. We went closer to the cart and I spoke to him. Ralph opened his eyes and stared at us for a minute before he spoke, "Where did you guys come from? I thought you were dead." He was very pale from loss of blood, and I could see that he had been hit in both legs by 20mm shrapnel. The four of us were ordered to carry Ralph into the building and put him with the other captured airmen.

* * *

Thus, George McFall tells us his story of the plane crash and the capture of him and his crew. After the four officers were captured by the Germans, they met Ralph and his German escorts just arriving, and they were ordered to carry him into the building where they were being temporarily placed. Later all the airmen were removed from the building and sent to different POW camps. George McFall was sent to Stalag Luft III and Ralph Sirianni was sent to Stalag Luft I.

Index